Praise for *Called into the Mission of God*

"As the discipline of missional hermeneutics begins to explode, it is exciting to see this careful, perceptive study of the Thessalonian correspondence that is sensitive to the letters' original purposes and sharply focused on mission. Roji T. George's groundbreaking work speaks both from and to the Indian context. But it also addresses the global church, highlighting the missional implications—especially among the marginalized and in the context of oppressive political power—of the church's public, cruciform, risk-taking identity that participates in the mission of the Triune God. I highly recommend this important book to scholars and practitioners alike."

—Michael J. Gorman,
Raymond E. Brown Professor of Biblical Studies and Theology,
St. Mary's Seminary & University

"The value of any hermeneutical approach to Scripture can only be measured by its fruit. By this standard, Roji T. George's application of a missional hermeneutic to the Thessalonian correspondence is substantially valuable and fruitful, while his exploration of its relevance to the church in India carries salutary lessons for the wider global church. With close attention to the text and its original context, he illuminates the subversively counter-cultural meaning and power of the gospel, the missional nature of the church's existence and the Holy Spirit's presence, and the crucial importance of ethical formation within Christian communities. This is the wholesome fruit of disciplined missional hermeneutics in action."

—Christopher J. H. Wright,
Langham Partnership,
author of *The Mission of God* and *The Mission of God's People*

"The application of new approaches to the age-old task of understanding Scripture often yields surprising beneficial insights. Writing from outside the bubble of the global West, Roji T. George successfully employs a recently developed missional hermeneutic to the eschatological confusion addressed by Paul in his first letter to the Thessalonians. The results prove helpful for both the church and the academy."

—James Miller,
professor of inductive bible study and New Testament,
Asbury Theological Seminary

"This is an unusual study of Paul's letters to the Thessalonians that brings together various aspects of Pauline thought. Beginning with the observation that Scripture is missional in intent, Roji T. George examines these letters from a missional perspective. He sets out the relevant contours of the context in which the Apostle founded the church in the city, and then highlights how Paul challenges the Thessalonians to fulfill God's purpose for them by living lives of faith and love, in the power of the Spirit and in the hope of the eschatological consummation of God's saving work in Christ. To this end, he encourages them to follow his example and that of his partners in mission, even as they seek to translate the gospel in their everyday lives. This study provides very worthwhile reading, and I am delighted to endorse it as such."

—Brian C. Wintle,
professor emeritus,
Union Biblical Seminary, Pune

"This is a remarkable addition to the recent attempts at engaging in Scripture through the lens of God's mission. Employing mission as the hermeneutical key, the author has quite skillfully unearthed the missional vision that Paul had woven into his eschatological epistles. This book combines scholarly erudition and unapologetic commitment to Christian mission."

—P. V. Joseph,
professor of theology and mission,
Luther W. New Jr. Theological College, Dehradun

"In teaching us to read the New Testament missionally, Roji T. George is restoring to us, in insightful and powerful ways, the original context of the apostolic writers, who understood all doctrine and ethics within the larger context of the world mission of the church, lived out in real contexts and settings that must receive the gospel."

—Timothy C. Tennent,
professor and president,
Asbury Theological Seminary

CALLED INTO THE MISSION OF GOD

CALLED INTO THE MISSION OF GOD

A MISSIONAL READING OF PAUL'S THESSALONIAN CORRESPONDENCE

ROJI T. GEORGE

FORTRESS PRESS
MINNEAPOLIS

CALLED INTO THE MISSION OF GOD
A Missional Reading of Paul's Thessalonian Correspondence

Cover image: Kristin Miller

Cover design: Corinthia terrain in North Peloponnese from airplane / Memitina / iStock

Paperback ISBN: 978-1-5064-3365-3

eBook ISBN: 978-1-5064-3366-0

Dedicated to my loving daughters,

Joanne and Janet,

for their love, care, and encouragement.

I am proud to be called their father

as they grow up to be God's children in this world.

CONTENTS

ACKNOWLEDGMENTS

Looking back at the time spent in the process of writing this book, I gratefully acknowledge God's enabling grace that sustained me during the difficult hours of this whole project. This journey had its own share of difficulties due to illness and mental and physical fatigue after long hours of burning the midnight lamp at the end of a normal working day. But the voice whispering within me, encouraging me to persist tirelessly, kept me moving forward. I am grateful to God who called me to be a partner in his mission and is active in me to accomplish his purpose in and through my life every day. If I had not recognized and sensed his assuring presence throughout, a journey such as this would have been impossible. I am also grateful to Dr. Jesudas Athyal for the invitation to contribute a volume on a theme that has been close to my heart for some time now. His encouragement and periodic inquiries on the progress helped me to meet the scheduled deadline. I also praise God for friends, church members, and family members who have been continually praying for me. Finally, I am grateful to my wife, two daughters, and my mother, who have extended encouragement and sacrificial support to me. Despite all odds, they graciously allowed me to spend the necessary time for the completion of this book.

INTRODUCTION

Every year as I teach the course called "Hermeneutical Trends and Methods of Interpretation in New Testament Studies," a question that comes up at times during the class discussions hints at the key contention against the modernistic hermeneutical logic. Out of curiosity, students ask: How can one be sure of methods and approaches founded upon different philosophical premises, cultural contexts, times, and worldviews and produce *the* author-intended meaning of an ancient text here and now? As an academician predominantly lenient, yet critical, toward reader-oriented interpretation, I have maintained that while producing *the* author-intended meaning of the text could be the ideal goal of interpretation, the role of subjectivity in all our interpretations cannot be denied or even avoided completely.

As human beings conditioned by the sociocultural and religiopolitical environment that we are born into, no one can avoid personal hermeneutical priorities and biases from playing out at one's interpretation of any text. Whether they are ancient or modern texts, ultimately it makes no difference to an interpreter's biases. All of them come with certain set of preconceived notions consciously or unconsciously. While such an understanding is now common knowledge among the majority of the biblical scholars, it has not gone down well with many who are preoccupied with the author-intention-oriented interpretation. Well, there is some truth in their claims and arguments. But, the problem is that neither can anyone do away with a desire to exhume the original authorial intention in producing a text nor can one yield oneself completely to draw meaning based on the whims and fancies of a modern reader. While the former option of interpretation is hypocritical and secretive, with personal biases brought in with claims of objectivity and innocence, the latter can be too dangerous for faith and practice. In practicing the latter interpretive approach, unless one is intentionally responsible toward the text, the interpreter has unlimited space to drag the text and operate it irresponsibly. It can throw innovative ideas and contextually authentic meanings from the modern interpreter's specific location without doing justice to the text. In other words, it is universally true that a certain degree of subjectivity is inevitable in every effort of interpretation. But, it cannot be a license to undo an interpreter's responsibility toward the biblical text. The reason is simple: The text we are choosing for interpretation is a document of faith, sacred Scripture, and not a fiction or a story that is produced for leisure-time reading. Thereby, interpretation of the Bible is not inconsequential. The biblical text deserves better hermeneutical efforts without denying the reality that there is a huge gap of time and space between the text and us. Hence, one needs to be constantly on the move for a hermeneutical tool that seems to balance between our conclusion and the author's intent, and the meaning of the text to the original readers and the meaning and significance of the Scripture for us here and now.

Probably, with such words of caution ringing in my mind, I find missional hermeneutics to be a good option for my hermeneutical engagement with the text practiced creatively but responsibly, here and now in my historical context. Missional hermeneutics is practiced by many biblical scholars in the last one and a half decades to read the Bible in the light of the nature and purpose of the Scripture, the authorial intent in producing any text, and the contextual nature of the significance of the text for both the original and the modern readers. As it will be discussed in Chapter 1, missional hermeneutics intentionally prioritizes the mission of God as a theological lens to engage with the Bible. The Bible is understood as the tool to fashion the community of God by teaching and exhorting them to recognize, engage as partners of God, and accomplish the missional purpose of its origin and existence at all times. The modern readers are expected to identify the missional intent, techniques, and manner in which the desired missional goal is achieved through the biblical text in the first-century context and then make an attempt to replicate the principles creatively and contextually in a particular historical context here and now. Thereby, I see the origin, purpose, and goal of producing these documents in the Bible being fulfilled both in the original context and now. It allows us to escape from pursuing narrow ideological interests in drawing the meaning of any biblical passage and rather include them under the larger umbrella of missional hermeneutics to address them responsibly in the light of the ongoing mission of God in the world and missional self-understanding. Such an exercise leaves minimum room for Christian activism to be about human efforts riding on stray theological stance to achieve some temporary goals proposed by short-term vision and understanding of the history. Instead, under the missional lens, such ideologically bent Christian activism gets theologically absorbed into the eternal plan, purpose, and activity of God. It nurtures a consciousness that with God his elect ones in the world are working out a wholistic liberation until the consummation of the eschatological age to come.

Hence, having been persuaded by the hermeneutical assumptions and premises of the missional reading strategy, my interest in reading Paul's Thessalonian correspondence through the missional lens began to take shape. As the present study attempts to read Paul's Thessalonian correspondence through the missional hermeneutical perspective, my interest is not to engage with every literary or theological debate associated with 1 and 2 Thessalonians in Pauline scholarship. So, though many of the issues vehemently debated are important to the overall theological engagement, they are inconsequential to my contention; thereby, they are not central to my study. However, several of these important debates are carefully used in the study to elaborate the missional thrust of the two letters. I count them important and use them to conclude whenever required, but they do not set my interpretive agenda in the book. The interest, at first, is to recognize the instrumental role and nature of Paul's letters in the then gentile missionary context and then identify the same instrumental role of these letters as part of Scripture, for us today both within and outside the ecclesial context. *Missio Dei* forms the metanarrative that characterizes the beginning and end of the interpretive praxis of the text, both in words and the being of the missional community itself.

I see the uniqueness of my work in highlighting the missional tenor of the letters and not in establishing the world behind the text or in resolving the textual issues. It neither traces the development nor contradictions in Paul's thinking on major theological themes like eschatology in the Thessalonian correspondence. As I read, for me the final text in my hand is the divine tool through which God is at work both in the first century and today, inside the church and in the world. The intended role of Scripture must be viewed as forming, shaping, and establishing communities for his ultimate redemptive purpose. Probably, that must primarily set the agenda for our textual engagement. It must not be read as a rejection of critical scholarship as practiced in the biblical studies favoring missional hermeneutics. Perhaps, more serious and deeper critical discussion on historical and literary critical studies may be kept aside for some other occasion.

Select studies on Paul's Thessalonian correspondence

First and Second Thessalonians have been in discussion among the Pauline scholars primarily for reasons other than their missional significance. The survey that ensues below does not intend to be exhaustive. Instead, it only intends to set the present study in its present academic context. Theologically, it has been undertaken to understand the apostle's earliest understanding of eschatology and its development in relation to the eschatological teachings in his later letters. Pelser, investigating the idea of resurrection of the dead in Paul's letters, deals with a century-old question about the development of Paul's idea on eschatology. He finds that it is beyond doubt that an important shift did take place in Paul's thought about the resurrection idea. While he expected an imminent return of the Messiah when he wrote 1 Thessalonians, Paul in 1 Corinthians appears to have moved on from such an understanding. Initially, he did not think about the possible death of believers before the Parousia happens. He revised such a position in the light of the delay of the Parousia and death of some of the believers teaching that resurrection will happen while they are still awaiting the immediate return of the Messiah (cf. 2 Cor 15). However, finally, moving away from his earliest understanding of eschatology in Thessalonians, Paul taught in 2 Corinthians 5 and surely in Philippians 1:23 that the death of the believers is a reality in the process of their eternal salvation.[1] Unlike Pelser's interest, Woodbridge has sought to discuss various alleged discrepancies in Pauline eschatology, indicating the change of Paul's mind on crucial points. For Woodbridge, death of believers was always on Paul's mind while the Parousia was imminent as Paul would have believed. He rejects scholarly contentions that discrepancies are evidence of contradictions in Paul's thought on eschatology and argues that a proper exegesis of his words prove that there exist coherence and consistency in his writings on the topic. The use of new imageries and a sort of different reflection on the topic is merely his emphasis upon certain aspects in response to the need of the situation he was addressing.[2] Recently, on a different note, Garrow contends that the tradition behind 1 Thessalonians is *Didache* 16.[3]

Some others have undertaken to study the two letters from the sociological perspective seeking to reconstruct the sociohistorical world behind them or to hear the rhetorical significance of Paul's words within

1 G. M. M. Pelser, "Resurrection and Eschatology in Paul's Letters," *Neotestamentica* 20 (1986): 37–46.

2 Paul Woodbridge, "Did Paul Change His Mind?: An Examination of Some Aspects of Pauline Eschatology," *Themelios* 28, no. 3 (2003): 5–18.

3 Alan John Philip Garrow, "The Eschatological Tradition behind 1 Thessalonians: Didache 16," *Journal for the Study of the New Testament* 32, no. 2 (2009): 191–215.

the then-real situation. For example, Robert Jewett has done an extensive study on the social, political, religious, and cultural context to elucidate the words of the apostle. It is a significant contribution to hear Paul's words loud and clear within the sociohistorical context. However, the entire work is interested in reconstructing the world behind the text to return to the text and explain its meaning based on sociological realities. In Chapter 9 of his book, he even employs "The Millenarian Model" to explain the emerging Christianity in Thessalonica.[4] Recently, Ascough too, resorting to the then-existing social organization, has attempted to equate the Thessalonian community to the professional voluntary association in Greco-Roman antiquity. He finds shreds of evidence for his contention in Paul's use of professional association language in 1 Thessalonians along with the seeming voluntary association analogies shared by the community of believers in Thessalonica. Thus, the church in Thessalonica not only looked to the outsiders like a professional association, but they functioned internally in the same manner.[5] Similarly, Malherbe has expended his energy to explain the form and shape that the early Christian communities took in the Greco-Roman world based on 1 Thessalonians. He uses 1 Thessalonians as a test case to understand the social phenomenon because no other documents from Paul, for him, throw so much detail to explain the social process of community establishment and the apostle's intentional use of native Thessalonian traditions to elucidate his content (e.g., 1 Thess 2:1–8). He says, "rather than simply organize a church, Paul founded, shaped, and nurtured a community. In so doing, he was sensitive to the needs of the individuals within the community who had committed themselves to new beliefs and a new way of life. Paul was, in fact, engaged in pastoral care, although he does not describe the enterprise in that manner."[6]

Donfried's collection of his important articles is, in a sense, representational of the trends prevailing in the study of Thessalonian correspondence. The articles collected in a single volume covers a wide field of studies: (i) politics, socio-religious situation prevailing in first-century Thessalonica and their importance to understand the content of the two letters under investigation, (ii) the vital theological themes related to the Thessalonian correspondence, and (iii) the questions dealing with the literary nature—the epistolary and rhetorical aspects—of Paul's letters to the Thessalonians. The collection includes his groundbreaking work

4 Robert Jewett, *The Thessalonian Correspondence: Pauline Rhetoric and Millenarian Piety*, Foundations and Facets (Philadelphia, PA: Fortress Press, 1986).

5 Richard S. Ascough, "The Thessalonian Christian Community as a Professional Voluntary Association," *Journal of Biblical Literature* 119, no. 2 (2000): 311–28.

6 Abraham J. Malherbe, *Paul and the Thessalonians: The Philosophical Tradition of Pastoral Care* (Philadelphia, PA: Fortress Press, 1987), 1–109, cited from 1.

suggesting the significance of Cabirus cult to understand the context of the ethical directives within the socioreligious context of Thessalonica.[7] In fact, in a later publication coedited by Donfried and Beutler, two vital aspects of the Thessalonian studies are debated from multiple angles. They represent two important areas of discussion continuing in the study of Paul's letter to the Thessalonians. The two areas of discussion are the debate about the rhetorical context of the letters based on 1 Thessalonians 2:1–12 and the methodology related debate arguing and counterarguing the importance of epistolary analysis over rhetorical analysis of the letters or vice versa. The debate carried out in the earlier section ends loosely by pointing toward a possible synthesis of the two methods of analysis in studying the two letters.[8] However, Witherington's commentary on 1 and 2 Thessalonians, written from a socio-rhetorical perspective, rejects the synthesis approach to favor rhetorical analysis, although recognizing the presence of some epistolary elements in the letters that he mentions parallel to the rhetorical structure. He attempts to explain the rhetorical character of Paul's words with their social and theological significance. He maintains that while 1 Thessalonians is an epideictic rhetoric, 2 Thessalonians belongs to the deliberative rhetorical genre. Although it is a resourceful work for various reasons, one would seldom find the author highlighting the missional significances.[9]

Similarly, in recent years, interest in imperial studies has led some to read the Thessalonian correspondence within the Roman imperial context. Harrison, in his article, argues that the traditionally pronounced eschatology in 1 Thessalonians is inherently flawed due to the excessive mirror reading of the text. Laying forward positive evidence for the Thessalonian eschatology, Harrison contends that Paul's gospel was loaded with high imperial language in order to counter the Roman imperial

---

7 Karl P. Donfried, *Paul, Thessalonians, and Early Christianity* (Grand Rapids, MI: William B. Eerdmans Publishing, 2002). There are fifteen articles collected and republished in this volume. A few significant contributions are: For social and political context see "The Cult of Thessalonica and the Thessalonian Correspondence." For the important theological themes see "The Theology of 1 Thessalonians as a Reflection of its Purpose," "The Assembly of the Thessalonians: Reflections on the Ecclesiology of the Earliest Christian Letter," "The Kingdom of God in Paul," and "Justification and Last Judgment in Paul." For epistolary and rhetorical analysis see "The Epistolary and Rhetorical Context of 1 Thess. 2:1–12."

8 Karl P. Donfried and Johannes Beutler, eds., *The Thessalonians Debate: Methodological Discord or Methodological Sysnthesis?* (Grand Rapids, MI: William B. Eerdmans Publishing, 2000).

9 Ben Witherington, *1 and 2 Thessalonians: A Socio-Rhetorical Commentary* (Grand Rapids, MI: William B. Eerdmans Publishing, 2006). Witherington's identification of 1 Thessalonians as epideictic and 2 Thessalonians as deliberative rhetoric are mentioned in page 21.

eschatology that was aggressively propagated during the Augustan era. For him, Paul by doing that had gone ahead preaching a subversive gospel scuttling the Roman political discursive supremacy.[10] Later, Peter Oakes in a similar fashion argues that Paul in 1 Thessalonians 4:15–17 and 5:3, by inflating his language with Roman imperial terminologies redraws the map of the universe concerning the power structure. He places Jesus as the real power at the center against the Roman imperial claim, while placing Caesar at the center of the world power structure. For Paul, Jesus is above the Roman Caesar, though it does not seem to be so in the then existing earthly power structure. Paul's intention by doing that was not to preach an anti-imperial gospel but to encourage the persecuted community of Christians. He did not want them to view themselves as alienated and weak people but as people who are close to the real supreme power. In short, Paul in 1 Thessalonians (also Phil 2:9–11) is rearranging the order of power placing Jesus at the center and decentering Caesar.[11] I have argued that in 1 Thessalonians, Paul's relationship pattern, ethics, and the gospel of Christ could be read through a transcultural hybrid postcolonial lens. Paul as a transcultural hybrid figure articulates his gospel of Christ in the interstitial space of the Jewish, Greek, and Roman cultures in affiliative-disruptive fluid terms. For me, when reading in the Roman colonial context, Paul's ethical directives and social structure of relationship are at home culturally in the Greco-Roman cultural context in Thessalonica, but it is disruptive in demanding unflinching loyalty and obedience to the absolute demand of Christ as the real supreme power.[12]

None of the representational works mentioned pay due attention to the missional significance of Paul's letters to the Thessalonians. My missional reading implies that Paul's letters are instrumental in forming and shaping a community of God in Thessalonica according to the grand narrative of God's universal mission beginning at the Genesis account of creation to the end times, as the apocalyptic visionary describes it in the book of Revelation. I am not aware of any significant work published in this area, except Johnson Andy's missional commentary on 1 and 2 Thessalonians. However, Johnson's work is primarily an exegetical exploration of the words of the apostle and their missional implications.

10 J. R. Harrison, "Paul and the Imperial Gospel at Thessaloniki," *Journal for the Study of the New Testament* 25, no. 1 (2002): 71–96.

11 Peter Oakes, "Re-Mapping the Universe: Paul and the Emperor in 1 Thessalonians and Philippians," *Journal for the Study of the New Testament* 27, no. 3 (2005): 301–22.

12 Roji T. George, "Situation in Thessalonica and Paul's Advice to The Community in 1 Thessalonians: A Postcolonial Reading for Contextual Significance in India Today" (Paper presented at the Soceity for New Testament Studies Asia Pacific Lesioning Regional Conference, Kottayam, October 22, 2016), 1–27.

Ideas like election receive sufficient attention in its Jewish background, but areas of missional exploration like the elect community's missional engagement as an interpretive community do not find space in the work. Discussing the theme, Johnson has also done a thematic study of eschatology and related concepts, but the missional pneumatology, imitation as a strategy of discipleship, the letters as a missional tool, etc., are not elaborated.[13] However, his work is important in making a significant shift from the earlier academic engagements with the Thessalonian correspondence focused on learning his mission strategies and highlighting the making of Paul the missionary. Whether it is Roland Allen's work (reprint, 1962)[14] or the much-celebrated work of David Bosch, *Transforming Mission* (1991), both reflect the general trend of their times. Allen and Bosch dealing with Paul's theology and practice of mission treat his letters as evidence to draw the apostle's mission strategies.

In this context, undertaking a missional reading of Paul's correspondence in the following chapters, I ask certain key questions that function as the guiding compass in the rest of my journey:

1. What is the theological framework Paul employs to interpret the theological themes and traditions missionally?
2. Do the theological themes and ethical exhortations in the Thessalonian correspondence betray missional motif?
3. How did Paul the apostle comprehend and strategize his missional purpose through the letter writing in the light of the unique historical context of the community in Thessalonica?
4. Did Paul use creatively Jewish and Greco-Roman social and religious traditions to create missional consciousness in the community?
5. If yes, what were those traditions and how were they reinterpreted contextually to create a missional community?

Plan of the Book

In the following discussion, in Chapter 1, the method of interpretation employed, the missional hermeneutic is first discussed in detail. As it is of recent origin and has vital disagreements persisting among the proponents about its nature and the exact steps of interpretation, the chapter enables the reader to attain a wider view of the field of study. The

13 Andy Johnson, *1 and 2 Thessalonians*, The Two Horizons New Testament Commentary (Grand Rapids, MI: William B. Eerdmans Publishing, 2016).

14 However, there have been studies interested in explaining Paul the missionary and his works. For example, Roland Allen, *Missionary Methods: Saint Paul's or Ours?* (Grand Rapids, MI: William B. Eerdmans Publishing, 1962).

discussion includes with a brief clarification on important words like "mission," "missional," or "church." Though they are commonly used in mission studies, they represent some unique emphasis in the missional hermeneutical reading strategy. A less familiar reader in the field requires a short description of these terms to gain a clearer understanding of the emerging discussion. Other important hermeneutical presuppositions, its definition, premises of the engagement, the goal of the interpretive exercise, and the four major trends of missional hermeneutics prevailing in the current academic discourse are briefly discussed and clarified. The critical discussion that ensues in understanding the similarities and uniqueness of the four trends proves that none of them is complete in itself to carry out a missional interpretation comprehensively. Hence, a tentative combination of all four trends is attempted in good faith as a viable approach to study Paul's two letters to the Thessalonians in this work.

If the goal of Chapter 1 is to facilitate a better understanding of the missional thrust of the two letters, Chapter 2 attempts to set the two letters of Paul to the Thessalonians in their original setting. Thessalonica, a Roman city, during Paul's time, was under Roman imperial domination. As a result, Thessalonica witnessed cultural, ethnic, and religious cross-pollination that directly impacted every aspect of its private and public life. Although the city successfully retained its Greek heritage for a longer period than Philippi, mixing of religion and politics for selfish Roman imperial gains provided opportunities to the native population to negotiate power from the other end. Besides, the newfound community of the gentile believers too underwent a complex time characterized by persecution, moral issues, and disillusionment due to delay in the Parousia, and so on, which required Paul's urgent attention. The discussion carried out helps to appreciate the real situation in which Paul the apostle, entered the city in 49–51 C.E., preaching and forming the missional community according to the gospel of Christ. Paul's reply in the letters was pastoral and missional by nature. Paul repeatedly reminds the community that they ought to live a life worthy of their calling and must win the respect of the outsiders, while praising them for their role in the spread of the gospel.

The subsequent chapters (chapters 3–6) seek to deal with the four key theological-ethical themes from a missional perspective. While eschatology, a very dominant theme in the two letters, is explained as a framework of the apostle to reflect missionally upon the other theological themes and ideas in his writings, the content of Paul's earliest eschatological thought itself seems to be engrained with the desired seeds of missional transformation. Similarly, Paul's understanding of God and his community is also missional. The study attempts to underline the fact that Paul presents God to the believers in Thessalonica as the prime initiator and doer of rescue mission in the world through the call and establishment of a community for himself in Thessalonica. The relationship of the church with God and Christ and their special status as the elect people from among the rest of the Thessalonians are understood in the light of partnering with God in his mission. Probably, Paul's appreciation and encouragement to them to continue in the triad of Christian virtues—faith, love, and hope—is thoroughly missional in essence. The study also discusses the prophetic role of the church as a risk-taking community in the local context.

In the same way, the discussion on "the gospel and the missional pneumatology," in two parts, highlight the missional content and the active missional role of the gospel Paul preached. The Holy Spirit as the eschatological blessing of God to the church and his effective role not only in the preaching of the gospel, but also as the sustaining joy giver to the community and the distributor of the essential charismatic gifts for missional reason will be discussed. If so, Chapter 6 discusses imitation as the apostles' strategy of discipleship, adopted from the Jewish and Greco-Roman social context, to build, nurture and establish the local community to be effective partners in *missio Dei* with universal ramifications.

The readers would notice that almost every chapter has a section discussing the relevance of the topic's studies for the life and mission of the church in India. These sections are only intended to spark thoughts on necessary areas of ecclesial life in India requiring urgent attention from all to intentionally pursue transformation, fulfilling God's missional purpose in our corporate life.

Finally, the study concludes by answering the key guiding questions raised in the beginning and discussed in the following chapters.

1

READING A TEXT MISSIONALLY

In a church context, mission-oriented sermons are preached with the primary intention to encourage a cross-cultural evangelistic activity. The grand motto, "reaching the unreached for Jesus," inspires such enthusiastic sermons. Jesus's words, "Go into all the world and preach the gospel to all creation" (Mark 16:15 or the Matthean version of the Great Commission in Matt 28:19–20) have been invoked time and again to underline the mandate given to every Christian. In addition, examples of the biblical figures (like Paul and the early apostles) and the sacrificial lives of illustrious missionaries in the past and present centuries are brought alive in words before the congregations as perfect models for all to imitate in fulfilling God's plan for humanity. Such zeal has led to a stereotypical treatment of the Bible. While the select biblical passages have at times been termed central to Christian faith practices, some others have received a proof text treatment. The Bible is believed to contain pieces of evidences for the mission that justifies our ecclesial plans and programs. Thus, such an approach violates the true understanding of the nature of the Bible by narrowly limiting the idea of mission to select passages alone (e.g., Gen 12:1–4; Isa 6:1–8; Matt 28:18–20; Acts 1:8; Rom 9:16; 10:14).

Even in academic discussions, the dominant interests were to discuss "Biblical Foundations of Mission in the Old and New Testament." This was especially so in the study of the New Testament, where each book was discussed elucidating its unique contribution to draw a broad picture of mission in the New Testament. However, "in recent decades, a more promising way of relating mission and the Bible has begun to emerge. It seeks to engage in an intentional, self-involved, *missional* reading of

Scripture as a whole."[1] According to Flemming, the reasons are fourfold: (i) A growing understanding that mission involves much more than a mere cross-cultural mission. (ii) Interpretation of the Scripture requires greater appreciation of the meaning of the text in its original context. It recognizes the very formative missional environment, the missional nature of the Bible, and the interpretive function of the Bible in the missional formation of the community. (iii) Mission-sensitive majority world voices as conversation partners of those in Western academia increasingly determine the real agenda of theological discourse. (iv) The emergence of a new hermeneutical trend called missional hermeneutics.[2]

The advantage of undertaking a missional interpretation of the Bible is not just enlisting select biblical passages teaching about the mission of God. Instead, missional interpretation redefines the very nature, origin, and purpose of the composition of the Bible. Then, the mission of God is not just a component of the larger biblical teaching, but also the interpretive lens to unravel the true meaning of the biblical text. It means every major theological theme in the Bible must be read and understood through the missional lens. Thus, a tectonic shift in our missional-theological engagement with Scripture is initiated, which also necessitates a major shift in the understanding of important terms for our further discussion.

1.1. Important Terms and Definitions

Mission

Traditionally, the term has been widely understood, owing to its Latin root, as "to send." Biblical scholars have used the two terms "mission" and "sending" as parallel terms for *Shalach* in Hebrew and *apostello* in the Greek New Testament and the LXX.[3] Such an understanding played a greater role in defining the self-consciousness of the church, through the centuries, as God's chosen community sent out into the world. So, mission entailed a human initiative of undertaking cross-cultural journeys to people in geographical regions unfamiliar to the gospel. In doing this, God is viewed as the prime sender and the task of the one being sent, the church or a missionary, is to save the unsaved. The sent out agent of God functions as God's obedient servant who is commissioned to be his witness. According to Hedlund, "Mission is a special kind of sending. It

[1] Dean E. Flemming, *Why Mission?*, Reframing New Testament Theology 4, ed. Joel B. Green, 1st ed. (Nashville: Abingdon Press, 2015), xvi.

[2] Flemming, *Why Mission?*, xvi–xvii.

[3] Joy Thomas, "The Evolution of the Concept of Mission in the Bible," in *Bible and Mission in India Today*, ed. Jacob Kavunkal and F. Hrangkhuma (Bandra, Bombay: St. Pauls, 1993), 38.

is always towards those outside. Mission is beyond the existing Church."[4] In the words of John Stott, "'Mission' concerns his redeemed people, and what he sends *them* into the world to do."[5] It "describes rather everything the church is sent into the world to do. 'Mission' embraces the church's double vocation of service to be 'the salt of the earth' and 'the light of the world'. For Christ *sends* his people into the earth to be its salt, and *sends* his people into the world to be its light (Matt 5:13–16)."[6]

In the recent missional readings, biblical scholars have explicitly expressed their dissatisfaction with the narrow application of the term in bearing Christian witness. Though the narrow understanding of "mission" limited to mere "sendness of the church" is not completely rejected, it has been viewed to be insufficient to comprehend the wider significance of the mission. In fact, Bosch opines that "mission remains undefinable; it should never be incarcerated in the narrow confines of our own predilections."[7] Wright uses "the term mission in its more general sense of a long-term purpose or goal that is to be achieved through proximate objectives and planned action."[8] He defines "mission" saying: "*Fundamentally, our mission (if it is biblically informed and validated) means our committed participation as God's people, at God's invitation and command, in God's own mission within the history of God's world for the redemption of God's creation.*"[9] In other words, it is not just a God's chosen individual's activity to extend salvation to those beyond the reach of God's saving act "but the vocation of a whole people who play part in God's salvation on behalf of the whole world."[10] In doing so, according to Goheen, the church situates herself in the direction of the biblical narrative, that is, "from the particular to the universal." Then, God's election of his people is not an end in itself but a means to bless all the nations.[11]

---

4 Roger E. Hedlund, *Evangelization and Church Growth: Issues from the Asian Context* (India: CGRC McGavran Institute, 1992), 11.

5 John R. W. Stott, *Christian Mission in the Modern World* (Bombay: Gospel Literature Service, 1993), 19.

6 Stott, *Christian Mission,* 30–31.

7 David Jacobus Bosch, *Transforming Mission: Paradigm Shifts in Theology of Mission*, American Society of Missiology Series no. 16 (Maryknoll, NY: Orbis Books, 1991), 9.

8 Christopher J. H. Wright, *The Mission of God: Unlocking the Bible's Grand Narrative* (Downers Grove, IL: IVP Academic, 2006), 23.

9 Wright, *Mission of God*, 22–23 (emphasis original).

10 Michael W. Goheen, "A History and Introduction to a Missional Reading of the Bible," in *Reading the Bible Missionally*, ed. Michael W. Goheen (Grand Rapids, MI: William B. Eerdmans Publishing, 2016), 21.

11 Goheen, "Missional Reading of the Bible," 22.

Missional

In recent discussions, the term *missional* is used in "a less technical and broader sense as something characterized by mission and related to the mission of God."[12] However, when used as a qualifier of the following referent in a sentence, it assumes a technical nature. For example, when used as a qualifier of "church," it redefines the term *church*. On such occasions, the term highlights the mission character of the referent. It is an adjective that "describes not a specific *activity* of the church but the very *essence and identity* of the church as it takes up its role in God's story in the context of its culture and participates in God's mission to the world."[13] For this reason, some scholars like Flemming have preferred to use the term *missional* over *missionary* because the latter is often understood in a limited sense underlining a cross-cultural movement with the gospel.[14]

Church

In the light of the paradigmatic shift in the current missiological studies, the missional *redefining* of the New Testament ecclesiology is vital. Unlike in the Christendom of the Western church, since 1930, there emerged a greater consensus that "the church must be defined and must act as part of the larger mission of God."[15] A *missional church* may be defined as a community of God formed and fashioned by its participation in the mission of God to redeem, heal, and restore the world marred by human sin. It recognizes itself primarily not as a sending agency but as the one being sent to participate in the continuous activity of God in the world from the beginning to the eschatological end. In short, no aspect of its life and activity is untouched by God's redemptive mission.[16] At the foundation of this newer understanding of the theology of mission of God lies the doctrine of the Trinity, which is essential for a right ecclesiology. The true understanding of the church is ultimately rooted in understanding the God of the Bible as a missionary God who sends the church to be Christ's witness.[17] No doubt, to speak of a missional church is to speak of the church whose essence and purpose of existence is defined in the light of

---

12 Dean E. Flemming, *Recovering the Full Mission of God: A Biblical Perspective on Being, Doing, and Telling* (Downers Grove, IL: IVP Academic, 2013), 18.

13 Michael W. Goheen, *A Light to the Nations: The Missional Church and the Biblical Story* (Grand Rapids, MI: Baker Academic, 2011), 2.

14 Flemming, *Full Mission of God*, 17.

15 Darrell L. Guder, *Called to Witness: Doing Missional Theology*, The Gospel and Our Culture Series (Grand Rapids, MI: William B. Eerdmans Publishing, 2015), 74.

16 "So We Do Not Lose Heart," in *Treasure in Clay Jars: Patterns in Missional Faithfulness*, ed. Lois Y. Barrett, The Gospel and Our Culture Series (Grand Rapids, MI: William B. Eerdmans Publishing, 2004), x.

17 Guder, *Called to Witness*, 74.

the mission of God. Even the testimony of the New Testament about the apostles founding the communities of God in the Roman world was "to found missional communities to continue the witness that had brought them into being."[18]

Hobbs enumerates twelve important indicators from the working draft prepared by the Developing Congregational Models Team under GOCN explaining what a missional church might look like in the present (American) context. They are:

1. The missional church proclaims the gospel.
2. The missional church is a community where all members are involved in learning to become disciples of Jesus.
3. The Bible is normative in this church's life.
4. The church understands itself as different from the world because of its participation in the life, death, and resurrection of its Lord.
5. The church seeks to discern God's specific missional vocation for the entire community and all of its members.
6. A missional community is indicated by how Christians behave toward one another.
7. It is a community that practices reconciliation.
8. People within the community hold themselves accountable to one another in love.
9. The church practices hospitality.
10. Worship is the central act by which the community celebrates with joy and thanksgiving both God's presence and God's promised future.
11. This community has a vital public witness.
12. There is a recognition that the church itself is an incomplete expression of the reign of God.[19]

Scripture/The Bible

As part of a missional reading of the Bible, recent missional readers have called for a shift in recognizing the original purpose, nature, and role of the Bible in the life and mission of the community of God. The Bible is not thought to bear merely positive mission commandments, but it is the product, tool, and witness to God's continual mission in and through the life and mission of the community of God. The Bible is authoritative with

18 Guder, *Called to Witness*, 66.

19 Walter C. Hobbs, "Appendix: Method," in *Treasure in Clay Jars: Patterns in Missional Faithfulness*, ed. Lois Y. Barrett, The Gospel and Our Culture Series (Grand Rapids, MI: William B. Eerdmans Publishing, 2004), 160–72.

its variety of literary genre for they all authorize a missional community on the earth to function in freedom and responsibility within the set boundary. Unlike the traditional understanding of the authority of the Bible as the foundation for the binding authority of the mission imperatives in the Bible, the missional interpretation of the Bible "explores the nature of biblical authority itself in relation to mission."[20]

The authority is not inherent to Scripture, but it is authoritative because, as Wright would explain, it brings us in contact with the threefold reality in parallel to Christ Jesus: (i) The reality of the God, Yahweh, who is known only through the Bible evokes multiple forms of responses from us in perfect alliance to his nature and work in the world. Similarly, as we recognize Jesus in the New Testament as the one sharing in the identity of Yahweh himself, it is authoritative to us by laying a framework for our life and conduct in the world. (ii) Ultimately the Bible is the grand story with a universal scope that invites us to embrace and engage in the biblical metanarrative here and now. The story of Jesus is the climax of the grand story that begins in the Old Testament. Between the two of these, we need to locate ourselves relying on the promises of God to Israel in the past and the hope of the future in Christ. (iii) The story of the election and the continued relationship of Israel with Yahweh renders meaning, goal, and vitality to us as the people of God in and through Christ. The missional authority of the Christian mission is derived out of the call of Israel to be the light of the nations. As we live for, belong to, and bear God among us in Christ, the New Testament narrates our ethical and missional responsibilities toward the world.[21]

1.2. A DEFINITION OF MISSIONAL HERMENEUTICS

What is missional hermeneutics? *Missional hermeneutics*, a relatively new term in circulation among the biblical interpreters, is understood and defined differently based on the approach adopted by an interpreter. It makes stating a clear definition of the method of reading the Bible difficult and complicated but not impossible. In simple terms, "it is a holistic understanding of mission from a holistic reading of the biblical texts," in which one reads both "the indicative and the imperative of the biblical revelation with equal seriousness, and interprets each in the light of the other."[22] Missional hermeneutics draws mission to the heart of the Bible in an unprecedented manner to interpret it. It broadens the scope of mission from a narrow understanding of treating it as equal to evangelism

20 Wright, *Mission of God*, 51.
21 Wright, *Mission of God*, 54–58.
22 Wright, *Mission of God*, 61.

based on a limited span of biblical passages like the Great Commission in Matthew 28:18–20. Bauckham defines missional hermeneutics as:

> A way of reading the whole of Scripture with mission as its central interest and goal.... A missionary hermeneutic would be a way of reading Scripture that sought to understand what the church's mission really is in the world as Scripture depicts that mission, and thereby to inspire and inform the church's missionary praxis. Such a hermeneutic, one that reads the Bible with a view to mission, should properly be developed in reciprocal relationship with the practice of mission as itself a practice of interpreting Scripture.[23]

This definition assumes that Scripture is all about mission. For Bauckham, the mission of God is the central golden thread, the metanarrative, that connects the whole story of the Bible as one story of God's purposeful dealing with humanity. The story of God's missional engagement in the Bible develops from one particular event and expands in its scope to include the whole universe. So, for him, two important methods already in circulation among the biblical scholars, the canonical interpretation and narrative interpretation, must be employed. While missional hermeneutics seeks to read the whole story of the Bible as one metanarrative in which many other mini-narratives may be read missionally in connexion, the narrative nature of the Bible reminds us that in the narrative development from the particular to the universal, both God and his people acquire a narrative identity on the go. Notably, in the New Testament, this progression toward the universal level at the climax happens through the three hyperbole: the temporal, spatial, and numerical.[24]

Flemming expands the scope of the hermeneutical engagement by adding another dimension to the understanding of Bauckham. Flemming maintains that there are two foundational elements necessary to practice missional hermeneutics meaningfully: "First, a missional hermeneutic consciously reads Scripture as a *witness* to the gracious mission of the triune God, that is, the *missio Dei* . . . . Secondly, missional interpretation is also concerned with how Scripture functions as an *instrument* of the *missio Dei*."[25] Hence, Bauckham states, "A missional hermeneutic, then, invites us to listen to Scripture with our ears attuned to the cadences of God's mission. At the same time, it asks: How do these texts shape God's

[23] Richard Bauckham, "Mission as Hermeneutic for Scriptural Interpretation," in *Reading the Bible Missionally*, ed. Michael W. Goheen (Grand Rapids, MI: William B. Eerdmans Publishing, 2016), 28–29.

[24] Bauckham, "Mission as Hermeneutic," 29–34; Richard Bauckham, *Bible and Mission: Christian Witness in a Postmodern World* (Grand Rapids, MI: Baker Academic, 2003), 11-12.

[25] Dean E. Flemming, "Revelation and the *Missio Dei*: Toward a Missional Reading of the Apocalypse," *Journal for Theological Interpretation* 6, no. 2 (2012): 162.

people into faithful communities that are caught up in the mission of God in their local contexts?" [26] Guder too agrees with the addition of the second aspect of the missional interpretation. He argues for a missional "interpretation of the Scriptures in terms of the fundamentally missional vocation of the church of Jesus Christ. This approach to biblical interpretation is rooted in a consensus about the character of the apostolic strategy—what the apostles were actually intending as they carried out the pentecostal mission (Acts 2 leading into the rest of Acts)."[27]

However, some recent discussions have highlighted *culture* as a third but a vital aspect of missional hermeneutics. Barram placing the prime interpretive location at the center maintains that missional hermeneutics requires posing critical questions "in order to discern the faith community's calling and task within the *missio Dei*." For him, the missional questions are inherently rooted in a particular interpretive location to enable us to read Scripture faithfully here and now.[28] Cautioning against the threat to be dictated by one's own cultural bias and preferences when interpreting Scripture, Franke, in line with Newbigin's call to involve Christians from other culture who read the Bible differently, as the third interlocutor proposes to adopt an interdisciplinary approach called "Intercultural hermeneutics." It enables drawing recontextualized insights from an already contextualized text out of mutual interaction between all the partners. Thus, the missional hermeneutic would be "*open* to the witness of Christians in other cultures, *resisting* the temptation to absolutize our own culturally shaped theological models."[29]

In short, the above discussion enables us to briefly state that a missional hermeneutic prioritizes mission in reading the Bible because the latter is the product, instrument, and the result of the missional intention of a missional God. While missional motif is a dominant thread running across the two Testaments binding them together along with all other narratives in them in order to form a missional community of God, they are inevitably formed within the original culture of the author, which needs to be openly recognized. Hence, the task of hermeneutics is to hear the meaning of the text, appreciate the role of the missional Scripture within the recipient culture, and to seek to hear the Truth in the Bible in recontextualized terms, here and now.

---

26 Flemming, "Revelation and the *Missio Dei*," 163.

27 Guder, *Called to Witness*, 90.

28 Michael D. Barram, "The Bible, Mission, and Social Location: Toward a Missional Hermeneutic," *Interpretation* 61, no. 1 (2007): 58.

29 John R. Franke, "Intercultural Hermeneutics and the Shape of Missional Theology," in *Reading the Bible Missionally*, ed. Michael W. Goheen (Grand Rapids, MI: William B. Eerdmans Publishing, 2016), 87–91, cited from 91 (emphasis added).

1.3. Why missional hermeneutics in biblical studies?

The urgency to undertake a missional reading of Scripture lays both in the method's inherent strength to explain the meaning, nature, and role of the Bible in the life of the church and the need of corrective to the lopsided post-enlightenment hermeneutical practices intensely pursued in biblical studies. First, despite all its useful contributions, the origin of higher critical scholarship in the atheistic and rationalistic environment of the Western academia crippled it from upholding the significance of Scripture in defining and directing the missional purpose of the church in the world. The highly specialized critical study of the text, at times, became an end in itself without real significance for the church at present. In fact, mission was not part of the theological discussion until Karl Barth, and the others began to speak about the relationship between mission and theology.[30] Sadly, from Schleiermacher's era, mission was relegated, with a bias, to the area of practical theology[31] and missiologists merely devoted themselves "to teach the practical side of outreach and refused to engage the theological curriculum at a deep level."[32] It widened the gulf between the enlightenment-oriented biblical studies and the ongoing missiological studies that generally kept itself aloof from the higher critical discussions in biblical studies. While biblical studies remained obsessed with a detached reading of Scripture to bridge the gap between the ancient biblical text and the present context, missiological studies failed to critically engage with the text bridging the cultural gap between the ancient text and the present context in deriving relevant biblical insights for mission.[33]

The twentieth century witnessed great interest in investigating every literary unit in order to reconstruct the world behind the text instead of highlighting the unique way in which God is speaking to his people. Goheen rightly observes that the "attention to the historical, cultural, literary, and even theological details of the text was separated from hearing God speak to his people in the text."[34] Biblical scholarship driven by the higher critical approach claimed to be neutral and objective in studying, analyzing, and interpreting a text by its non-committal detached reading, but it subtly promoted a culturally and doctrinally biased modern reading of the Bible. Even Bultmann, an insider of a such interpretive legacy, recognized this truth when he boldly confessed, "no exegesis is without presuppositions, inasmuch as the exegete is not a *tabula rasa*, but on the contrary, approaches the text with specific questions or with a specific

30 Guder, *Called to Witness*, 6–12.

31 Guder, *Called to Witness*, 21.

32 Goheen, "Missional Reading of the Bible," 4.

33 Goheen, "Missional Reading of the Bible," 5.

34 Goheen, "Missional Reading of the Bible," 9.

way of raising questions and this has a certain idea of the subject matter with which the text is concerned."[35]

Second, on a positive note, missional hermeneutics is necessary to do a committed reading of the Bible. It attempts to do justice to Scripture by treating every part of it as integral to the larger missional narrative, while it also provides the central place to mission in all biblical discourses. It is not limited to select mission commandments found in the New Testament or passage that concern with mission and evangelism explicitly. Missional hermeneutics restores missional theology to the strategic position it indisputably deserves and affirms the actual significance of the Bible in the life and mission of the church. In fact, Barram justifies the vitality of missional hermeneutics for us today by harking back to Paul, the apostle, as an example of a missional interpreter from within the canon. For him, our missional interpretation of Paul's letter to the Corinthians helps us to understand Paul as a missional interpreter who "attempts to reshape the Corinthian Christians' hermeneutical assumptions and proclivities in light of the gospel [that] may thus prove to be especially useful and significant in the ongoing missional formation of Christian communities today."[36] In other words, missional hermeneutics appears to serve the formation of a community of God based on scriptural directives in order to serve the ultimate purpose of God through their election to save or redeem the whole humanity.

In the same way, missional hermeneutics helps in reconstructing our identity as the elect ones of God in Christ for the twenty-first century in the light of God's election of Abraham and his descendants to be a blessing to the nations. In fact, the same lens of the early Christian missional self-consciousness evident in the New Testament becomes the content of our identity and mission today. The more the Bible is interpreted through the missional lens, the more the creative engagement of the canonical authors with their own cultural context becomes evident before us. It opens up the possibility of forming new creative models of biblically sound missional interaction with our own culture. A direct benefit of it within a local context would be to distinguish the gospel from the culture of a missionary. It will surely embolden local Christian communities to reinvent their own unique sociocultural space within a context while assuming a biblically sound assimilative-disruptive Christian identity. In short, we are not speaking merely about contextualization of Christianity, but about an

35 Rudolf Bultmann, "Is Exegesis Without Presuppositions Possible?," in *Existence and Faith: Short Writings of Rudolf Bultmann*, trans. Schubert M. Ogden (London: Fortana Library, 1964), 342.

36 Michael D. Barram, "'Fools for the Sake of Christ': Missional Hermeneutics and Praxis in the Corinthian Correspondence," *Missiology* 43, no. 2 (2015): 196–97 (parenthesis added).

authentic incarnation of the Christian gospel with missional purpose in a non-Christian world like Paul did, rejecting the validity of the works of the law for the Galatian Christians (Gal 2:15–4:20).

1.4. Competing or Complementary Trends in Missional Reading

Identifying and delineating trends in a fast-emerging field called missional hermeneutics is difficult, though not impossible. The reasons are obvious; it is a complex and reasonably new field of study among biblical scholars with unresolved points of dispute. It has still not gained the due acceptance among biblical scholars that it rightly deserves. Hence, the effort to make its presence recognized among other established interpretive approaches as a viable tool of interpretation still continues. According to Michael W. Goheen, the ambiguity of the meaning of the term *mission*, the naive approach of missiologists to formulate the biblical basis for the foundation of mission, and the prevailing enlightenment-oriented non-missional hermeneutical practices in the field of biblical studies hinder it from gaining wider acceptance among biblical scholars.[37] Further, issues such as: (i) prevailing different presuppositions and prioritizations of what is integral to a robust missional hermeneutic among the missional hermeneuts, and (ii) the manner and role assigned to important constituents[38] in interpretation make a straightforward description of the current state in the field of study very difficult.

In such a situation, Hunsberger's identification of "four streams of emphasis"[39] in missional hermeneutics is quite insightful to gain an overview of the field of study. The discussion that follows is not intended to be exhaustive but representational to help in recognizing the current state of missional interpretive engagement. Hunsberger's effort is based on the recognizable "gravitational pull towards what is believed by the proponents to be the most essential aspect of what makes biblical interpretation missional."[40] Hence, a critical survey of various studies carried out to interpret the Bible through a missional lens shall be undertaken based on Hunsberger's classification.

---

37 Goheen, "Missional Reading of the Bible," 3–6.

38 Such as, the original authorial intent, reader's sociocultural location, the overarching theological theme unifying and defining the Bible, and the role of cultures and traditions intertwined within the text to equip the church in the mission of God.

39 George R. Hunsberger, "Proposals for a Missional Hermeneutic: Mapping a Conversation," *Missiology* 39, no. 3 (2011): 310–18.

40 Hunsberger, "Missional Hermeneutic," 310.

1.4.1. Missional metanarrative of the Bible: An interpretive framework

Hunsberger calls the first stream, "the missional direction of the story" because, for him, in this particular stream "the *framework* for biblical interpretation is the story it tells of the mission of God and the formation of a community sent to participate in it."[41] Goheen maintains that the Bible only tells one single story of redemption that has universal validity and "there is much to be gained from the recovery of reading the Bible as a grand narrative."[42] It begins with the fall of humanity into sin in Genesis 3 and continues until the establishment of the New Jerusalem. What lies between the beginning and the end of the story is the "interpretation of the meaning of cosmic history."[43] For him, if the Bible is understood as one single story, it exercises authority over our lives by fashioning it missionally.[44] The grand narrative of the Bible is the mission of God into which the community of God, down through the centuries, is called to participate. The fundamental assumption underlying this stream of hermeneutical engagement, in the words of Christopher J. H. Wright, is that "*the whole Bible renders to us the story of God's mission through God's people in their engagement with God's world for the sake of the whole of God's creation.*"[45] For Michael W. Goheen, "the heart of a missional hermeneutic is the recognition that God chooses and covenants with a *particular people* to fulfill his universal purpose of restoration."[46] Hence, Wright contends that unlike in the earlier discussion about "the biblical basis of mission," what is more important in missional hermeneutics is to recognize that "*the whole Bible is itself a 'missional' phenomenon.*"[47] Such an understanding of the Bible implies three vital hermeneutical presuppositions: (i) the Bible is *not* just a *record* of God's continual saving act through his people in human history, (ii) the canon *itself is* an *instrument* of God's creative and renewing act of forming and equipping his people for God's mission, and (iii) the Bible is the "*product*" of God's ultimate mission.[48]

41 Hunsberger, "Missional Hermeneutic," 310.

42 Craig G. Bartholomew and Michael W. Goheen, "Story and Biblical Theology," in *Out of Egypt: Biblical Theology and Biblical Interpretation*, ed. Craig G. Bartholomew et al., *Scripture and Hermeneutics Series*, vol. 5 (Milton Keynes: Paternoster Press, 2004), 144.

43 Michael W. Goheen, "The Urgency of Reading the Bible as One Story," *Theology Today* 64, no. 4 (2008): 471.

44 Goheen, "Bible as One Story," 473.

45 Christopher J. H. Wright, *The Mission of God: Unlocking the Bible's Grand Narrative* (Downers Grove, IL: IVP Academic, 2006), 51 (emphasis original).

46 Goheen, "Missional Reading of the Bible," 15–16 (emphasis original).

47 Wright, *Mission of God*, 22 (emphasis original).

48 Michael W. Goheen and Christopher J. H. Wright, "Mission and Theological Interpretation," in *A Manifesto for Theological Interpretation*, ed. Craig G.

In his essay, "Mission as a Matrix for Hermeneutics and Biblical Theology" (2004), he describes missional hermeneutics in relation to other existing interpretive models: "biblical foundations for mission," "multicultural hermeneutical perspectives," and "advocacy readings and postmodern hermeneutics."[49] First, the effort to build a scriptural basis for mission is fulfilled by developing an exhaustive catalogue of biblical texts, those providing a legitimate basis for mission (e.g., Matt 28:18–20). It could also be called the "biblical apologetics for mission"[50] because the primary goal is to defend Christian mission based on the scriptural foundation. Hence, the approach inherently suffers with "suspicion of circularity."[51]

Second, the multiplicity of cultures is a reality that cannot be ignored in interpretation as it gives birth to multiple ways of looking at biblical texts. Nevertheless, the "plurality of interpretation" must not be misconstrued as "a hermeneutical ideology" nor "a relative charter."[52] The desired coherence in interpretation in a pluralistic context, according to Wright, comes through from the whole Bible by a bifocal reading approach: "messianic reading" and "missional reading." He illustrates his hermeneutical proposal as authentic based on Jesus' interpretation in Luke 24.[53] For him, the *messianic reading* supplies "the hermeneutical matrix for our reading of the whole Bible," while the *missional reading* includes four vital areas of critical exploration: (i) "the purpose for which the Bible exists," (ii) "the God the Bible renders to us," (iii) "the people whose identity and mission the Bible invites us to share," and (iv) "the story the Bible tells about this God and this people and indeed about the whole world and its future."[54]

Third, converging and diverging, simultaneously, from varied advocacy and postmodernistic readings, the missional reading recognizes the liberative thrust of the biblical narrative for itself (saying, not all missionaries are agents of colonialism) and for others from oppression. It does not deny the Bible as "*the* story," while celebrating "localness," diversity,

---

Bartholomew and Heath A. Thomas (Grand Rapids, MI: Baker Academic, 2016), 174, 189; Wright, *Mission of God*, 22.

49 Christopher J. H. Wright, "Mission as a Matrix for Hermeneutics and Biblical Theology," in *Out of Egypt: Biblical Theology and Biblical Interpretation*, ed. Craig G. Bartholomew et al., *Scripture and Hermeneutics Series* (Milton Keynes: Paternoster Press, 2004), 109–20. The subsequent in-text references mentioned within parenthesis concerning Wright's proposal are from this source. The same is re-published with little modification in Wright, *Mission of God*, 33–47.

50 Wright, "Mission as a Matrix," 109.

51 Wright, "Mission as a Matrix," 112.

52 Wright, *Mission of God*, 40.

53 Wright, "Mission as a Matrix," 115.

54 Wright, *Mission of God*, 31.

and cultural plurality, both within the canon and in the present context of interpretation.[55]

If so, the vital hermeneutical question to ask would be: How can the Bible be interpreted in the matrix of mission? Goheen and Wright, justifying missional interpretation, argue that mission is "thematically central to and historically generative of the scriptural text."[56] The mission of God lies central to the whole biblical account that cannot be overlooked in our interpretation. Such a mission-focused interpretive approach offers a corrective to the mistaken non-missional dogmatic reading practice of the Enlightenment. The reason is obvious; the role of the Bible is understood as "a *mean of missional grace*" because the canon does not just bless God's people, but it also extends the "salvation to God's people *for the sake of the world*."[57] Goheen maintains that the Bible as one story defines our true missional identity and role as participants in God's mission to redeem fallen humanity.[58] The Scripture as a whole, the Old Testament and New Testament, is a means to save, fashion, and enable the people of God to reach out to the rest of God's creation as part of God's continued salvific mission.[59] Our failure to recognize this significant role of the Bible will not only deprive us of adequate understanding of the nature, origin, and authority of the Bible over us, but it will also blind us from a proper self-understanding in God's perspective, gaining broader vision to live as God's partners in the world, and fulfilling God's ultimate purpose in and through us today . Thereby, the theological reading of the Bible with mission at its center will be lost.

How do the Bible, its nature, and authority relate to the mission of God? Wright and Goheen explain them differently. For Goheen, the authority lies in the "formative role" of the Bible to powerfully shape the community of God's people and extends the "healing to the world."[60] He states that it is not the equipping of people to go out to preach the gospel, but "the vocation of God's people is to be a distinctive people for the sake of the world. God works first of all *in* his people and only thereafter *through* his people, for the sake of the nations."[61] Wright, a biblical scholar with missiological leniency in interpreting the Bible, argues that

---

55 Wright, "Mission as a Matrix," 115–20 (emphasis original).

56 Goheen and Wright, "Mission and Theological Interpretation," 172.

57 Goheen and Wright, "Mission and Theological Interpretation," 190 (emphasis original).

58 Goheen, "Bible as One Story," 475.

59 Goheen and Wright, "Mission and Theological Interpretation," 189–92.

60 Goheen, "Missional Reading of the Bible," 25; Michael W. Goheen, "A Missional Reading of Scripture and Preaching," in *Reading the Bible Missionally*, ed. Michael W. Goheen (Grand Rapids, MI: William B. Eerdmans Publishing, 2016), 243.

61 Goheen, "Missional Reading of the Bible," 26 (emphasis original).

the authority of the Bible is based on its missional context of origin. If "mission is what the Bible is all about,"[62] the Bible is a witness to God's dealing with the whole of creation including fallen humanity. However, it originated within the context of struggles, both internal and external, of God's people to live among others. While the elect community of God struggled to comprehend God's revelatory act, the confession of God's revelation in the world faced challenges from other conflicting and competing religio-cultural claims. Hence, the biblical narrative itself is a missional narrative, "a product of mission in action."[63] Such an understanding of the Bible is relevant to our reading of Paul's letters to the Thessalonians written in the middle of the first century C.E. Later, we will discuss the pluralistic social and religious contexts and the crisscrossing of conflicting discourses in Thessalonica. Those contexts and conflicting traditions must have directly or indirectly determined the content of the apostle's letter that shaped and equipped the Thessalonian community to participate in God's continuing universal mission. We would seek to understand the missional thrust of the "contingency"[64] of Paul's letter contributing to narrate a story of God's continuous activity in the world in and through the new converts in Thessalonica.

In this respect, the grand biblical story authorizes our participation in the mission of God, not just the mission imperatives scattered in the Bible. Unlike few mission commands, the Bible is a collection of seemingly non-missional stories that "authorize our action in mission. They make our mission appropriate, legitimate, and indeed necessary and inevitable. The authority for our mission flows from the Bible because the Bible reveals the reality on which our mission is based."[65] The realities Wright mentions are: (i) the identity of God as the biblical God, (ii) the story of the beginning of human history at creation via the great fall of humanity leading to the point of the new creation in Christ, and (iii) the story of his people sharing and replicating God's character and identity (e.g., holiness) to the nations.[66] Hence, "biblical *imperatives* are characteristically founded on biblical *indicatives,*" thereby, "the Bible effectively grounds their authority (i.e., the mission imperatives) in that reality."[67] In other words, in missional hermeneutics, the mission imperatives in Scripture and biblical indicatives help reading one in the light of the other. They lead to a radical shift of understanding from an anthropocentric to a theocentric (*missio*

62 Wright, *Mission of God*, 29.

63 Wright, "Mission as a Matrix," 121.

64 J. Christiaan Beker, *Paul the Apostle: The Triumph of God in Life and Thought* (Philadelphia, PA: Fortress Press, 1980), 11–12.

65 Wright, "Mission as a Matrix," 125.

66 Wright, "Mission as a Matrix," 125–29.

67 Wright, "Mission as a Matrix," 129 (emphasis original and parenthesis added).

Dei) understanding of mission in which we human beings are graciously invited to participate with God. In missional hermeneutics, the theocentric understanding of mission provides the fundamental interpretive assumption with which the entire Scripture must be read today.

A possible critique of this stream is evident in the postmodern suspicion of all types of metanarratives. A postmodern critic celebrating mini-biblical narratives for liberation would reject the mission of God as an oppressive and homogenizing metanarrative. Goheen rejects such a generalized critique of biblical metanarrative by giving two main reasons: (i) Unlike other metanarratives subtly furthering their agenda of victory and domination in the intra-historical period, the biblical metanarrative envisions the final victory at the end of history. The pursuit of the final victory at the return of the Messiah is accomplished only through the nonconformist self-sacrificial mission modelled after the self-giving death of Jesus. It consciously refuses "to be co-opted into the death-dealing powers of the dominant story."[68] (ii) In its journey from the Jewish capital, Jerusalem, to the imperial capital, Rome, and finally to the ends of the earth, the gospel has not annihilated the cultural diversity, but it has celebrated "the splendor and treasures in all local stories" by refining and purifying.[69] Bauckham rejects the postmodern objection against the metanarrative based on the content of preaching about God's narrative identity known through the history of Israel and Jesus. In a context of the global contest for truth among the idols of tyranny, the content of missional metanarrative is solely the cross of Christ in and through which God intervenes in person in human history. Such a divine act of self-identification for universal salvation is "not with humanity in its self-aggrandizement, but with humanity in its degradation, humanity victimized by the human will to power."[70] Thereby, the content of witness and the mission of the church is replicating the cross here and now today amidst the human quest for domination and self-aggrandizement. Moreover, the "corrosive cynicism" of postmodernism must realize in the light of the cross that "the will to power is not the ultimate reality of things," but it is "the true God" we know through the cross "who is different."[71]

1.4.2. Knowing the original purpose of the books: A key to missional interpretation

The prime proponent of the second trend is Darrell L. Guder. Hansberger mentions this trend as "the missional purpose of the writings," because

68 Goheen, "Bible as One Story," 481–82, cited from 482.

69 Goheen, "Bible as One Story," 482.

70 Bauckham, "Mission as Hermeneutic," 38–39, cited from 39.

71 Bauckham, "Mission as Hermeneutic," 40.

unlike the first trend it is concerned with the "character of the biblical literature itself" and is primarily concerned with the "purpose and aim of the biblical writings, and the canonical authority by virtue of their formative effect."[72] Guder maintains that the missional hermeneutic is to interpret Scripture based on the apostolic strategy of forming a missional communities. The New Testament as a document performs the task of forming a missional community, both in its original context and today in the modern times, by "affirmation, correction, encouragement, and always continuing evangelization and edification. We, therefore, need to read and respond to Scriptures in the same way."[73] For example, the apostles like Paul wrote letters to various local Christian congregations in order to continue the formation of witnessing communities to further the apostolic task. The gospel narratives perform this task of community formation by narrating the earthly ministry of Jesus inviting people to "follow him" in order to become the apostles. He states, "the actual task of these Scriptures, then, was to deal with the problems and the conflicts, the challenges and the doubts as they emerged in particular contexts, so that these communities could be faithful to their calling."[74] In other words, "the epistles' authors, through their writings, were continuing the formation of the congregations they had founded. The purpose of that founding was to continue the apostolic mission ignited at Pentecost, which often entailed cross-cultural translation and the forming of new expressions of apostolic mission communities."[75]

The key hermeneutical question raised is, "How did this particular text continue the formation of witnessing communities then, and how does it do that today?" The secret to translate the missional faithfulness known in the biblical accounts is to recognize the vitality of context in biblical narratives. Knowing how the biblical writers undertook the task to equip the early Christian communities to live as witnessing communities teaches us to learn together as a community to live worthy of the gospel (Phil 1:27). Guder calls it a witnessing community's continuing act of "interpretive translation with missional connectedness." He explains this interconnectedness between the two by defining the "interpretive translation" as:

> The gospel is constantly being interpreted into and for a particular context. In that process, however, it is the same gospel, the continuation of

---

72 Hunsberger, "Missional Hermeneutic," 313.

73 Darrell L. Guder, "Missional Theology for a Missionary Church," *Journal for Preachers* 22, no. 1 (1998): 6.

74 Guder, *Called to Witness*, 90–92, cited from 91.

75 Darrell L. Guder, "The Implication of a Missional Hermeneutic for Theological Education," in *Reading the Bible Missionally*, ed. Michael W. Goheen, The Gospel and Our Culture Series (Grand Rapids, MI: William B. Eerdmans Publishing, 2016), 286.

> the same story, the good news that connects every community to each other. In this nexus of interpretive translation and missional connectedness, we see in particular situations how the universal, multicultural, multi-organizational, multilingual church continues to carry out its apostolic strategy to be Christ's witnesses.[76]

Hence, Scripture is read with a total commitment to positively highlight its authoritative function over our lives in encountering Christ through the written letters. The Holy Spirit enables us to respond in obedience, the Spirit "enabled obedience," to the written testimony and continue witnessing both by being discipled ourselves and discipling others.[77] In fact, elsewhere as he states, the authority of Scripture is recognized not in "a set of prepositions" but "in the way the Spirit works through them to continue the apostolic mission through the formation of witnessing communities." The written testimony equips the communities to bear witness for Christ in the world.[78] The other aspect of this positive commitment to the authority of Scripture in witnessing community formation is also to oppose every other scriptural reading approach that dilutes the importance of bearing witness to the divine self-revelation.[79] For Guder, the Western individualistic understanding of salvation, which is reductionist in its very nature, obstructs the building of a missional community and the reading and hearing of the Bible in a communal context. In other words, Christian salvation of an individual is not a static event but an ongoing process, for there exists a continuity from the individual's conversion to the formation of a witnessing community.[80]

Guder contends that the challenge is to recognize that there is a biblical emphasis upon the followers of Christ, the church, to carry on the public witness. In Pauline letters, the burden upon Christians to bear public witness is primarily taught to fulfill by learning to live a life worthy of the gospel of Christ (e.g., Phil 1:27). In other words, their personal transformation, according to God's absolute will is thoroughly missional, which they must practically live out before others. The gospel of God's love for the whole world must be preached in action by living in love.

Thus, "the primary task of a missional hermeneutic then is to provide a particular congregation the formation it needs to be able to live out both its gathered life and its scattered life faithfully."[81] The reason is that "the theme 'vocation'" is the "defining centre" of the biblical teaching on

---

76 Guder, *Called to Witness*, 92.

77 Guder, *Called to Witness*, 101–3, cited from 102.

78 Guder, "Implication of a Missional Hermeneutic," 286.

79 Guder, *Called to Witness*, 91–92.

80 Guder, *Called to Witness*, 107–11; Guder, "Missional Theology," 7.

81 Guder, *Called to Witness*, 113–17, cited from 116.

ecclesia in which we are saved only to save others.[82] This task is possible only by a determined daily effort enabled by the Spirit to walk worthy of the gospel. In no way is it a perfected community but a community in and through which God is at work to complete the pilgrimage. Similar to Brownson for whom "the gospel" as the matrix of interpretation effects coherence amidst a diversity of experiences, Guder maintains that learning to "walk worthy" brings congruence between their preaching and practice.[83]

1.4.3. Reading from the reader's location: The hermeneutical lens

Unlike Guder's contention to read the Bible in the light of the original missional purpose of the author, the third trend in missional hermeneutics seeks to read the Bible from the other end of the interpretive spectrum, that is, from the social location of the readers called out to function as a missional community of God. A missional community's "sent-ness" in its social location is an absolute necessity for missional hermeneutics.[84] The fundamental question asked by the community of faithful requiring missional hermeneutics is: "How do we read the Bible faithfully today?"[85] It "privileges the missiological 'location' of the Christian community in the world as a hermeneutical key."[86] Hansberger terms this trend led by Michael Barram as "the missional locatedness of the readers."[87]

Justifying his proposal to practice missional hermeneutics faithfully, Barram contends that right in the first century Paul already practiced it correcting those in Corinth who wrongly construed the implication of the gospel in wisdom, knowledge, power, and freedom. Paul in 1 and 2 Corinthians deconstructs "an inadequate Corinthian hermeneutic" based on foolishness, slavery, weakness, and love founded upon the cross in order to give "strong correctives designed to foster in them a faithful missional identity and conduct."[88] Paul employs counterintuitive metaphors based on the cross to rectify the mistaken non-missional and counter-productive implications of the gospel by the Corinthians with the sole aim "to give rise to inherently missional hermeneutics, rooted in and faithful to the *mission Dei* in specific, located contexts."[89]

---

82 Guder, *Called to Witness*, 130.

83 Guder, *Called to Witness*, 125–39.

84 Michael D. Barram, "'Occupying' Genesis 1–3: Missionally Located Reflections on Biblical Values and Economic Justice," *Missiology* 42, no. 4 (2014): 386–87.

85 Barram, "Bible, Mission, and Social Location," 42.

86 Barram, "Bible, Mission, and Social Location," 43.

87 Hunsberger, "Missional Hermeneutic," 314.

88 Barram, "'Fools for the Sake of Christ,'" 196–198, cited from 197.

89 Barram, "'Fools for the Sake of Christ,'" 205.

Barram argues that "a missional hermeneutic should not be characterized primarily by methodology per se" but by "asking missional questions—fundamentally, questions about purpose—God's and ours."[90] In fact, "a missional hermeneutic will appropriate any and all methods that help to clarify the purposes of God and vocation of God's people" who are brought into the mission of God.[91] Barram maintains that asking missional questions of the purpose of God and ours must "form the context of our questions...articulated in the broadest and least restrictive sense possible," and is vital for missional hermeneutics.[92] Then, the hermeneutical questions from readers' location are essentially missional questions. To the core, such questions not only arise from the specific context of the readers but they also have vital implications to their life and mission because they defy the local social conditioning that forces us to neglect them otherwise. "In that sense, the social location of the people of God is at the very heart of a missional hermeneutic" for they enable us "to read the Bible more faithfully today."[93] In the words of Barram:

> A missional hermeneutic should be understood as an approach to Scripture that self-consciously, intentionally, and persistently bring[s] to the biblical text a range of focused, critical, and located questions regarding church's purpose in order to discern the faith community's calling and task within the *mission [sic] Dei*. Such questions will be inherently contextual—rooted in the fundamental conviction that we read the biblical text as those who have been drawn into the larger purpose of God.[94]

In his book, *Mission and Moral Reflection in Paul*, Barram brings both the missiological and biblical scholarship on a common board dialoguing with each other in order to demonstrate the close missional implications of Paul's moral exhortations. His primary contention is that the letters of Paul "serve a missional function for the apostle,"[95] because "Paul's understanding of his mission provides the texture and context for his instruction."[96] It proves that for Paul mission is much broader than the narrow modern view of mission as merely evangelism and church planting. It involves nurturing Christian communities (also by his ethical instructions) "constitutive of his missional vocation as are initial evangelism

---

90 Michael D. Barram, "'Located' Questions for a Missional Hermeneutic: The Gospel and Our Culture Network," 2006, accessed June 1, 2020, https://gocn.org/library/95/.

91 Barram, "'Located' Questions."

92 Barram, "'Located' Questions."

93 Barram, "'Located' Questions."

94 Barram, "'Located' Questions." Cf. Barram, "Bible, Mission, and Social Location," 58.

95 Michael D. Barram, *Mission and Moral Reflection in Paul*, Studies in Biblical Literature vol. 75 (Frankfurt am Main: Peter Lang, 2006), 135.

96 Barram, *Mission and Moral Reflection in Paul*, 148.

and community formation. So defined, Paul's 'mission' can function as a principal rubric for interpreting everything that he writes, thinks, and does."[97] In short, Barram states that "he exhorts his communities in such a way that he may fulfill his own mission ('in order that all people may be saved' [e.g., 1 Cor 9:19–23; 10:32–33])."[98] Thus, when Paul exhorts to encourage by modelling or exhortation a behavior of choice, the underlying motivation is to bring salvation to all. They enable Paul to accomplish his missional vocation because, for Paul, Christian behavior in a social context is evangelistic in function. Hence, on one hand, inappropriate behavior could damage the cause of mission; on the other hand, appropriate Christian conduct can further Christian witness.[99]

So, the biblical text must be approached with missiological questions that originate from the locatedness of the missional community caught up and involved in the mission of God here and now. The sharp missional questions are dialogical by their nature; in a sense, they interrogate the text and our interpretation of them. In other words, the interest lies not just in reading a text by asking missional questions from one's specific context but also how the text interprets its reader at a given time is vital in the formation of questions of interpretation. For example, one of the many possible questions that Barram asks is: "Does our reading of this text acknowledge and confess our complicity and culpability in personal as well as structural sin?"[100] Note that the missional question is bifocal; it grants freedom to raise questions unique to the reader's context to interpret a text, and it also requires a reader to be open to the reverse interpretation from the side of the text of the reader's intent and act.

1.4.4. Gospel in conversation with culture: A critical hermeneutical engagement

The fourth stream is termed as "the missional engagement with cultures" by Hunsberger, because in it "the gospel functions as the interpretive matrix within which the received biblical tradition is brought into critical conversation with a particular human context."[101] Reconstructing missional hermeneutics within a pluralistic context, James W. Brownson concedes the inevitability of diversity in interpretation and the necessity of having a hermeneutic of coherence based on the gospel as a new matrix of missional interpretation. For him, the diversity of interpretation is not an evidence of flawed hermeneutical engagement. Instead, it is "the sign

97 Barram, *Mission and Moral Reflection in Paul*, 1-10, cited from 10 (parenthesis added).

98 Barram, *Mission and Moral Reflection in Paul*, 148.

99 Barram, *Mission and Moral Reflection in Paul*, 149–73.

100 Barram, "'Located' Questions."

101 Hunsberger, "Missional Hermeneutic," 316.

of an unfinished task" of interpretation that the early Christian canonical writers did with their hermeneutical biases relating the text and context that the modern interpreters too must do likewise.[102] He draws the legitimacy of such an approach by locating the primacy of the close relationship between early Christianity and pluralistic cultural contexts as a fertile ground of beginning scriptural interpretation.[103]

Brownson's proposed missional hermeneutics celebrates the diversity of interpretation, but he suggests a need for commitment to dialogue with other biblical readers in order to correct the possible defective idiosyncratic interpretations that do not "connect with our common humanity," that is, a "cultural construct" arising out of "interaction of different cultural perspectives."[104] In other words, the diversity of interpretation is healthy when it is born out of human diversity without distorting "our common text" and connecting "with our common humanity."[105]

For Brownson, biblically, at the heart of the method lies the dialectic between cultural specificities of any biblical event or character and the universal scope of the narrative uniquely in both the Testaments (e.g., Gen 12:2–3; Isa 2:2–4; Matt 8:10–11 cf. 15:24). Theologically, it notices God's presence in every culture as no culture exhausts God's revelation. In other words, though one God, one salvation story, and one scripture are assumed, it does not subscribe to a monoculture and monoreligious perspective. Hence, it sees the availability of God's grace and mercy to all, while appreciating God's glory among all people, cultures, and nations. Salvation is made available to all in a multicultural context both by affirming the local cultures and calling them to repentance by critiquing them.[106] He says,

> It also involves a heightened sense of connectedness to other diverse cultural settings where praise is also given to God. The Christian experience of salvation not only purifies and enriches one's distinctive cultural identity; it also deepens the awareness that one participates with all of humanity in a multicultural worship of God that transcends any particular context. Hence, *the Christian experience of salvation creates a dual*

[102] James V. Brownson, "Speaking the Truth in Love: Elements of a Missional Hermeneutic," *International Review of Mission* 83, no. 330 (1994): 481–83, cited from 481. An enlarged version of it has been published later in 1998. See James V. Brownson, *Speaking the Truth in Love: New Testament Resources for a Missional Hermeneutic*, Christian Mission and Modern Culture (Harrisburg, PA: Trinity Press International, 1998).

[103] Brownson, "Speaking the Truth," 482.

[104] Brownson, "Speaking the Truth," 483.

[105] Brownson, "Speaking the Truth," 483.

[106] Brownson, "Speaking the Truth," 484–87. Brownson maintains that the call to repentance is not annihilation of a local culture but sanctification of it to evoke greater praise to God.

> *identity*: on the one hand, I am a member of a particular community that offers its own distinctive praise of God, and on the other hand, I am a member of a diverse human community that offers a much more powerful, indeed astonishing, array of voices, singing a form of doxology that radically transcends my own distinctive voice.[107]

For him, the strength and uniqueness of the missional reading are found precisely in the interaction between the local and the multilayered communal belongingness of oneself that evokes praises to God. Explaining the complex interplay between the twine-forked Christian identities, Brownson employs the image of a choir. He says that in such a hermeneutical engagement, each missional interpreter is invited to lend one's own unique and valuable voice into the group that nourishes the polyphonic witness.[108]

In this context, affirming the necessity for a balance between the centrifugal and centripetal movement in interpretation and seeking a coherence founded on the Bible is crucial for an efficient hermeneutical model. Such an effort to balance the diversity of cultural experiences in the f irst-century Christianity is visible in the essence of the gospel preserved by every canonical author.[109] For us to find coherence amidst diversity, there needs to be a "dialectic between exegesis and hermeneutics," which means to search for "recurring motifs and themes, common structures, patterns of narratives, lines of development, 'trajectories' and the like" exegetically without ceasing to be self-critical toward one's own conceptualization of faith and practice in the light of the discovered coherence.[110] To this end, for Brownson, the gospel itself is "the hermeneutical perspective or matrix through which the Christian tradition and specific historical contexts are *interpreted*,"[111] where in doing so the three elements of interaction—the literary context, the Jewish and Christian traditions, and the particular historical context of an author forming the interpretive matrix—must be analyzed.[112] To answer how the gospel forms a hermeneutical framework, it is argued that one must recognize three basic features: (i) the demand to accept and appropriate the soteriological significance of Jesus effecting life transformation (i.e., the locutionary and illocutionary aspect of the gospel), (ii) the invariable implicit universality of the gospel, and (iii) the death and resurrection event of Christ shaping the whole tradition with a

---

107 Brownson, "Speaking the Truth," 487 (emphasis added).

108 Brownson, "Speaking the Truth," 487.

109 Brownson, "Speaking the Truth," 488–90.

110 Brownson, "Speaking the Truth," 490.

111 Brownson, "Speaking the Truth," 499.

112 Brownson, "Speaking the Truth," 495.

vivid understanding of how God is at work in making his claim over the world.[113]

Thus, the four principal questions guiding our missional reading of the Bible are:

1. What is the specific situation that prompts this writing and to which is it addressed?
2. How are the Jewish and Christian traditions being brought to bear in this specific situation?
3. What are the literary dynamics and contexts that lend shape to this coalescence of tradition and situation?
4. What are the hermeneutical assumptions that guide this bringing together of tradition and situation in literary form, and how are these assumptions related to basic Christian affirmations about the center of the gospel?[114]

The most important strength of the model is that it allows us to hear the uniqueness of the missional thrust of each of the biblical author while appreciating the universal significance of the gospel. It renders greater freedom to appropriate the gospel in different cultural contexts, even today, while remaining essentially coherent to the transcultural missional context. Thus, similar to Wright and Goheen's refutation of postmodern critique, Brownson claims that the missional interpretation speaks in the language of truth in love without a desire to dominate. It allows discovering "its true voice and its own distinctive experience of full humanity as the gospel takes root in fresh and diverse ways."[115]

A fine example of illustrating the interaction of Scripture, culture-historical context, and mission in the hermeneutical engagement of Paul is found in the PhD dissertation of J. Ross Wagner. Wagner maintains that in his letter to the Romans, Paul interplays all the three shaping and reshaping each other constantly in his "ongoing struggle to make sense of God's design for Israel and to faithfully fulfill his own divinely-ordained role in the outworking of that plan."[116] Thus, the key questions Wagner seeks to answer are:

> First, how did Paul, as an ancient reader, approach the book of Isaiah. In what form (or forms) did he encounter the book? What were the interpretive assumptions and techniques with which he read and appropriated

[113] Brownson, "Speaking the Truth," 499–502.

[114] Brownson, "Speaking the Truth," 502.

[115] Brownson, "Speaking the Truth," 503.

[116] J. Ross Wagner, *Heralds of the Good News: Isaiah and Paul in Concert in the Letter to the Romans* (Boston, MA: Brill, 2003), 1.

> the prophet's words? Second, how did Paul's understanding of the gospel and of his own particular calling as an apostle shape his reading of Isiah, and, conversely, how did Isaiah's oracles help to form Paul's conception of his own message and mission? Finally, how does this interplay of scripture, theology, and mission come to expression in the particular argument of the letter to the Romans, and to what extent can attention to these questions enrich a reading of the letter?[117]

When Paul wrote the letter to the churches in Rome, the issue of God's faithfulness to the Jews, in general, their rejection of the Messiah, and their final destiny in the light of an increasing number of gentiles joining the eschatological community of God, appeared to be a critical theological riddle. His reflection on his mission by reading the Isaianic text in the particular cultural and historical context insures to him that it is a script written by God. He believed that Isaiah, like his fellow preacher, spoke "concerning his own (Paul's) role in the eschatological restoration of Israel."[118] It becomes evident to us as we unravel how Paul carefully quoted and alluded to the words of Isaiah while speaking about his mission to the gentiles. In Romans 9–11, Paul read Isaiah within his cultural and historical context and believed that the hope of Israel for deliverance is realized in Christ. However, the gentiles are also incorporated in it. In fact, for Paul, the gentiles have a prominent role in the formation of the community of God that puts Israel's salvation in two stages: in the present a remnant of Israel believes in Christ, but finally the incorporation of the gentiles will make Israel jealous and cause them to return to YHWH by believing in Christ. As a result, "Paul finds himself playing a pivotal role in this drama of cosmic redemption: he is not only a herald bearing the message of redemption to the gentiles, but also a chosen instrument through whom God will provoke his own people to jealousy and to effect their salvation."[119]

1.5. Missional hermeneutics: A reader-oriented interpretive strategy?

Is missional hermeneutics (including the one proposed by Brownson) just another reader-oriented interpretive strategy similar to several other advocacy reading strategies currently in circulation among several biblical scholars? The answer is a firm "No" with a qualification added to it. Our discussion on the current competing trends in missional hermeneutics makes us consider the term *missional hermeneutics* as an umbrella term that reflects a seemingly mixed character of both reader-oriented and

---

117 Wagner, *Heralds of the Good News*, 2–3.
118 Wagner, *Heralds of the Good News*, 33.
119 Wagner, *Heralds of the Good News*, 353–59, cited from 359.

author-intention-oriented interpretive approaches. My impression is that it is primarily the latter due to unanimity among scholars on mission as a central theme of the Bible, but it also inherits subjectivity through the preferential choice of an interpreter to choose mission as the theological lens to read Scripture out of self-conscious missional ecclesiology.

In the last quarter of the nineteenth century, biblical studies witnessed the rise of a host of identity-oriented advocacy reading practices (like feminist, dalit, and tribal hermeneutics). They were received by many in biblical studies with wide open arms because of their ability to translate the significance of the ancient biblical narratives for modern readers' day-to-day experiences in the world. They approached the Bible with existential concerns born outside of the text for varied reasons such as, to recover the liberative insights embedded in them. The goal is to articulate a biblical response to those concerns that are real to a reader here and now. They either unravel the cultural bias embedded within the text justifying the oppressive socio-cultural and religiopolitical systems or use the Bible to speak prophetically against the dark social structural realities confronted by the people of God in the world. At times such approaches have questioned the authority of the Bible over us by turning it merely into a literary product of a particular culture.

In missional interpretation, Wright, Goheen, Guder, and others, focus on the nature and role of the Bible as a tool in forming and fashioning the community of God, whereas Barram and Brownson call for reading the Bible with contextually loaded questions about the purpose of God and the cultural location of a reader. The former group of scholars identify mission as the biblical metanarrative that arguably sets the framework for biblical interpretation, while the latter like Brownson celebrate the diversity of interpretations. In the former group, both the Old and the New Testaments are viewed theologically as one continuous story of God's mission, which warrants a missional reading. All other important theological themes are brought under the grand missional narrative of Scripture. It reduces the possibility of looking at the Bible through a single window called mission. Hence, despite strongly arguing for missional metanarrative of the Bible, Bauckham states: "Of course, such a missionary hermeneutic could and should be *only one way of reading Scripture* among others, since mission itself is not the comprehensive subject of the whole Bible."[120]

Missional hermeneutics approaches the Bible to understand its meaning, purpose, and role of the church in the world. It does not claim that *the* interpretive approach is capable of providing the scientific and objective

120 Bauckham, "Mission as Hermeneutic for Scriptural Interpretation," 28 (emphasis added).

biblical truth with universal validity. Craig Bartholomew is right in maintaining that the missional hermeneutic is "a subset of a theological hermeneutic" because mission originates from the Triune God and Scripture encompasses much more than mere missional motif that is subject to a broader theological discussion.[121] However, Goheen and Wright frankly concede its limitation by saying that "it is *not the only lens* we employ to read the entire canon of Scripture since mission does not constitute the comprehensive subject matter of the biblical narrative."[122] In short, unlike currently trending postmodern advocacy readings, missional hermeneutics depends on a biblically-based lens for interpretation along with the church's missional self-consciousness. It equips the hermeneutical exercise with a strong antidote to radical subjectivity imposed from outside the text, as promoted in recent postmodern readings of the Bible. It begins with a frank recognition that it is a purposeful prioritization of one theological theme over others found in Scripture because of a fresh understanding of the nature, function, and role of Scripture. In short, the choice to read the Scripture is based on missional self-consciousness authenticated by the biblical metanarrative, mission.

As a subset of theological hermeneutics, missional hermeneutics acknowledges the authority of the Bible to define, control, and direct the missional role of the community of God. Missional hermeneutics recognizes that the unfolding of the incomplete story of the ever expanding universal church in the present not only begins in the Bible but it "anticipates the literal fulfillment of hope of universal salvation" in future.[123] In this grand narrative of ever-widening spiral from the particular to the universal salvation story, "the church of the post-biblical time until the present [not only] begins to read Scripture in the light of her identity and mission as defined in them"[124] but, in addition, it also factors in the need of the cultural context of the reader for a faithful reading of the Bible. It lends the church a "missional-theological lens" that helps in reading the Scripture with a prior commitment of submission to its authority and reverence to it as the word of God that is given with a specific purpose and role to shape her effective participation in God's holistic universal mission.[125] Hence, a missional lens with theological interest can be understood only by a fine balance between the missional nature of the Bible and the

121 Craig G. Bartholomew, "Theological Interpretation and a Missional Hermeneutic," in *Reading the Bible Missionally*, ed. Michael W. Goheen (Grand Rapids, MI: William B. Eerdmans Publishing, 2016), 80.

122 Goheen and Wright, "Mission and Theological Interpretation," 15 (emphasis added).

123 Bauckham, "Mission as Hermeneutic," 34.

124 Bauckham, "Mission as Hermeneutic," 34 (parenthesis added).

125 Bauckham, "Mission as Hermeneutic," 34.

questions of the church's missional existence in the twenty-first century. In short, missional hermeneutical exercise constantly oscillates between the biblically founded missional-theological lens and the cultural locatedness of the reader's community to read the Bible faithfully and effectively today. In fact, its inherent ability to balance between the core theological theme of the Bible and the living experience of the church makes it theologically authentic, and contextually and missonally relevant.

1.6. Reading the Thessalonian correspondence missionally

As our discussion on the trends in missional hermeneutics makes clear that scholars practice missional hermeneutics with vast difference despite the current broad consensus among them to interpret the Bible through a missional lens. It proves that missional hermeneutics exists without any one particular interpretive strategy. Hunsberger succinctly states, "none of these is sufficient on its own to provide a robust hermeneutic."[126] If so, it is inevitable for me to explain the method of study undertaken in this book.

I intend to employ a broad combination of the four major emphases currently argued as vital in biblical interpretation. There is no dispute that mission is a pivotal metanarrative that holds together several other vital theological motifs like salvation, eschatology, and so on. When we seek to read Paul's Letter to the Thessalonians through a missional lens, it doesn't downplay the importance of eschatology found in the letter. However, the vital questions asked are:

1. What is the significance of Paul's Thessalonian correspondence within the grand interpretive framework of *missio Dei* in the Bible?
2. Did Paul have a missional purpose in sending the Letter(s)? If yes, how does it apply to us today?
3. Does the apostolic correspondence form, nurture, and guard the community, according to God's ultimate purpose, as they lived in a hostile environment?
4. How does his apostolic mission to form a missional community of God in Thessalonica get fulfilled through the letter(s)? How are they included to continue the universal mission of God in their own context?

126 Hunsberger, "Missional Hermeneutic," 310.

5. How does the gospel—built on hermeneutical assumptions creating a blend of traditions and situation in the letter(s)—correspond to the specific sociopolitical and cultural situation of the readers?

Answering these questions through the study to a satisfactory end requires us to appreciate a dynamic relation between the author, text, and context. Neither of them is to be viewed as an absolute in the process of meaning-making. Instead, each one is determined by the other two realities. First, Paul, as the author, is not independent of Scripture, the text. The text has always fashioned his self-consciousness, character, and meaning of life. Living as a Pharisee, Paul fulfilled the requirements of the Jewish laws head and shoulders above his contemporaries. He did recognize its importance in defining himself and the purpose of his life under Judaism. However, in the post-conversion context, Paul reread the Old Testament through the christological lens to understand his own calling on the road to Damascus, the missional responsibility laid upon him by election, and the renewed knowledge of God's universal purpose of unifying the whole humanity "in Christ" to share in the blessings promised through Abraham. Such self-understanding made it inevitable for Paul to become a preacher of the gospel to the gentiles. Second, Paul's experience of Christ on the road of Damascus compelled him to read the text quite differently from how he read it earlier. His experience of Christ radically transformed his vision of Scripture. Earlier his vision of Scripture was colored by an ethnocentric reading lens that forced him to understand the mission of God in its narrowest form. However, he could do so no more after encountering Christ. As a result, his letters are born out of his firm self-consciousness as the one co-opted by God into the *missio Dei* to fulfill the Abrahamic promise to bless the nations. In other words, Paul's letters are born out of his mission and are vital instruments in fulfilling the missional mandate upon him.

Finally, Paul, the apostle, was conscious of the cultural realities, his own and his readers'. Hence, Paul articulated his words and missional practices in tandem with the sociopolitical and religio-cultural dynamic of the Greco-Roman cities, like Thessalonica, that he visited. He relied upon the Old Testament narrative and viewed the divine story unravelling in and through Jesus Christ as an extension of God's promise to bless the nations. He did view the church as the agency of God in accomplishing his eternal plan in this eschatological time. However, it was not without recognizing the significance of the specific cultural context and traditions of his readers that he could explain his mind contextually. For example, on the one hand, in emphasizing his extreme disapproval of the Galatian opponents' law-observing mission among the gentile Galatians, Paul in 5:12 alludes to the popular cultic practice of the Cybele cult in the region to parallel the worthlessness of the necessity of circumcision preached by some in the churches.[127] The missional dimension of Paul's allusion to such negative cultural parallel in order to disapprove certain actions is that he wants to correct either a potential or prevailing threat to their right missional formation in Christ. On the other hand, Paul employed Hellenistic rhetorical, philosophical, and ethical traditions apart from imageries from athletics, slave market, and daily household practices to educate, fashion, and establish a culturally rooted native community of disciples in line with God's ultimate purpose for them.

If so, a missional reading of 1 and 2 Thessalonians requires a satisfactory exploration and reconstruction of the sociocultural context of the community of God in Thessalonica. A clear understanding of the sociocultural, economic, religious, and political context of the believers would enhance our understanding of the immediate context that necessitated a letter(s) from him. It will in turn also highlight the missional purpose of the sender and how he intends to fine tune his readers' self-understanding in the light of the eternal salvific plan of God, known in the Jewish scriptures, to nurture a community of participants in the mission of God.

To sum up, a relatively new trend in biblical interpretation called missional hermeneutics draws to the center, as never before, the question of mission as the key factor in biblical interpretation. It seeks to treat the variety of genre found in the Bible through a single window in order to understand how they all together facilitate our self-understanding, role, and purpose of existence in the light of God's mission. It promises a corrective to the post-Enlightenment driven logic of hermeneutical methods, which promoted their unique cultural biases under the guise of claims for neutrality, objectivity, universality, and scientific explorations. While they were born in an atheistic environment of the Western academia decentering God from their so-called scientific investigation and turning Scripture merely into an ancient literary piece available to us today for analysis; the missional hermeneutics begins by acknowledging the Bible as the authoritative word of God instrumental in fashioning the elect ones of God. The Bible is treated not just as a witness to God's activity in the past but also as the product and instrument to continue the mission of God through the church.

With this underlying consensus, the biblical scholars who intentionally depart from continuing in the intellectual legacy of the Enlightenment-era espouse and promote methods of interpretation with at least four major emphases to encourage a faithful reading of Scripture today. The study undertaken in the remainder of the book recognizes the

127 Roji T. George, *Paul's Identity in Galatians: A Postcolonial Appraisal* (New Delhi: Christian World Imprints, 2016), 216.

inadequacy of any one hermeneutical emphasis to do justice in reading 1 and 2 Thessalonians. Hence, the best possible combination of the prevailing four major emphases in missional hermeneutics to understand Paul's correspondence from all possible multiple angles is adopted.

2

LOCATING THESSALONIAN CORRESPONDENCE IN ITS MISSIONAL CONTEXT

Missional hermeneutics provides a new set of lenses for us to interpret the Bible. The Bible as a whole is now approached and read as a document that is missional by nature. So, every single book is arguably understood not just as one originating within the missional context of the early church in the first century, but it is also viewed as a vital tool that has played an active function in the origin, growth, and formation of the missional community in the then context. Hence, it is vital for us to reconstruct the original context and other issues discussed and debated in relation to the general background of the 1 and 2 Thessalonians. Further, the added significance for us, the twenty-first-century readers, is that it allows us to bridge the gap between the sociocultural and religiopolitical contexts of the modern readers and the text. Hence, the discussion in the present chapter shall aim to discuss vital issues like the date, occasion, literary dependence, purpose, the authenticity of the documents, etc. The aim of the discussion is not to undertake an elaborate study of every aspect discussed and debated in the study of the Thessalonian correspondence. Instead, the attempt is only intended to clear the deck on these issues reasonably and moderately before carrying out a missional reading of the Thessalonian correspondence for the better understanding of my readers.

Hence, at first, the story behind the text shall be reconstructed by studying the social, cultural, religious, and political context of the city of Thessalonica. Then, in addition to questions related to authorship, the date, authenticity, the immediate life situation that occasioned the sending of the letters by the apostle and the purpose of the letters shall be critically discussed. It is hoped that the discussion will finally facilitate us to recognize and highlight the missional meaning, content, and function of 1 and 2 Thessalonians in the remaining chapters.

2.1. The city of Thessalonica: Social, cultural, religious, and political context

Thessalonica, a prominent city of Macedonia, was named after Thessaloniki, the daughter of Philip of Macedon, by her husband Cassander, a trusted general of Alexander. She was the half-sister of Alexander. Thessalonica was located at the tip of the Thermaic Gulf. As part of Roman favor upon Thessalonica, the city was connected directly to Rome when the *Via Egnatia* was built in 130 B.C.E. The unique geographical location not only enhanced its chances for economic prosperity but it also played a significant role in making Thessalonica the leading city in the region, the capital of Macedonia, and a strategic location for the Roman military movements. In the first century C.E., Thessalonica had the reputation of being the metropolis (mother city) of the whole region.[1]

2.2.1. Socio-political context

The political history of Thessalonica, during the Roman times, is primarily of submission and subordination with a keen interest among the elite native/Greek citizens to turn the prevailing Roman domination into a good fortune for the city and for oneself individually. After its founding in 316–315 B.C.E., it came under a Roman provincial rule in 146 B.C.E. after rebelling against the Romans under the instigation of Andriscus. The rebellion was quelled successfully by the Romans under the leadership of Caecilius Metellus.[2] However, later out of her tactful support to Anthony and Octavian against Brutus and Cassius, unlike other Greek cities, in 42 B.C.E., the city earned a privileged status as a free city under the Roman rule. Such a privileged position continued into the time of Paul, except for a short spell of its revocation by Tiberius in 15 C.E., after which Emperor Claudius reinstated its status as a free city.[3]

Thus, at the time when Paul first visited the city, Thessalonica enjoyed the status of being a free city. It ensured Thessalonica its right to be self-governed by five or six politarchs, who were annually chosen, freedom from paying tax and tributes to Rome, the authority to mint coins,

---

1 M. Eugene Boring, *I & II Thessalonians: A Commentary*, The New Testament Library, 1st ed. (Louisville, KY: Westminster John Knox Press, 2015), 15; Witherington, *1 and 2 Thessalonians*, 2–3.

2 Todd D. Still, "Paul's Thessalonian Mission," *Southwestern Journal of Theology* 42, no. 1 (1999): 5–7; Jewett, *Thessalonian Correspondence*, 123.

3 Still, "Paul's Thessalonian Mission," 6–7.

and the absence of the Roman army within its four walls.[4] Such a political arrangement did not imply her independence from Roman domination but only subservience, with limited freedom, under the Roman goodwill that she had mastered well to live with by instilling "the habit of obedience, or, at least, the avoidance of open opposition."[5] In some sense, in the first century, the Thessalonians' obedience to Rome was inevitable in the light of their earlier rapid, tactful, politically intelligent switching of political allegiance between Roman army generals "at the drop of a hat." The earlier opportunist approach had made her loyalty toward Rome questionable in the first century,[6] which, then, made the Roman response of favor toward the city dependent upon the native subjects' submissive attitude and enthusiastic approval of the Roman imperial interests. In other words, "their 'freedom' was relative, dependent on continued loyalty to the Roman regime and support of Roman policy."[7]

2.2.2. Religio-cultural context

More importantly, the consequence of Roman colonization of Greek Thessalonica was the cross-pollination of cultures, religions, and politics of the colonizer and the colonized. Although Thessalonica, unlike Philippi, successfully retained its Greek heritage until the fourth century by retaining the Greek language over Latin as its administrative or official language and other ancient native languages, "in 200 years of Roman domination, the perspectives and mind-set of the superpower had inevitably influenced virtually every aspect of life, including religion."[8] Within a (post)colonial context, it yielded a complex, dynamic, and fluid transcultural hybrid space of power negotiations. The colonial administrative system in Thessalonica was a form of Roman adaptation of the former Greek democratic model of native administration including the demos, a council, the politarchs, the city treasurer, etc., but the native officials "functioned as agents of Roman rule."[9] In other words, "the Roman overlordship functioned in Thessalonica *under the guise of conserving*

4 Still, "Paul's Thessalonian Mission," 8; Boring, *I & II Thessalonians*, 15; Jewett, *The Thessalonian Correspondence*, 123;Witherington, *1 and 2 Thessalonians*, 3–4; Charles A. Wanamaker, *The Epistles to the Thessalonians: A Commentary on the Greek Text*, The New International Greek Testament Commentary (Grand Rapids, MI: William B. Eerdmans Publishing, 1990), 3.

5 Martin Goodman, *The Roman World 44 B.C.–A.D. 180* (London: Routledge, 1997), 232.

6 Callia Rulmu, "Between Ambition and Quietism: The Socio-Political Background of 1 Thessalonians 4,9-12," *Biblica* 91, no. 3 (2010): 397.

7 Boring, *I & II Thessalonians*, 15.

8 Boring, *I & II Thessalonians*, 16.

9 Jewett, *Thessalonian Correspondence*, 123. See also Still, "Paul's Thessalonian Mission," 8.

democratic ideals,"[10] while the native elites lavishly reciprocated Roman benefaction by "mixing" religion with politics in a hybrid religio-political system called the imperial cult. It must be borne in mind that the imperial cult in Thessalonica was not thrust upon the natives by Rome,[11] but the native subjects purely engineered it as part of their effort to eulogize the powerful and superior with strong anticipation of favors outflowing from the latter. Rome exploited such subservient religio-political response to naturalize her colonial domination, superiority, and selfish interests. In it, according to Jewett, the Greek ideals articulated in their religious tongue

> were coopted in Thessalonica to legitimate Roman colonialism, and although the populace of Thessalonica had not experienced any form of democracy for centuries, the force of the ideals remained sufficiently alive to be useful at the propagandistic level. *The goal of the imperial cult was to sustain Roman power, so the religious and political ideals it celebrated functioned as an ideology.*[12]

The temple dedicated to the emperor with priests of the cult was built toward the west of the city, probably, the site from where the statue of Augustus was unearthed.[13] The local mass support to the imperial cult indicated the enthusiastic support to the stable Roman imperial rule.[14] The numismatic evidences found in the city bear the image of deified Julius Caesar minted on the obverse, while on the reverse Augustus appears as *divi filius*. Although the title *theos* is used only for Julius, and Augustus is not mentioned as the "son of god," the placing of the two juxtaposed testifies the awareness among Thessalonians about the *divi filius* status of the emperor.[15] Further, the coins found in Thessalonica bore slogans about "freedom and harmony" engraved on them, which testified to the

---

10 Jewett, *Thessalonian Correspondence*, 124 (emphasis added).

11 Boring, *I & II Thessalonians*, 18.

12 Jewett, *Thessalonian Correspondence*, 124–25 (emphasis added).

13 David W. J. Gill, "Macedonia," in *The Book of Acts in Its Graeco-Roman Setting*, ed. David W. G. Gill and Conrad Gempf, *The Book of Acts in Its First Century Setting*, vol. 2 (Grand Rapids, MI/Carlisle: William B. Eerdmans, 1994), 415; Witherington, *1 and 2 Thessalonians*, 5; Boring, *I & II Thessalonians*, 18.

14 Boring, *I & II Thessalonians*, 16.

15 Witherington, *1 and 2 Thessalonians*, 5. See also, Still, "Paul's Thessalonian Mission," 9; Harrison, "Paul and the Imperial Gospel," 81–82; Abraham Smith, "Unmasking the Powers: Towards a Postcolonial Analysis of 1 Thessalonians," in *Paul and the Roman Imperial Order*, ed. Richard A. Horsley (Harrisburg: Trinity Press International, 2004), 57; Karl P. Donfried, "The Assembly of the Thessalonians: Reflections on the Ecclesiology of the Earliest Christian Letter," in *Paul, Thessalonica, and Early Christianity* (Grand Rapids, MI: William B. Eerdmans Publishing, 2002), 140.

democratic values enmeshed in the imperial cult as represented by the Roman benefaction.[16]

Another significant aspect of religio-cultural hybridization was the cross-fertilization of the native Cabirus cult and the persona of the emperor where he appears like divine Cabirus. Thereby, he was included as their personal deity, closely identified with Cabirus, who protects them from all dangers even beyond this life within the dominant religious cult of Thessalonica in the first century.[17] According to Riesner, the archaeological pieces of evidence prove that "the Cabirus-cult was absorbed by the official city cult since the Augustan period."[18] Within a transcultural context, it is a religious cross-fertilization of traditions of both the colonizer and colonized, a fusion encouraged by both, as a part of the larger (post)colonial ideological discourse bargaining power. For the Romans, such a fusion or absorption of religious traditions into one dominant religio-political system, that is, the imperial cult, affirmed and naturalized their political domination, racial superiority, and functional hierarchy in order to protect their selfish colonial interests, while for the colonized subjects of Thessalonica it is a native idiosyncratic expression of loyalty toward Rome. A similar expression of political loyalty of the Thessalonians to Rome is also evident in their fusion of the imperial cult with the goddess Roma that undergirds the *Pax* and *Securitas* brought by Rome in Thessalonica.[19] Further, it was also a fusion of personal religious piety with the accepted pattern of social relationship defined under Greco-Roman clientelia where the patron's favor is reciprocated with appropriate eulogy by the client, in this case the Thessalonians. Among the Thessalonians, those who were left without benefit from it were the lower class of laborers, craftsmen, etc., as their protector god Cabirus is co-opted by Rome into a hybrid civic cult (i.e., a "mixture" of native and Roman divine and political figures forming a civic cult) in which the "Roman rule placed advantage in the hand of a small elite who acted as the chief instigators of the cult."[20]

---

16 Jewett, *Thessalonian Correspondence*, 124.

17 Witherington, *1 and 2 Thessalonians*, 5–6. Boring, *I & II Thessalonians*, 18; Jewett, *Thessalonian Correspondence*, 129; E. Randolph Richards, "Ministering in a Tough Place: Paul's Pattern in Thessalonica," *Southwestern Journal of Theology*. 42, no. 1 (1999): 21.

18 Rainer Riesner, *Paul's Early Period: Chronology, Mission Strategy, Theology*, trans. Doug Stott (Grand Rapids, MI: William B. Eerdmans Publishing, 1998), 379.

19 Boring, *I & II Thessalonians*, 18.

20 Jewett, *Thessalonian Correspondence*, 126, 131–32, cited from 126; cf. Karl P. Donfried, "The Cults of Thessalonica and the Thessalonian Correspondence," in *Paul, Thessalonica, and Early Christianity* (Grand Rapids, MI: William B. Eerdmans Publishing, 2002), 31–38; Richards, "Ministering in a Tough Place," 22.

In terms of religion, Thessalonica was a pluralistic society in which, during the time of Paul, multiple religious/cultic groups like the cult of Serapis, the cult of Dionysus, Zeus, Demeter, Aphrodite, the Imperial cult, etc., coexisted mutually influencing each other with the most dominant Cabirus cult in Thessalonica.[21] By the time Paul arrived in Thessalonica, it was saturated with the Roman patronage system defining every form of relationships. The city had a mixed population that included Macedonians with Greek identity along with later entrants like Jews, Italians, Celts, etc.[22] According to Jewett,

> the population of Thessalonica was largely of Greek descent, the Macedonians having long been integrated into a rather coherent nation with Greek identity. The city has been founded as an amalgamation of Greek immigrants with the local Macedonian inhabitants of a number of surrounding villages on the site of the ancient city of Therme. The recollection of the origins of the city and the continued settlement of descendants from some of these previous urban centers in specific neighborhoods of the city indicates a measure of continuity in population despite later immigration. During the Roman period there were numerous Italians who had followed the Roman legions into Thessalonica, as well as a few Celts and other minorities. The hordes of barbarians that Cicero had complained about in Thessalonica a century before Paul's arrival were likely well integrated into the Greek population of the city by the time of the Thessalonian correspondence, though some of them were probably the descendants of the Macedonian villagers who retained a measure of distinctiveness down to Cicero's time.[23]

The ethnic diversity in Thessalonica is also attested by Paul's own reference to the persecution of believers in Thessalonica by the term *symphyletai* ("your own countrymen" 1 Thess 2:14) referring to the people of the same race or tribe.[24] So, the persecution that befalls the believers was from the native pro-imperial subjects in Thessalonica from different

---

21 Donfried, "Cults of Thessalonica," 22–31; Charles A. Gieschen, "Christian Identity in a Pagan Thessalonica: The Imitation of Paul's Cruciform Life," *Concordia Theological Quarterly* 72, no. 1 (2008): 4; Charles Edson, "Cults of Thessalonica (Macedonica III)," *Harvard Theological Review* 41, no. 3 (1948): 153–204.

22 Wanamaker, *Epistles to the Thessalonians*, 4.

23 Jewett, *Thessalonian Correspondence*, 119. Cf. Richards, "Ministering in a Tough Place," 19–20.

24 BDAG, "συμφυλέτης, κτλ," 960. The term can be understood in two senses—ethnic and local. However, the ethnic sense appears to be more logical and acceptable in the light of the parallel drawn between the situation in Thessalonica and Judea. Abraham J. Malherbe, *The Letters to the Thessalonians: A New Translation with Introduction and Commentary*, *Anchor Bible*, vol. 32B (New York: Doubleday, 2000), 168; Wanamaker, *Epistles to the Thessalonians*, 113.

ethnic, social, and cultural backgrounds,[25] though according to Luke, it originated from the Jews in Acts 17:5.

If so, in such a hybrid postcolonial context, both the colonizer and the colonized influence each other creating a web of intersections, absorption, and "oneness" in uneasy terms. It is contended that Paul's advice to the Thessalonian community must be fixed within this larger discursive context where interreligious, interethnic, intercultural, etc., negotiations of power occurred at every level of relationships. However, what were the immediate circumstances that triggered Paul's response? What are those determining factors of the Thessalonian community that controlled Paul's paraenesis? A clearer understanding of them will enhance our appreciation of Paul's nuanced cultural posture in a postcolonial context.

2.2. Authenticity and date of Paul's Thessalonian correspondence

For us to read Paul's Thessalonian correspondence faithfully today, it is vital to state clearly at the outset the positions taken with regard to the critical issues that are intensely debated among the biblical scholars. They help us to put the correspondence in perspective to discuss Paul's purpose of sending the two letters in quick succession and their missional significance to the community of God in Thessalonica. In the past, though some from the Tübingen School have questioned the authenticity of the letters, in contemporary scholarly discussions 1 Thessalonians is universally agreed to have originated from the pen of Paul. However, the authenticity of 2 Thessalonians is intensely debated in contemporary discussions.

Both 1 and 2 Thessalonians give an impression that the letters were by Paul, Silas, and Timothy, equally (1 Thess 1:1; 2 Thess 1:1). The three are mentioned together as senders of the letters without any distinction. Hence, Witherington allows the possibility of Silas and Timothy to be scribes of Paul, who dictated the letters in the light of the constant use of "we" in the letter. For him, the high-frequency use of "we" against "I" (i.e., 96.7 percent) in 1 Thessalonians, and similarly, 93.9 percent in 2 Thessalonians prove Paul as the main speaker on behalf of the team to the new converts in Thessalonica. There are significant pieces of evidence in the letters like the use of the first person singular to advise the congregation in 1 Thessalonians 5:27 and Paul's unique signature line in 2 Thessalonians 3:17.[26] Even the shreds of external evidences strongly support the second-century testimony for Paul's authorship. In 140 C.E., Marcion included it in the collections of Paul's letters. Similarly,

25 Witherington, *1 and 2 Thessalonians*, 87–88; Boring, *I & II Thessalonians*, 99–101.

26 Ben Witherington, *1 and 2 Thessalonians: A Socio-Rhetorical Commentary* (Grand Rapids, MI: William B. Eerdmans Publishing, 2006), 9-10.

Muratorian Canon (180 C.E.), Irenaeus, Tertullian, and others, have accepted it as originating from Paul.[27]

However, Guthrie enumerates the reasons why some disputed Pauline authorship in the past: (i) the alleged differences between Acts 17:2 and 1 Thessalonians 2:7–11 concerning the duration of Paul's stay in Thessalonica, (ii) the question of the impression that Paul's description of the composition of the community in the city as predominantly gentile converts (1 Thess 1:9; 2:14; 4:1–5) contradicts Luke's portrait, and (iii) the possible non-Pauline interpolations of passages in 1 Thessalonians (e.g., 1 Thess 2:13–16 on the basis of implied historical context and linguistic dissimilarity,[28] or 5:1–11 that seemingly contain a different set of vocabulary and theological themes). The arguments in favor of a non-Pauline origin—alleging an act of forgery committed by an unknown person at a later date by sending the letter in the name of Paul—are not beyond dispute. None of the above stated arguments are tenable because: (i) the seeming difference in mentioning the exact duration of Paul's stay in the city is because while Luke provides specific details about Paul's visits to the synagogue, Paul speaks about his ministry among the gentiles; (ii) Paul's mention of his readers in Thessalonica as gentile converts (1 Thess 1:9; 2:14; 4:1–5) complements Luke's mention of many God-fearers who joined the apostle as a result of his ministry in the city (Acts 17:4); and (iii) the later scholarship (like Weatherly[29] refuting Schmidt and Plevnik's[30] supporting of the authenticity of 1 Thessalonians 2:13–16 and 5:1–11, respectively) has rejected the interpolation theories by comparing the disputed passages within 1 Thessalonians.[31] Moreover, Carson, Moo, and Morris state that "the vocabulary and style are Pauline, as are the ideas put forward."[32] In cases where some have argued otherwise, if the letter is not written by Paul addressing the specific pastoral need of the community, it is unclear "why should anyone write a letter like this and claim that it came from Paul?"[33] Especially if Paul had already died and it was known to the church, it is difficult to explain the nature and purpose of the Letter

---

27 Donald Guthrie, *New Testament Introduction*, 4th ed. (rev.) (Leicester: Apollos, 1990), 589.

28 For example, Daryl Schmidt, "1 Thess 2:13-16: Linguistic Evidence for an Interpolation," *Journal of Biblical Literature* 102, no. 2 (1983): 269–79.

29 Jon A. Weatherly, "The Authenticity of 1 Thessalonians 2:13-16: Additional Evidence," *Journal for the Study of the New Testament* 13, no. 42 (1991): 79–98.

30 Joseph Plevnik, "1 Thess 5:1-11: Its Authenticity, Intention and Message," *Biblica* 60, no. 1 (1979): 71–90.

31 Guthrie, *New Testament Introduction*, 589–92.

32 Donald A. Carson, Douglas J. Moo, and Leon Morris, *An Introduction to the New Testament* (Grand Rapids, MI: Zondervan, 1995), 344.

33 Carson, Moo, and Morris, *Introduction to the New Testament*, 344.

adequately. Hence, modern scholarship has come to treat 1 Thessalonians unanimously as an undisputed letter of Paul.

Concerning 2 Thessalonians, the question of authenticity is much more complex and disputed. Though it is inconclusive till date, unlike 1 Thessalonians, based on shreds of evidence ranging from its different literary style to its seeming literary dependence upon 1 Thessalonians, a large number of recent scholars prefer to term it a pseudonymous (or deuteropauline) work. Jewett and Marshall, in their work, trace back the history of serious argument against Pauline authorship to F. C. Baur. The two other significant works arguing for an alleged forgery came from William Wrede and Wolfgang Trilling, which were adopted by many in the following years to dispute their authenticity.[34] Stacy summarizes the basis of Trilling's theological and literary objections as:

- perceived dependence upon 1 Thessalonians;
- perceived contradictory eschatologies (e.g., 1 Thessalonians is characterized by the belief in an imminent Parousia whereas 2 Thessalonians has an elaborate Jewish apocalypticism; cf. 1 Thess 5:1–11 with 2 Thess 2:1–12);
- lack of personal references in 2 Thessalonians;
- references to forgery in 2 Thessalonians 2:2 and 3:17 (some scholars suggest that this amounts to special pleading—the forger is attempting to deflect attention from the fact that 2 Thessalonians is, in fact, a forgery); and
- the vocabulary, style, and tone of 2 Thessalonians are noticeably different from 1 Thessalonians.[35]

Scholars like Beale, Jewett, Stacy, et al., do not consider these objections to the letter's authenticity formidable. The question of its slavish literary dependence upon 1 Thessalonians by imitating the literary structure, vocabulary, and style of the latter is rejected on two accounts: (i) the imitation argued is not as serious as it is made seemingly, and (ii) it is unclear why an author cannot repeat the pattern of one's earlier letter to the same group for some reasons is completely unknown to the modern readers.[36] This leads us to the alleged skill of the forger to insert 2 Thessalonians 3:17 and 2:2 in order to deflect the attention of his readers

34 Jewett, *Thessalonian Correspondence*, 3–16; I. Howard Marshall, *1 and 2 Thessalonians: Based on the Revised Standard Version*, New Century Bible Commentary (Grand Rapids, MI: William B. Eerdmans Publishing, 1983), 28–45.

35 R. Wayne Stacy, "Introduction to the Thessalonian Correspondences," *Review & Expositor* 96, no. 2 (1999): 178.

36 G. K. Beale, *1–2 Thessalonians*, The IVP New Testament Commentary Series (Downer Grove, IL: IVP Academic, 2003), 31.

from the forgery attempted. If it is really a forgery attempt, then the very letter, as Jewett contends, that the forger seeks to imitate for authenticity runs the risk of being discredited as inauthentic. For him, the implication of reading the two references together is to reject the undisputed letters (except 1 Corinthians [16:21], Galatians [6:11], and Philemon [19]) of Paul as inauthentic because they do not bear his handwriting.[37]

Even the question of a lack of personal reference in the Letter is unacceptable because it overlooks 2 Thessalonians 3:7 and 9, where Paul appeals to the believers in Thessalonica to imitate his model. Similarly, after repeatedly pointing out Trilling's predisposition toward its inauthenticity despite the possibility of concluding otherwise based on the prevailing ambiguity in the evidence, Jewett demonstrates how a serious look into the possible social situation of the audience and tracing of similar points in other undisputed letters of Paul could thwart the seemingly strong arguments. For example, Trilling's treatment of 2 Thessalonians as a tract unrelated to any specific situation due to its significant difference from the vocabulary and style of 1 Thessalonians is feeble and weak when compared with the vast difference between the undisputed authenticity of 1 and 2 Corinthians. He rejects Trilling's contention stating that "it is compelling only on the assumption that a single mode of discourse is constitutive for Pauline letters, which is completely untenable."[38] Hence, he concludes that 2 Thessalonians along with 1 Thessalonians must be accepted as authentic letters of Paul for the weight of arguments lay in favor of its authenticity. He states, "the marks of authentic use of Pauline vocabulary, style, and argumentative form are sufficiently extensive that any forgery hypothesis is hard to sustain."[39]

Stacy refutes Trilling's contention based on the following arguments: (i) If the use of seventeen unique words in 2 Thessalonians is a reason to refute its authenticity, then it must be borne in mind that despite unique terms in 1 Thessalonians, all including Trilling accept its authenticity; and (ii) The argument is problematic if the absence of standard Pauline theological themes like justification by faith in the letter along with apparent inconsistent teaching on eschatology between 1and 2 Thessalonians are viewed as evidences for the inauthenticity of 2 Thessalonians. While the former is highlighted due to the individual scholar's theological bias, the latter disregards the uniqueness of the situations of the two letters demanding a specifically different response from the apostle.[40] Moreover, the demand for consistency on eschatological teachings in the two letters

---

37 Jewett, *Thessalonian Correspondence*, 17.

38 Jewett, *Thessalonian Correspondence*, 10–15, cited from 12–13.

39 Jewett, *Thessalonian Correspondence*, 17.

40 Stacy, "Thessalonian Correspondences," 178–79.

contradicts the fundamental character of "the apocalypses, which often combine the thoughts of the imminence of the End and of preparatory signs."[41]

In short, the two letters are Paul's letters sent to the same community. If so, when did Paul send the letters to the community of God in Thessalonica? Scholars who view the two letters as originating from the pen of Paul have credited 1 Thessalonians to be one of the earliest letters of Paul, if not the earliest. Although Donfried has argued for early 40s C.E. date for the first Letter,[42] the general consensus among the scholars who support Paul's authorship has been to date it between 50–52 C.E.[43] The problem with the early date for 1 Thessalonians as argued by Donfried is that it makes two important assumptions that: (i) Galathians 1:21 implies Paul's early visit to Thessalonica and to Corinth that the Lukan account in Acts does not mention, and (ii) it is possible to date the event mentioned in Acts 18:1, reading in continuation to Acts 18:5, as referring to Claudius's edict in 41 C.E. instead of 49/50 C.E. In this case, Acts 18:2–4 is viewed as a mistaken reference to a later event; in fact, a "retrojection made from a later period."[44]

However, Donfried's appeal to a possible retrojection is not widely accepted. Scholars have maintained that Paul visited Thessalonica, after the Jerusalem Council (Acts 15), during his second missionary journey. The edict of Claudius mentioned in Acts 18:2–4 is understood as the event mentioned by Suetonious, which is supported by other ancient historians like Orosius.[45] If so, the first letter to the Thessalonians must have been sent shortly after Paul reached Corinth in 50/51 C.E., which makes it one of the earliest letters of Paul along with Galatians. Then, shortly after that, Paul wrote another letter to them, 2 Thessalonians.[46] Although a

---

41 Carson, Moo, and Morris, *An Introduction to the New Testament*, 345.

42 Karl P. Donfried, "1 Thessalonians, Acts and the Early Paul," in *Paul, Thessalonica, and Early Christianity* (Grand Rapids, MI: William B. Eerdmans Publishing, 2002), 71–76; Karl P. Donfried, "The Theology of 1 Thessalonians," in *The Theology of the Shorter Pauline Letters*, New Testament Theology (Cambridge: Cambridge University Press, 1993), 9–12.

43 For example, Witherington, *1 and 2 Thessalonians*, 10; F. F. Bruce, *1 and 2 Thessalonians*, *Word Biblical Commentary*, vol. 45 (Waco, TX: Word Books, 1982), xxxv.

44 Donfried, "The Theology of 1 Thessalonians," 10–12, cited from 12.

45 See for an elaborate discussion on this topic, Ben Witherington, *The Acts of the Apostles: A Socio-Rhetorical Commentary* (Grand Rapids, MI: William B. Eerdmans Publishing, 1998), 539–44.

46 See for an extensive discussion on the prevailing broad range of opinions on the authenticity of 2 Thessalonians Paul Foster, "Who Wrote 2 Thessalonian?: A Fresh Look at an Old Problem," *Journal for the Study of the New Testament* 35, no. 2 (2012): 150–75. Foster maintains Pauline authorship of the letter with some fresh reasons.

definite gap of time between the two letters cannot be exactly mentioned, Paul's repetition of similar literary structure in composing the Letters, the language, style, and vocabulary, and the seeming increase of intensity of the problem of persecution and idleness among the members of the community explains that the second letter must have followed without much delay within a few weeks or a couple of months. The internal evidence to an earlier letter in 2 Thessalonians 2:2 and 15, and 3:17 most probably refers to 1 Thessalonians. Beale maintains that "while it is possible that 2:15 could refer to some other earlier epistle to the Thessalonians other than '1 Thessalonians,' it is improbable that this is the case."[47]

If the above discussion gives us sufficient reasons to treat the two letters as originating from the pen of Paul between 50–51 C.E., then the reconstruction of the story of the formation of the community of God in Thessalonica and the immediate occasion giving birth to the two quick letters must be carefully reconstructed.

2.3. The Question of Sequence and Occasion of 1 and 2 Thessalonians

An important question related to the reconstruction of the occasion of Paul sending the two letters to the community of Christians in Thessalonica is: Did Paul write 2 Thessalonians before 1 Thessalonians unlike the order of their appearance in the New Testament would seemingly suggest? Scholars like J. C. West,[48] T. W. Manson,[49] Charles A. Wanamaker,[50] and others, have contended based on the internal evidences that Paul had sent 2 Thessalonians at first and then 1 Thessalonians. The underlying foundation giving birth to the argument for the chronological priority of 2 Thessalonians is that the canonical order is set not based on chronology but "in general the longer epistles come first."[51] Hence, enumerating the arguments in favor of this position from Johannes Weiss, Manson enlists five major internal evidences in support. They are: (i) the mention of persecution as continuing at the time of writing 2 Thessalonians (1:4–7), against the same mentioned as a past event in 1 Thessalonians (2:14), proves the chronological priority of the former. (ii) While the internal problems of the community like disorder, idleness, etc., are already seemingly known concerns in 1 Thessalonians 4:10–12, in 2 Thessalonians

---

47 Beale, *1–2 Thessalonians*, 17.

48 J. C. West, "The Order of 1 and 2 Thessalonians," *Journal of Theological Studies*, 15, no. 57 (1913): 66–74.

49 T. W. Manson, "St Paul in Greece: The Letters to the Thessalonians," *Bulletin of John Rylands Library* 35, no. 2 (1953): 12.

50 Wanamaker, *Epistles to the Thessalonians*, 37–45.

51 West, "Order of 1 and 2 Thessalonians," 66.

3:11–15 it appears to be a new phenomenon plaguing the community. (iii) If 2 Thessalonians was not written before 1 Thessalonians, then the signature line (2 Thess 3:17) proving the genuineness of the letter is meaningless. (iv) 1 Thessalonians 5:1 mentioning the needlessness of teaching about the time and occasion of the Parousia would make sense openly if the readers are already familiar with the discussion on it done earlier in 2 Thessalonians 2:1–12. (v) Adding the fifth point to the four already contributed by Weiss, Manson maintains that the thrice repeated expression "Now concerning" in 1 Thessalonians 4:9, 4:13, and 5:1 when seen in the light of 1 Corinthians 7:1 proves that Paul is replying to the questions raised by the Thessalonians in the light of his statement in 2 Thessalonians.[52]

However, most scholars today reject the arguments enlisted in favor of the sequential priority of 2 Thessalonians over 1 Thessalonians despite its certain weaknesses. In other words, most despite recognizing its limitations still prefer a position upholding the canonical order of writing the letters as a better option that is historically logical and less speculative. Robert Jewett, arguing in favor of the canonical sequence, contends that "there is an intrinsic historical logic in the traditional sequence."[53] He supplies three vital reasons for his contention: (i) It is important to notice that never in 1 Thessalonians does Paul make any reference to a letter sent earlier, whereas 2 Thessalonians has three notable instances (2 Thess 2:2, 15; 3:17) that require a letter to precede it. While 2 Thessalonians 2:2 and 15 explicitly refer to a letter sent earlier, which must be 1 Thessalonians in the light of lack of any sort of evidence for a letter that is not available to us today, 2 Thessalonians 3:17 requires at least one letter to have been sent earlier both for Paul to claim a signature line as his unique authenticating evidence and for the Thessalonian believers to verify the claim. (ii) Reference to persecution is common in both the letters. However, 1 Thessalonians explains the apocalyptic significance of the letter as something to be anticipated without fail for believers in Christ who belong to the new age but are living in the shadow of old age. In contrast, 2 Thessalonians assumes a doctrinal instruction while speaking about persecution only as an indicator of God's eschatological judgment. Undoubtedly, the canonical sequence must be logically consistent. (iii) Assuming that the epistolary rhetoric involving reference to a past contact is usually to the last contact, 1 Thessalonians 2:1–2 when read in conjunction with 1 Thessalonians 2:17 and 1:5, 9–10 indicates that Paul is referring to his first visit with them. Unlike it, the sole reference in 2

---

52 Manson, "St Paul in Greece," 428–47.

53 Jewett, *Thessalonian Correspondence*, 26–27.

Thessalonians (2:15) to the founding mission of Paul in Thessalonica is concerning the most recent contact with them through a letter.[54]

Further, Witherington refuting the sequential priority of 2 Thessalonians over 1 Thessalonians argues that the "aorist of *edidachthete* in that verse (2:15) likely goes with *di'epistolēshēmōn*, which surely indicates that the letter referred to was written in the past and hence is likely to be our 1 Thessalonians." Further, the question common to both the letters implies that the initially raised queries during Paul's first visit to Thessalonica were addressed in 1 Thessalonians and later in 2 Thessalonians he gives more details due to the new situation arising in the congregation.[55] Hence, the present discussion favors canonical sequence to understand the epistolary situation that gave rise to both the letters.

If Paul wrote both the letters between 50 C.E. and 51 C.E., what must have been the immediate need(s) of the community that formed the occasion for writing them? What are those reasons that compelled Paul to take due cognizance of the situation arising in order to facilitate nurturing a healthy life and growth of the community?

The Lukan account in Acts tells us that Paul visited Thessalonica, in the region of Macedonia, during his second missionary journey. This journey was made after attending the Jerusalem council (Acts 15:5–35) and the confrontation with Peter in Syrian Antioch (Gal 2:11–14). Unlike in his earlier missionary tour, the difference of opinion with Barnabas, a fellow gentile missionary, over John Mark, Paul decided to continue his missionary journey along with Silas (Acts 15:36–41). At first, he travelled to the churches founded during his first missionary journey in the south Galatian region, strengthening them in the word. It was at this stage that Timothy went along with Paul and Silas in mission. Paul along with his companions, travelled through Derbe, Lystra, Phrygia and Galatia, and Mysia and reached Troas. While in Troas, through divine intervention, he might have received the Macedonian call in a dream. Thus, Paul and his companions embarked on a transcontinental missionary trip for the first time (Acts 16:1–10). The first city in the European continent that they stayed and did mission in was Philippi, a leading city and a prominent Roman colony. Here, despite initial success in finding converts and the establishment of a flourishing church that faithfully participated with the apostle in all his ups and downs in mission, Paul and his team had to leave the city owing to the opposition they faced there (Acts 16:11–40).

The next leading urban center for multiple reasons where they based themselves to preach the gospel was Thessalonica. It was "the largest and most important city of Macedonia, a port and commercial center" and

54 Jewett, *Thessalonian Correspondence*, 27–30.

55 Witherington, *1 and 2 Thessalonians*, 15.

"the seat of a Roman proconsul."[56] The initial ministry that Paul did in the city was among the Jews. They succeeded in establishing a church. Luke says, "some of the Jews were persuaded and joined Paul and Silas, as did a large number of God-fearing Greeks and quite a few prominent women" (Acts 17:4). But, this evoked opposition from some Jews in Thessalonica who continued to chase them even in Berea when they heard about the success of these missionaries among the Jews in the synagogue and Greek men and women (Acts 17:10–13). Hence, leaving behind Silas and Timothy, Paul was escorted to Athens immediately where he moved around and preached about the living creator God (Acts 17:14–34). After this, Paul travelled to Corinth and lived in the city, ministering for not less than eighteen months (Acts 17:11, 18).

During his stay in Corinth, his colleagues, Silas and Timothy, rejoined him after returning from Macedonia (Acts 18:5). Probably, at first, Paul, and later, Silas and Timothy arrived in Corinth in 50 C.E. as mentioned earlier. Paul's long stay in Corinth must have given ample time for Timothy to arrive and for the apostle to quickly send two letters to the recently founded church in Thessalonica. Timothy arrived in Corinth with a mixed report about the Thessalonian believers' state of affair after Paul was aborted from the city prematurely during his first mission stay among them. This must have left a huge vacuum in their learning of the details of the new faith that they received through Paul and his companions, while there must have also been something in the report to rejoice about. The encouraging report by Timothy included their standing firm in the faith, which is nothing less than regaining life and their affection toward him. Paul says, "For now we really live, since you are standing firm in the Lord" (1 Thess 3:8). Paul does not say it without any reason. Despite lacking fuller understanding of the faith (cf. 1 Thess 3:10 "what is lacking in your faith") they have received through the apostle's ministry; it is no less a report of great importance that the new converts of Thessalonica are loyal to the gospel amidst persecution. It was no small reason for Paul and his companions to rejoice. However, a positive report about them from Timothy did not mean that there were no other concerns that required Paul's immediate attention. According to Koester,

> 1 Thessalonians mirrors throughout the problems that might result in a young congregation that was firm in its conviction, but would be confronted by difficulties in the exposition and defense of its new faith within a matter of a few weeks and months. These include such questions as the credibility and integrity of the apostle, hostilities from the

[56] Helmut Koester, *Introduction to the New Testament Vol 2: History and Literature of Early Christianity*, 3rd print, Foundations and Facets: New Testament (New York, NY: Fortress Press, 1984), 108.

outside, consequences for Christian conduct, and the significance for life in the present of the newly acquired status of salvation.[57]

Koester's summarization of the occasion of sending 1 Thessalonians suggests a multipronged situation, where questions about Paul, the Thessalonian believers' faith and ethics, outsiders' attitude toward them, the spread of over-realized eschatology among some in the church, and so on, are pertinent. According to Stacy, the direct consequence of misunderstanding Paul's gospel by the Thessalonian believers amidst unexpected twists of events around them was that they "misunderstood Paul's eschatological emphasis on the 'new age' of the kingdom of God and the imminence of the Parousia of Christ to mean that they were already children of the new age and, as such, were exempt from life's exigencies, demands, and vicissitudes," such as: (i) they did not expect persecution as an integral lot of a true Christian which shocked them completely; (ii) their over-realized eschatology made them believe that no member of the community would die before the Parousia; and (iii) the ripple effect of the misunderstood eschatology became evident in moral laxness and idleness.[58] We shall undertake a short discussion about them to highlight their importance to learn Paul's missional intention in sending 1 and 2 Thessalonians quickly in succession.

2.3.1. Immediate context: Persecution of the Thessalonian community

In his first letter to the Thessalonians, Paul repeatedly refers to the situation of his readers facing intense persecution and opposition (e.g., 1 Thess 1:6; 2:14). Paul's concern for the new converts in Thessalonica is reflected in his twofold attempts to preserve them in the faith: (i) Paul sends Timothy to Thessalonica in order "to strengthen and encourage" the Thessalonians in their faith (1 Thess 3:2). (ii) Paul does not want any of them to get unsettled desires to remind his readers that "we are destined for them (trials)" (1 Thess 3:3). Beale rightly observes that "no one seriously disputes that Paul was worried about the welfare of his readers' faith and wrote to encourage his new converts (cf. 3:1–5)."[59] Perhaps, Paul wants to tell them that their new found faith in Christ Jesus is a call to suffer for their loyalty to Jesus, the Lord. It must not surprise them because as they already know, Paul and his companions have been previously "treated outrageously in Philippi" (1 Thess 2:2) and he both taught and practically demonstrated among them that persecution is inevitable for those who believe in Christ (1 Thess 3:4). Most probably, the persecution

57 Koester, *History and Literature of Early Christianity*, 112–13.

58 Stacy, "Thessalonian Correspondences," 186–87, cited from 186.

59 Beale, *1–2 Thessalonians*, 15.

that began while Paul was there with them continued even after his departure. The main opposition to the earliest missionaries and their converts was not merely public irk toward their idiosyncratic behavior (like Paul's). Rather, it was because of the gospel itself, that is, the gospel was interpreted as a political gospel by some Thessalonians (Jews).

The context of persecution corresponds well with Luke's description of Paul's initial ministry in Thessalonica—staying at the house of Jason, where he faced violent protest from the native Jews and others (Acts 17:1–9). Paul and his companions reached Thessalonica from Philippi, where they preached in "a synagogue of the Jews" (Acts 17:1). As a result, some of the Jews along with "a great multitude of the God-fearing Greeks and a number of the leading women" joined with Paul and Silas (Acts 17:4). This was an occasion that some Jews out of "jealousy" (Acts 17:5), with the support of men from *agora,* protested against Jason, the host of Paul in the city. The direct accusation against them levelled both by the gentiles and Jews in Thessalonica was of treason/disloyalty toward the Roman emperor for they speak about "another king, Jesus" (Acts 17:7). Beale states, "according to Acts 17:7, the pagans of the city viewed Paul as a traitor to Caesar both politically (as head of state) and religiously (as head of the imperial cult)."[60]

E. A. Judge's study of the decrees of Caesar gives us the reason behind the uproar created in the city and the logic of interpreting the gospel that Paul preached in political terms. Judge, citing examples of oaths of loyalty to Caesar administered by the city authorities in Paphlagonia and Cyprus, maintains that it could have been a similar situation in Thessalonica.[61] He states that "in some respect the politarchs were obliged to take cognizance of offences against the 'decrees of Caesar'" based on the oath of loyalty (especially Paphlagonian) to Caesar, his family, and descendants that they had taken to fulfill throughout their life, even at the peril of their own death.[62] However, the addition to it in the oath of loyalty to Tiberius, as it was practiced in Paphos to Cyprus demanding support, reverence, and obedience on the part of the subjects, makes it possible for us to consider such a formula is sufficient enough to lead "the Thessalonians treating the oath as a 'decree' of Caesar."[63]

If so, the Thessalonians offered unconditional obedience to Rome and adopted a pro-colonial stance quite slavishly having been informed of the enslaving decree of Caesar. They created uproar against the new preachers

60 Beale, *1–2 Thessalonians*, 15.

61 Edwin A. Judge, "Decrees of Caesar at Thessalonica," *Reformed Theological Review* 30, no. 1 (1971): 1–7.

62 Judge, "Decrees of Caesar," 5–6, cited from 5.

63 Judge, "Decrees of Caesar," 7.

in the city. Although they protested in the light of the probable harsh consequences to follow, for even seeming to be condoning Paul's subversive gospel, their slavish/colonized mindset is evident beyond doubt in Luke's testimony in Acts 17:7. Further, the scenario becomes more poignant to us—if the instigators, at first, were Thessalonian Jews, those of a colonized race, who had known about the mission and message of Paul who preached about a rival king, Jesus (Acts 17:6–7). Interestingly, their zeal for the imperial interest, while protecting their own, compels them to follow Paul into the city of Berea in order to quell politically subversive "gospel" claims by the preacher (Acts 17:10–13). Thus, it is not merely an act of the law-abiding Roman citizens who seek the interest of the city but an example of the colonized "self" replicating the colonizing "self" in a different context with a strong urge to silence, dominate, and threaten the "other" within a postcolonial context.

Further, the Roman suspicion toward every voluntary association also forms the immediate context of Paul's advice. Although evidences for it are lacking in Asia Minor, the subservient nature of the associations' function and their regular affirmation of loyalty toward Rome explain their typical behavior as a response to Roman suspicion toward their activities.[64] Rulmu maintains that

> since the voluntary associations functioned as social supports for their members, it is hard to deny the heavy influence which patrons and benefactors had upon them. The guilds could have functioned, and as a matter of fact they did, as a means of displaying a patron's influence and honor, thus as a political entity. It is exactly for this reason that the civic magistrates and governors appointed by the Emperor regarded the *collegia* with suspicion.[65]

If so, the *ekklesia* in Thessalonica also could be viewed with suspicion in the then complex politico-cultural context. Most probably, the threatening situation was not only prolonged but it got aggravated. Donfried mentions that "the Thessalonian Christians' proclamation of the kingdom of God (2 Thess 1:15) generates hostility among non-Christians (2 Thess 1:8; 2:12)." To add, the mention of "*tois diōgmois* that always refers to persecution" is definitely indicative of the gravity of the continuing problem.[66]

64 Recently, Ascough and Rulmu have contended in favor of understanding the community in Thessalonica as a Voluntary Association. See, Richard S. Ascough, "The Thessalonian Christian Community as a Professional Voluntary Association," *Journal of Biblical Literature* 119, no. 2 (2000): 311–28, especially 398–99; Rulmu, "Between Ambition and Quietism," 397.

65 Rulmu, "Between Ambition and Quietism," 398.

66 Karl P. Donfried, "The Theology of 2 Thessalonians," in *The Theology of the Shorter Pauline Letters*, New Testament Theology (Cambridge: Cambridge University Press, 1993), 82.

2.3.2. Immediate context: The consequence of lack of teaching on eschatology and the Parousia

Due to Paul's sudden exit of Paul from Thessalonica during his first visit as a result of the opposition that broke out in the city, he could not complete his entire teaching on the Parousia with sufficient clarifications. This paved the way for the possible formation of a unique mixture of certain radical elements present in the Cabirus cult in Thessalonica and Paul's teaching on Christ's return. This worried Paul. Bruce maintains that the Thessalonian believers received the early Christian teachings on eschatology through Paul when he was with them. They had learned about the return of the resurrected Son of God from heaven when they would be saved from the end-time tribulation destined for the ungodly (1 Thess 1:9, 19; 5:9, 10). However, the question about the fate of "the dead in Christ" at the return of the Lord Jesus was not addressed before them.[67] Meanwhile, after the sudden departure of Paul and his companions from the city, some of the members in the community slept in the Lord. This had created confusion among them. Paul heard about the current dilemma that bothered them when Timothy returned from Athens after Paul had sent him to inquire about the well-being of the new converts.

Thus, based on the mixed report he received through Timothy, Paul wrote 1 Thessalonians assuring the believers that those who died in Christ will be first raised at Christ's return and then those who are still alive will be caught-up with the Lord mid-air (1 Thess 4:13–18). Apart from this, Paul also taught the suddenness of the coming of the day of the Lord "like a thief in the night" (1 Thess 5:1–3). However, Paul's letter was misunderstood. In fact, it caused an "opposite effect, heightening and further radicalizing the church's millenarian fervor."[68] If the chronological primacy of 1 Thessalonians over 2 Thessalonians is maintained, the complex situation arising in Thessalonica requiring Paul's immediate attention gets clearer. Paul's words regarding the indefinite timing of the Messiah's return in 1 Thessalonians (5:2), "led some readers to conclude that it was so imminent that there was no point in going on with the ordinary concerns of daily life; perhaps, indeed, it had already arrived."[69]

So, Paul corrects them by addressing the issue in 2 Thessalonians 2:1–12. He spells out specifically the order of events that necessarily precede the Parousia. Such teaching does not seem to contradict the secret and indefiniteness of the Messiah's return taught in the previous letter. While the ungodly alone would be taken by surprise when the Lord shall return, the believers would be ready all the time, says Paul in 1 Thessalonians 5:4–5.

67 Bruce, *1 and 2 Thessalonians*, xxxvii.

68 Stacy, "Thessalonian Correspondences," 188.

69 Bruce, *1 and 2 Thessalonians*, xlii.

They would definitely recognize the events as preceding the Messiah's return. Interestingly, Paul's interest in teaching them about the Parousia was purely to make them morally alert and to resist ethical degradation spreading among them.

2.3.3. Immediate context: Ethical degradation

Paul's appeal to live by a higher ethical standard among the gentile Thessalonians is directly connected with his understanding of the Parousia. The background for Paul's advice is the morally degrading native religio-cultural influences upon the new converts in the Christian community. There appears to have been certain forms of continuity-discontinuity among them with their pre-Christian life, which under particular circumstances corrupted their understanding of the vision of the apostle for the church in Thessalonica. For Donfried, rightly so, a deeper understanding of the pre-Christian gentile background of the Thessalonian believers explains the correlation between the Thessalonian context and Paul's use of varied terms in 1 Thessalonians 4:1–9. The advice of Paul, then, appears entirely intentional and context-specific in order to distinguish "the behavior of the Thessalonian Christians from that of their former heathen and pagan life which is still much alive in the various cults of the city." The specific meaning of the terms used, like *skeuos* and *ktaomai*, by Paul in the context of the then cultic practices "would surely not be lost on the Thessalonian audience nor its wider meaning of gaining control over the body with regard to sexual matters."[70]

Similarly, Paul ends his first letter to the believers in Thessalonica with a strong appeal for moral uprightness and soberness. For him, because we are to be prepared for the day of the Lord, believers must live as the children of light. They belong to the day, not darkness, which demands them to be sober in conduct (2 Thess 5:6–7). Such a strong appeal in 1 Thessalonians 5:5–7 and 19–22 by the apostle is triggered by the unique context of the Thessalonian mystery cults.[71] Riesner concludes that "Paul's ethical instructions to the Thessalonians are characterized largely by Jewish traditions, with the goal of giving the church an unmistakable identity of its own to ensure it would not be confused with other religious *collegia*."[72] There is an increasing consensus among the scholars that Paul's advice to the Thessalonians is caused by the threat created by the influence of the surrounding cults (syncretism) upon the community in Christ and the resultant moral degradation happening within the community.

---

70 Donfried, "Cults of Thessalonica," 29-31, cited from 30, and 31, respectively.

71 Donfried, "Cults of Thessalonica," 29–31. See also, Riesner, *Paul's Early Period*, 372–75.

72 Riesner, *Paul's Early Period*, 375.

Another closely associated issue threatening the communal life of the Christians in Thessalonica was idleness. Some among the believers had given up work and were depending upon others within the congregation to feed themselves (2 Thess 3:6–15). According to Paul's teaching, idleness has no room in Christian existence and the guiding rule of Christian work ethics is simple: "The one who is unwilling to work shall not eat" (2 Thess 3:10). In short, the problems threatening the community were multifaceted—moral uprightness, work ethics, and sexual purity.

2.3.4. Immediate context: The apostle's defence of self-integrity

Paul's seeming defence of his integrity before the new converts implies a possibility of some in Thessalonica misunderstanding him in the light of several other teachers of philosophy operating in the city. Koester states that Paul underlines this differentiation by drawing "a clear line between himself and the itinerant Cynic preacher."[73] In 1 Thessalonians 2:1–12, the line of difference that Paul emphatically draws is countercultural, and it places him on a higher moral pedestal. His interest is not pleasing people but God, not seeking to trick them but operating with pure intention, and not desiring authority over them but to nurture an affectionate relationship. According to Jewett, "the prominent place of this material in the narration of reasons for Paul's thanksgiving indicates its importance for the morale of the church which the rhetoric of 1 Thessalonians aims to sustain."[74] Jewett, in partial agreement with Schmithal, contends that some in Thessalonica critiqued Paul's leadership as the one who "merely proclaimed the spiritual message rather than demonstrating it." Knowing the gravity of the critique in causing a disturbance, possibly, among the believers, Paul affirms that his ministry among them was neither "without results" (1 Thess 2:1) nor was it "simply with words" (1 Thess 1:5).[75]

The justification to our assumption that some critiqued Paul and other local leaders' leadership is found in his exhortation to "acknowledge those who work hard among you" (1 Thess 5:12). The reason is simple: they "care for you in the Lord" (1 Thess 5:12). Hence, they deserved to be treated very high in love because of their work (admonishing). According to Jewett, Paul's words "justify the status and action of these leaders in the face of internal criticism" but without "any legal or institutional warrants, urging a willing submission from the good will of the congregation."[76] Paul's exhortation to do so is due to its potential to disrupt the intracommunity peace: "Live in peace with each other" (1 Thess 5:13).

---

73 Koester, *History and Literature of Early Christianity*, 113.

74 Jewett, *Thessalonian Correspondence*, 102.

75 Jewett, *Thessalonian Correspondence*, 102.

76 Jewett, *Thessalonian Correspondence*, 103.

It is in this context that one needs to read Paul's letter to the Thessalonians. Evidently, the situation in Thessalonica is not favorable to the Christian community to survive and flourish, while the visible moral degradation taking place within the community in a hybrid cultural context also needs to be dealt with.

2.4. The purpose of 1 and 2 Thessalonians

One cannot doubt that Paul's teaching on eschatology and the Parousia takes a larger share of space along with personal exhortations in the two letters. It does imply that the theological themes such as eschatology or the Parousia are vital to understand the letters, their occasions of writing, and the larger purpose of sending two letters in quick succession. However, Paul surely did not have a doctrinal interest to send the letters, for these letters do not exhaust his teaching on any of the doctrinal topics. Instead, he discussed the themes as much as they were thought to be relevant to the problems disrupting the corporate life of the community of God in Thessalonica. Rightly, Beker acknowledges the underlying truth about Paul's letters by contending that the letters are coherent to certain extent with the larger theological truth of the gospel but historically continent, simultaneously. So, they are authoritative yet occasional and personal in nature. They address specific situation arising within a community theologically and hermeneutically, which in the process "serve to make the truth of the gospel the effective word of God."[77] So, we ask: Did Paul merely envision resolution of problems disrupting the community in Thessalonica by his teachings as the sole purpose of his letter correspondence? Probably not! Resolution of the prevailing problems threatening the community was merely a means to achieve a larger purpose. Paul had an overarching larger purpose that required faithful interpretation of the truth of the gospel effectively in a multidimensional situation of the Thessalonian community.

Traditionally, as discussed as part of the occasion, Paul's seeming response based on the report he received through Timothy determined the immediate purpose of sending the two letters to the same community. Malherbe maintains that it was primarily a pastoral purpose that Paul had in writing these letters.[78] However, Paul's outburst in thanksgiving to God for the believers in 1 and 2 Thessalonians appears to reflect the overarching interest of the apostle concerning the new converts in Thessalonica. Paul's thanksgiving is centered around their conversion from the idols to the living God in the past, their unflinching persistence in the newfound faith despite persecution, Christian testimony of the Thessalonians

[77] Beker, *Paul the Apostle*, 23–24, cited from 24.

[78] Malherbe, *Paul and the Thessalonians*.

well-known among others, Christian formation consciously undertaken by imitation of Paul and the missionaries, and their endurance in Christ-inspired hope amidst present persecution (1 Thess 1:2–10; 2 Thess 1:3–10). They together indicate his larger interest in sending the letters, for they are not merely acknowledging what is good among them, but it is an encouragement by appreciation to continue in the same. Paul's prayer is that "God may make you worthy of his calling" (2 Thess 1:11). In other words, the apostle's primary interest despite his desire to resolve all the issues threatening the community in Thessalonica is that they may be worthy of God according to his ultimate purpose for them. Thus, he praises God for what they are today in Christ and how they live in love with one another, while praying for and encouraging them to live lives not only pleasing to God (1 Thess 4:1), but also worthy of their calling (2 Thess 1:11).

Interestingly, Paul's request for their prayer for himself and fellow missionaries is spoken in comparison with the Thessalonians. Paul says, "pray for us that the message of the Lord may spread rapidly and be honored, *just as it was with you*" (2 Thess 3:1, emphasis added). The missional purpose of Paul in sending the letters to the believers in Thessalonica becomes evident here. They have played an important role in honoring and rapidly spreading the gospel to their surrounding areas in the past, either by their steadfastness in faith or by personal testimony. In fact, the final goal of living worthy of God by maintaining sexual purity or working with their hands (not being busybodies—2 Thess 3:11) is only "to win the respect of outsiders" (1 Thess 4:12) or to restore the waivered by correction as of fellow believers (2 Thess 3:15). Even teaching on eschatology and the Parousia is vital for his mission in Thessalonica. Bruce maintains that not only the effectiveness of Paul's evangelization required clarity of his vision about the cosmic events at the eschatological times, but even the effectiveness of his missionary strategy also depended upon such things.[79] Similarly, Beale states that "Paul must write (in 2 Thessalonians concerning their over realized eschatological understanding) to set them straight because the consequences theologically and ethically will be disastrous for the witness of the Christian community in Thessalonica."[80]

2.5. Paul's Thessalonian community and the Christians in a pluralistic and hostile context in India

The primary intent of the discussion in the remainder of this chapter is to ensure not showing the present-day sociocultural and religio-political context of the church in India as parallel to the first-century context of the community in Thessalonica. Rather, the desired goal is to paint a broad

[79] Bruce, *1 and 2 Thessalonians*, xliii.

[80] Beale, *1–2 Thessalonians*, 30.

context of the church in India in line with the preceding discussion on the context of the Thessalonian community during the time of Paul. It is purported that the discussion will provide a broad basis to draw relevant implications of the missional-theological discussion on important themes in the Thessalonian correspondence carried out in the following chapters in the book.

Like Thessalonica of the first century, India is a land of a variety of people groups (ethnic groups), major world religions and their innumerable sects, cultures, economic classes, Christian denominations, etc. Probably, the pluralistic context of India is more complex and challenging for Christian mission today than it was at Thessalonica for Paul and his missionary companions in the first century. Without any exaggeration we can say that after a few 100 kilometers, one finds a different language, dialect, forms of cultures, and religions in India. Its pluralistic context poses varied forms of challenges before the church in India in actualizing her missional call. While the plurality of cultures challenges our effort to articulate the gospel in native worldviews and languages in order to be contextually relevant, the plurality of religions has evoked mixed responses from different religious communities on different occasions. In general, the Indian society has been peace-loving, intentionally pluralistic with mutual respect between the religious communities (*Sarwa dharma, Samabhava*), and harmonious.

However, in recent decades, especially in the last decade, we have witnessed a sharp resurgence of a majoritarian right-wing religio-cultural nationalism, with tacit support from the powerful political corners, which has threatened to break the fragile social web. Certain groups of the majority religion have resorted to violent reactions and ideological polarization breeding hatred toward other minority communities including the minority Christian community. At times, this has set the agenda for the national political debate. A religiously defined cultural identity in national discourse has caused unleashing of both verbal and physical violence against the minority communities by creating fear in them. The elected representatives in the parliament have resorted to communal and religiously polarizing language in their political speeches to define the religious "other" in India. In the name of the celebrated Hindu god, they call themselves *Ramzade* meaning "children of Ram." In contrast, all others, particularly those belonging to the Semitic religion, living in the Indian subcontinent are called *haramzade* meaning "illegitimate children."

Although opposition to the church and her missional activities is neither new nor unique to the history of independent India, it is beyond doubt that the right-wing Hindutva movement has aggressively perpetuated violence against the Christian minority in India. It is surely not a state sponsored persecution of the Christian minority, but the current regime's right-wing Hindu ideological leniency emboldens its political affiliates and other sister organizations to act boldly against the church. The government has generally either denied atrocities against the religious minority or has turned deaf ears to the persecuted minority. In the most recent Open Doors' 2019 World Watch List report, India appears in "The 10 Most Dangerous Places to be a Christian."[81] It has become common to hear daily news updates from various corners of the country reporting a mob lynching incident of Christian individuals; brutal murder of pastors, their families, and Christian converts; demolition of church buildings; desecration of the churches; atrocities against nuns and missionaries; prosecuting the faithful ones with false accusations under the anti-conversion laws; etc. It is an unprecedented phenomenon at such a large scale in the post-independent era in India.

Similarly, on the pretext of forced religious conversion or conversion by allurement—a criminal act under the anti-conversion bills promulgated in many states of India—an increasing number of Christian pastors and missionaries are harassed by false criminal police complaints being lodged against them. However, it is not rare to hear in national media reports about reconversion of the members of minority religious communities to the majority religion under the aggressively carried-out religious conversion program called *Ghar Wapsi* by some who belong to the latter group. The *Ghar Wapsi* movement has been successful to some extent among the economically poor and socially marginalized (dalits and tribals) groups of Christians. Moreover, we also hear about murderous attacks on Christian religious leaders and believers. In addition, in several instances, some mobs have desecrated Christian religious places, although very rarely have such miscreants been found to be guilty under the law. On the contrary, Christians have been accused of pursuing a political agenda due to their transnational loyalty to wrest power from Hindus in the name of God and destroying the Hindu culture by the spread of Western culture and religion.[82] Hence, Christian programs of evangelization and missionary works among the dalits and adivasis have always been viewed with suspicion. Often, the foreign funds received by the church in

---

81 Lindy Lowry, "The 10 Most Dangerous Places to Be a Christian" (Open Doors USA, January 16, 2019), accessed February 5, 2019, https://www.opendoorsusa.org/christian-persecution/stories/10-dangerous-places-christian-worldwatch-list/. See also, Harriet Sherwood, "One in Three Christians Face Persecution in Asia, Report Finds," *The Guardian*, n.d., accessed on February 8, 2019, https://www.theguardian.com/world/2019/jan/16/one-in-three-christians-face-persecution-in-asia-reportfinds.

82 Pralay Kanungo, *RSS's Tryst with Politics: From Hedgewar to Sudarshan* (Delhi: Manohar, 2003), 114.

India is viewed as evidence to prove their mischievous allegations against Christians in India. Such an environment created by a section of people in India has not only generated a huge amount of misinformation against the minority, but it has also given birth, nurtured, and caused the spread of hatred against them.

The ideology that vitiates the social environment and breathes threats against the minority community members is the ideology of Hindutva as promoted and propagated by the Hindu cultural organization named the *Rashtriya Swayamsevak Sangh* (RSS). Hindutva, a Hindu cultural nationalist movement, owes its origin to the insensitive missionary movement carried out in the pre- and post-independent India where every native belief, cultural practices, and value was uncritically condemned and rejected as sinful and ungodly.[83] It articulates the Hindu identity in both an inclusive and exclusive sense within the broad framework of territory, religion, Hindu *varnashrama* system, and language.[84] While in the territorial sense, all who lived toward the east of the Indus river are included in the group of original natives inhabitants of the land, the followers of Semitic religion are excluded considering them to be later invaders.[85] The Sangh "emphasizes that Hindu culture is the national culture. Hindu society is national society, Hindu art is national art. Hindu literature is national literature and Hindu history is national history. People belonging to various religions (excluding Christianity and Islam) in this country are all Hindus by culture and are nationals of this Hindu Rashtra."[86]

The other side of the story of the Christian community in India is the moral degradation, ethical corruption, and spiritual degeneration taking place within the church. In a shocking turn of events in Christianity in India, bishops and Christian leaders have been arrested and booked under atrocities against women (nuns)[87] and gross financial corruption

83 Robert Eric Frykenberg, "Hindutva and the Aftermath of Ayodhya: Dangers of Political Religion and Religious Nationalism," in *Nationalism and Hindutva: A Christian Response*, ed. Mark T. B. Laing (Delhi/Pune: ISPCK/CMS/UBS, 2005), 5–12; M. T. Cherian, *Hindutva Agenda and Minority Rights: A Christian Response* (Bangalore: Centre for Contemporary Christianity, 2007), 156–63.

84 T. K. Oommen, "Religious Nationalism and Democratic Polity in India: Impossibility of Reconciliation," in *Nationalism and Hindutva: A Christian Response*, ed. Mark T. B. Laing (Delhi/Pune: ISPCK/CMS/UBS, 2005), 36–37.

85 Kanungo, *RSS's Tryst with Politics*, 92.

86 Kanungo, *RSS's Tryst with Politics*, 126–27 (parenthesis added).

87 For example, Maria Thomas, "The AP Blows the Lid off Decades-Long Sexual Abuse of Nuns by Catholic Priests in India," *Quartz India*, n.d., accessed June 26, 2020, https://qz.com/india/1513007/how-catholic-priests-sexually-abused-nuns-in-kerala-india/; Aravind Gowda, "Pastor Held for Sexually Exploiting Minor Girls," *India Today*, n.d., accessed June 26, 2020, https://www.indiatoday.in/india/south/story/bangalore-pastor-held-for-sexually -exploiting-minors-135890-2011-06-19.

charges.[88] This not only marred Christian testimony in the public space, but has also at times left the devout believers in the lurch. Greed for a huge amount of wealth has led them to adopt fraudulent means against their Christian identity to act corruptly. It has hampered the Christian mission for it demolishes the validity of the gospel proclaimed to the non-Christian population. Often, the poor believers are deprived of pastoral care because the Christian conduct of the leaders within the church has been questionable. It has left the church morally bankrupt and, at times, has disqualified her of becoming the "light" and "salt" of the earth.

In addition, the innumerable proliferation of the independent churches without adequately trained pastors has also given rise to weird Christian practices and doctrines within the church. Often such groups have adopted a stance against theological education favoring the Spirit-inspired teachings within the church. Although such statements cannot be applied in general to implicate the charismatic and pentecostal denominations, it is an undeniable fact that at times, in some circles, the whims and fancies of the pastors are taught to the simple believers as the gospel truth. Prosperity theology has been taught at the cost of pursuing true Christian discipleship within the church. Even Christian faith in God and witness to Christ are encouraged in materialistic terms as a means to receive worldly blessings. Seldom do we hear sermons preached on the high Christian ethical demands upon the members of the church and the second coming of Christ as the judge of all.

In short, the church in India faces quite similar but unique challenges like the Thessalonian community of believers. In this context, a missional reading of Paul's Thessalonian correspondence becomes important not only to teach and encourage the church to partner with God in his universal mission but to also live her authentic identity in Christ amidst the other communities of people in India.

In short, Paul visited Thessalonica, a free Roman city in the first century, during his second missionary journey after he received in Troas the Macedonian call in a vision. After the city of Philippi, Thessalonica is the second major urban center that Paul visited during his mission in

88 For example, Anto Akkara, "Indian Campaign Against Church Corruption," *ChristianityToday.Com*, January 1, 2001, accessed on August 4, 2019, https://www.christianitytoday.com/ct/2001/januaryweb-only/14.0.html; "Bishop Warns against Illegal Sale of Church Property," *The Times of India*, n.d., accessed on August 4, 2019, https://timesofindia.indiatimes.com/city/allahabad/Bishop-warns-against-illegal-sale-of-church-property/articleshow/19553793.cms; "Land Scam of Rs 10,000 Crores Reported in Christian Organisations of Uttar Pradesh," *OpIndia*, 16 July 2019, accessed on August 4, 2019, https://www.opindia.com/2019/07/church-scam-fraudulent-land-deals-illegal-sale-of-over-10000-crores-reported-in-christian-organisations-of-uttar-pradesh/.

the region. The strategic geographical and commercial significance of the city during the Roman period invited people of different ethnic, religious, and cultural backgrounds into the city. This created a transcultural hybrid sociocultural context with a cross-fertilization of the different religions in Thessalonica. However, the dominant Roman presence as the unchallenged political power continued to make its presence felt not only through the presence of the army but also with the active Roman imperial cult. In this context, Paul initially preached the gospel of Christ among the Jews and succeeded in establishing a church. To this small body of believers soon, many native God-fearing Greek Thessalonians joined. However, Paul's quick success in winning converts in Thessalonica irked the local Jews who created a tumult in the city forcing him to cut short his mission work abruptly among them. Probably, the opposition by Jews against him and his companions continued even after his departure and was directed against the new community of Christians left behind. Paul's abrupt departure from the city not only created a lapse in teaching the Thessalonian believers the whole Christian doctrine on the second coming of Christ but it also evoked violent opposition from outside the church threatening the existence of the community of believers. To add, the early demise of the loved ones in Christ concerned the new converts about the dead ones' eternal destiny and the ethical degradation that began to happen with some Thessalonian Christians. These realities together formed the immediate occasion of sending the two letters from Corinth in 50–51 C.E. So, Paul's purpose of sending the two letters is on the one hand pastoral, that is, to strengthen the believers in their newfound faith despite suffering persecution, but on the other hand it is missional, appreciating them for their role in the spread of the gospel and for winning the respect of outsiders through their high moral living. They had to be reminded of their unique status in Christ and the promise of salvation in eternity by living as a community of disciples called to live a life worthy of the kingdom of God. Paul teaches them that their hope in Christ for both who have died already and those who are living is still valid until the coming of Christ. Hence, they ought to persist in suffering as the elect of God, through whom God is working out his eternal plan of salvation to all their neighbors.

3

ESCHATOLOGY: A FRAMEWORK FOR MISSIONAL THEOLOGY

A key interest in the study of Thessalonians, in the past, has been due to a significant amount of eschatological material found in the two small letters of Paul. Moreover, the letter has been interrogated, to go behind the text, to reconstruct the historical context in which Paul's eschatological thought took shape. However, it is interesting to notice that Paul's specific interest is not merely to provide a systematic exposition of the entire Christian eschatology to the Thessalonian readers but to also address the existential crisis—moral, social, and spiritual needs within the church requiring some more teaching on the last days events. Paul employs eschatology as a framework to address vital elements of their corporate existence as the community of God and gives them ethical exhortations so that they can fulfill divine purpose behind their election. "Eschatology suffuses the Thessalonian letters" so that it forms an integral part of Paul's theological vocabulary.[1]

Although in the past centuries, the term *eschatology* has been variedly interpreted by the students of Paul, in this chapter the term is employed with its most basic meaning. It refers to Paul's teaching on the last days including the events like the Lord's Parousia, the resurrection of the dead in Christ, Christians being caught in the air with the Christ, his judgment, destruction of the ultimate evil force, etc. He borrows apocalyptic categories of dualism to articulate his eschatological teachings in Thessalonian correspondence. In recent decades, Paul has been accused at times in modern scholarship that he has altered his position on various issues

1 Todd D. Still, "Eschatology in the Thessalonian Letters," *Review & Expositor* 96, no. 2 (1999): 195.

related to eschatology over his missionary career. However, this chapter does not seek to engage in resolving such contentious issues with evidence here.[2] Rather, the interest here is to recognize eschatology as Paul's theological framework in addressing major issues threatening the cohesive existence of the Thessalonian community. In doing that, their theological identity and its social implications, missional living, and formation as partners in the ongoing *missio Dei*, and the meaning of their suffering as Christians and God's justice in the light of the last judgment shall be included. The discussion in this chapter intends only to draw a broad framework for the discussion carried out in the remaining chapters. Such a discussion is important to avoid repetition of the content elsewhere in the book.

So, we engage in asking questions like: How central is eschatology in Paul's missional theology? What is the nature of Paul's language of eschatology? What are the major components of Paul's eschatology? What are the missional implications of Paul's eschatology?

3.1. The centrality of eschatology for Paul's missional theology in Thessalonian correspondence

Speaking in more general terms about eschatology in the New Testament, Beale maintains that "all doctrine in the New Testament is essentially eschatological in nature."[3] I believe it is right, especially with Paul. The importance of the idea of eschatology in Paul's theological vision about God and the destiny of the world cannot be over-estimated. According to D. E. Aune, apocalyptical thought "certainly provides a framework for this thought" whether or not it is the center of his theology.[4] While Still prefers to treat it as a "part of the warp and woof of the New Testament documents,"[5] for Gaventa it is "the raisins" of the "raisin toast."[6] To overlook the importance of eschatology in unravelling the heart and mind of the great missionary and apostle of Christ Jesus, Paul, would be to risk missing the very backbone of his thought, "the raisins" itself. Within the two letters,

2 For relevant discussion on Paul's consistent or inconsistent position on eschatology, see Woodbridge, "Did Paul Change His Mind?," 5–18. Woodbridge concludes in favour of Paul as a coherent thinker on the topic. He maintains that the seeming contradictions owe to the contextual needs that the letters sent were supposed to meet.

3 Beale, *1-2 Thessalonians*, 19.

4 D. E. Aune, "Eschatology (Early Christian)," *Anchor Bible Dictionary*, vol. 2 (New York: Doubleday, 1992), 602.

5 Still, "Eschatology in the Thessalonian Letters," 195.

6 Beverly Roberts Gaventa, *First and Second Thessalonians*, Interpretation: A Bible Commentary for Teaching and Preaching (Louisville, KY: John Knox Press, 1998), 76.

Paul speaks about God's intervention in human history in and through the death and resurrection of Jesus Christ as a mission to rescue and restore the alienated human beings to God's kingdom. As a part of it, Paul's mission in Thessalonica, the story of Thessalonian believers' conversion and their responsibility as the elect community of God to participate in his mission are both geared toward and driven by eschatological thinking. They ought to participate in God's mission by preaching in words, embodying the gospel within the local setting and fulfilling the mandate to be ethically formed as a Christlike community walking worthy of God's call upon them.

Paul saw the actualization of his call as "an apostle to the gentiles," gathering those outside of the Abrahamic blessings to share in the eternal blessings in Christ, by forming the community of Christian disciples across the cities in the Roman empire. These local communities had a larger corporate identity as one universal body participating in the *missio Die*. He preached, taught, and suffered hardships in his mission to equip, enrich, and enable them to fulfill the eternal missional purpose of their divine calling. However, as Hafemann states, "Paul's present joy over the Thessalonians' current life of faith does not satisfy him (cf. 4:1, 10); rather, he begs God more than ever to be able to see them again face to face in order to strengthen (καταριζω) what is still lacking in their faith (3:10)."[7]

But the question remains: What characterizes the theological vision of human history in Paul's mind that energizes him not only to persist relentlessly to spread the gospel he is divinely entrusted with, but also to teach and exhort his audience to capture the same vision with a sense of responsibility to continue in the same direction with him? Donfried answers the question succinctly by highlighting the significance of eschatology for mission in Thessalonian correspondence. He states, "eschatology is precisely that driving force behind Paul's vision of universality and catholicity which is for him nothing other than the mission of the church."[8] Paul feels an urgency to crisss-cross the empire with the gospel, forming and equipping believers to volunteer in the mission of God simply because he felt the return of the Son is certain and imminent (1 Thess 1:10). Hence, the impending end of the world necessitates greater missional push by the community of the elect of God beyond ethnic, racial, and cultural binaries. So, rightly Donfried maintains that "the church is universal because of its eschatological character reaching temporally and spatially in every

---

7 Scott J. Hafemann, "Divine Judgement and the Completion of the Missionary Task: Paul's Motivation for Ministry in 1-2 Thessalonians," in *Paul's Message and Ministry in Covenant Perspective: Selected Essays* (Bangalore: SAIACS Press, 2016), 192.

8 Donfried, "Theology of 1 Thessalonians," 78.

direction, crossing all frontiers of culture, class, race, religion, age, sex, and whatever else seems to erect walls of partition."[9]

If so, how does, according to Paul, eschatology help the church to fulfill God's mission in every sense? For Paul, it is possible only when "the eschatological word of God, the gospel, enters into the arena of human history. Only when Christ alone is recognised as the Lord of history and the victor of its ruling powers and principalities, is the church enabled and empowered to engage with the demons of our own time and place and to test everything, holding on to what is good and abstaining from every form of evil."[10] In fact, by inviting Christ as the Lord and victor over all visible and invisible created orders that we find the reason to participate in the eternally on-going missional engagement of God in the world. Hence, for the gospel to intervene in history in order to transform the power structures of the world, with Christ enthroned above them all, the community of God functioning as the agent of God here and now becomes vital. It is inevitable for us to overlook the eschatological basis of Paul's theology in order to understand the way it upholds the entire structure of his thought for missional significance.

The most explicit evidence of Paul's eschatological framework of theology is in 1 Thessalonians 1:9–10. Undoubtedly, here, Paul engrains "the gospel" he preached in Thessalonica in the eschatological framework. The three vital aspects of the early Christian eschatological thought "the themes of Parousia, resurrection, and judgement are interwoven."[11] That is to say, the Thessalonians waiting for the appearance of the Son from heaven is their unflinching hope in the Parousia (cf. 1 Thess 5:2). Further, while Jesus is mentioned as the one who is raised from the dead, it implies their bodily resurrection on the last day (cf. 1 Thess 4:14, 16; 5:10), the reference to Jesus as their rescuer "from the coming wrath" is a warning about the impending judgment upon those who oppose him in unbelief (cf. 1 Thess 2:14–16).

In the Thessalonian correspondence, Paul deals with eschatology in three major blocks of material (1 Thess 4:13–18; 5:1–11; 2 Thess 2:1–12), although the idea is suffused in the whole document with significant pointers scattered throughout. In the remainder of this chapter, an effort shall be made to revisit them through the missional lens to draw relevant insights for discussions in the following chapters. It requires us to undertake an overview of Paul's language of eschatology in order to set a direction for the remaining part of the discussion.

9 Donfried, "Theology of 1 Thessalonians," 78.
10 Donfried, "Theology of 1 Thessalonians," 79.
11 Aune, "Eschatology (Early Christian)," 602.

3.2. The Language of Eschatology

The language of eschatology in Thessalonian correspondence is "more theological and pastoral than predictive."[12] All the major theological themes in the Thessalonian correspondence are so immersed in Paul's eschatology that the nature of Paul's language of eschatology must be understood to recognize the fuller significance of all that he says. Paul employed the language specifically to respond to the local situation in line with the broad apocalyptic scheme of cosmic history in forming, shaping, and propelling the community of believers to ascent from their mere people of God consciousness to fulfill their missional role. According to Beker, the language that Paul employs is "the apocalyptic language of Judaism" by which he "expresses the Christ-event."[13] In it, for Beker, Paul employs his call as the "primordial experience" to form "his basal language" as a necessary component to speak about the Christ-event that "nourishes, intensifies, and modifies Paul's traditional apocalyptic language." So, the symbols like righteousness, reconciliation, etc., together make the symbolic structure of Paul's thought but they "in their particularity interpret the gospel according to the contingent needs of a particular situation."[14] Such a language when employed requires one to view the present time of the church as already a part of the coming of age. "The *character* of Paul's contingent hermeneutic is shaped by his apocalyptic core in that in nearly all cases the contingent interpretation of the gospel points—whether implicitly or explicitly—to the imminent cosmic triumph of God."[15]

In Thessalonians, Paul's eschatological language inherits and improvises the apocalyptic tradition of the Old Testament and the early Christian thought to exhort, teach, and establish the community of believers amidst the hostile environment. It uses a language that is much "bigger than life," as Beale says, to speak about the present realities of life.[16] Beale succinctly continues to say, "that is not to relegate eschatology to the realm of ethereal speculation, however, with no consequences for the present . . .. In 1 Thessalonians 5:1–11, for example, he does not exhort the Thessalonians to become 'children of the day,' rather, he declares that they are and urges them to act accordingly. The fact of God's coming triumph enables believers to look frankly on the dirt and grime that surround them but to live expectantly, leaning toward the future."[17] Paul constantly reminds them using his eschatological language that their present ethical life, faith and

12 Gaventa, *First and Second Thessalonians*, 79.

13 J. Christiaan Beker, *Paul the Apostle*, 15.

14 Beker, *Paul the Apostle*, 16.

15 Beker, *Paul the Apostle*, 19 (emphasis original).

16 Gaventa, *First and Second Thessalonians*, 78.

17 Gaventa, *First and Second Thessalonians*, 78–79.

conversion in Christ, suffering persecution, and perseverance have an impact beyond their temporal earthly existence. They ought to live in the present in light of the last days.

In doing that, as also Beale observes, the language of the New Testament shares the literary character of the Old Testament eschatological thought like the "latter rain." The Old Testament prophetically speaks about: (i) the tribulation that Israel is to undergo under her oppressors (Ezek 38:14–17), the gravity of her suffering persecution, and the threat of false teaching that lead many to apostacy (Dan 10:14; 11:27–12:10); (ii) the judgment of the enemies of Israel (Ezek 38:14–16); and (iii) the final victory of her Messiah leading to the establishment of his kingdom (Isa 2:2–4; Mic 4:1–3; Dan 2:28–45).[18] However, as also Beale mentions, unlike in the Old Testament, the New Testament speaks of the eschatology as a reality that has already begun in the present with the divine intervention in the birth, death, and resurrection of Jesus. If so,

> the resurrection marked the beginning of Jesus' messianic reign, the Spirit at Pentecost signalled the inauguration of his rule through the church (Acts 1:6–8; 2:1–43), and the persecution of Jesus and the church indicated the beginning of the final tribulation. What the Old Testament writers did not foresee so clearly from their vantage point was the reality that the kingdom and the tribulation could coexist at the same time (see Rev 1:9). Therefore, the latter days do not take place only at some point in the future but occur throughout the whole church age.[19]

Within the Thessalonian correspondence, the broad New Testament understanding of eschatology finds a vital reference, although they may not obtain an elaborate explanation. For example, first, the "latter days" idea does not get direct reference in the two letters to the Thessalonians, but it is clear that the Holy Spirit is given to the new converts in the city by God (1 Thess 4:8) in a similar manner to the event of Pentecost (Acts 2:1–43). The church in Thessalonica is born and continues in the ministry of Christ through the power of the Spirit displayed in and through the ministry and the content of the gospel of Christ that Paul and his companions preached (1 Thess 1:5). Amidst suffering, he fills them with joy (1 Thess 1:6) and sanctifies them for the eschatological salvation (2 Thess 2:13). Second, the church in Christ sharing in the blessings promised in the Old Testament suffers under her oppressors (1 Thess 3:3–4) and the believers are confused by the false teachers (1 Thess 5:21–22; 2 Thess 2:2–3). Although evildoers will be judged by the living and true God, their role in the present harms the corporate life and testimony of the people of God. Third, Paul teaches that the Lord Jesus will return to destroy "the

18 Beale, *1–2 Thessalonians*, 19.

19 Beale, *1–2 Thessalonians*, 20.

man of lawlessness" (2 Thess 2:8), who is "doomed to destruction" for his anti-God activities (2 Thess 2:4).

It requires us now to clarify the significance of Paul's eschatology for his personal missional consciousness and the missional formation of the Thessalonian believers. So, we ask: What are the significance and role of Paul's eschatology in forming the missional consciousness of Paul and the Thessalonian believers' missional call and purpose of existence? The resultant discussion in the following does not purport to be exhaustive. Different aspects of it shall be elaborated and analyzed in the following chapters along with the themes and ideas taken up for discussion in them. Instead, here, I shall seek to elucidate the pertinent points of Paul's eschatology that undergirds, structures, and builds his missional theology as evident in the two letters.

3.3. Eschatology, Paul's mission, and the Thessalonians

An important starting point to discuss the eschatological mooring of Paul's missional praxis and consciousness is his repeated earnest prayers offered to God for the Thessalonian believers (1 Thess 3:13; 5:23). In 1 Thessalonians 3:13, he prays that "when our Lord Jesus comes with all his holy ones" at the Parousia, may they be "blameless and holy" by the strengthening of *their hearts*. But in 1 Thessalonians 5:23, he prays for their *whole being*—the Spirit, soul and body—to "be kept blameless at the coming of our Lord Jesus Christ." The reason for this difference is that while in the first instance the prayer for blamelessness and holiness at heart is based on the good report about the Thessalonians (i.e., standing firm in faith amidst hostility) Paul received through Timothy, the second instance of prayer for their blamelessness in their whole being is triggered by the mention of the sanctifying act of God. In other words, while in the hostile context their hearts need to be absolutely grabbed by the sole desire to stand firm in their trust upon God, their worthiness to join in the victory parade of the Christ at his second coming is possible only by the sanctification of their whole being. The desire is that they may be rescued from the coming wrath.

However, what is the reason for Paul's intense concern for the believers in Thessalonica? The foundational reason for Paul is personal. That is, he does not want anyone to be lost by the deception of the tempter. He says, explaining the reason for sending Timothy to Thessalonica, that "I was afraid that in some way the tempter had tempted you and that *our labors might have been in vain*" (1 Thess 3:5). Paul suffered physical ailment (cf. Gal 4:13) during his second missionary journey and the violence unleashed against him and his companions. This made Paul worried about the spiritual well-being of the Thessalonian believers as he had stepped first in the European continent to preach in Thessalonica and the nearby cities, (Acts 17:1–9, 13–15; 1 Thess 2:2) amidst opposition and violence. According to Hafemann, "the goal of his prayers is that on this 'day' [the day of Parousia] Christ will be glorified in them and they in him through their ongoing, grace-created 'work of faith' (2 Thess 1:11–12). For God called them to salvation through Paul's gospel for the purpose of inheriting the glory of the Lord Jesus Christ (2 Thess 2:14)."[20]

In fact, for Paul, the community of the redeemed Thessalonians persevering until the last days is his "hope," "joy," or "the crown." He along with his fellow missionaries "will glory in the presence of our Lord Jesus when he comes" (1 Thess 2:19–20) just by seeing his loved ones in Thessalonica with him in God's presence. Witherington rightly observes that "Paul shows how much he treasures his converts by lavishing on them even eschatological significance." He calls them "the crown," (the *stephanos*), that is the laurel wreath, given by the Roman governor to the athlete who wins the race.[21] Paul envisions himself as an athlete in the Greco-Roman Olympics, where he runs to receive the *stephanos* from the Roman governor. However, in this case, his faithful race ensuring the successful presentation of the Thessalonian believers in the presence of our Lord Jesus Christ is everything to him; they are his hope, joy, crown, and glory. It is precisely for this eschatological reason that he himself was motivated to endure in the mission of God. Hafemann says, "the return of Christ as savior and vindicating judge thus plays a foundational role both in Paul's own motivation for ministry and in the Thessalonians' life of faith."[22] Hence, he continues even to include Paul's letter writing itself as "an essential continuing means of his missionary activity" in order to continue "strengthening of the church's faith in the present (i.e., the stipulation of the covenant relationship) in anticipation of the future (i.e., the promise of the covenant relationship; cf. 1 Thess 3:2)."[23]

Similarly, regarding the Thessalonians, Paul says that their divine election through the agency of the gospel is purposed so that they "might share in the glory of our Lord Jesus Christ" (2 Thess 2:14). The gospel proclaimed to his audience during his original visit to them was not merely him preaching to them, but God speaking through it to them.[24] What Paul means to say is that God was ultimately calling the Thessalonians through their preaching ministry "to share in the visible manifestation of

---

20 Hafemann, "Divine Judgement," 192.

21 Witherington, *1 and 2 Thessalonians*, 90–91.

22 Hafemann, "Divine Judgement," 192–93.

23 Hafemann, "Divine Judgemen," 193.

24 Witherington, *1 and 2 Thessalonians*, 233.

his holiness."[25] In other words, as the culmination of their salvation, the believers are to receive "the same glorious embodied condition Jesus himself has as a result of the resurrection (cf. 1 Cor 15). It is the very glory of Jesus that they will one day possess, and so they will have been made like him."[26] Hence, the relentless efforts of Paul, the apostle, in preaching and teaching the Thessalonians, in words and through letters, is "to continue to minister this gospel in the present order to prepare his churches for the judgment to come. It is because of the gospel's future focus on God's judgement that Paul sees the value of his own ministry at stake in the perseverance of his churches (1 Thess 2:19–20; 3:5; 2 Thess 1:4)."[27]

It is in this context that we need to mention the major components of Paul's eschatology in the Thessalonian correspondence.

3.3.1. The event of Parousia and the hope of resurrection

In 1 Thessalonians, Paul makes repeated direct references to the Parousia (2:19; 3:13; 4:15; 5:23), while on many other occasions he also makes indirect references to it in the other parts of the letter (1:10; 2:12; 4:6; 5:2). It proves the importance of the theme both for the Thessalonian believers and for Paul. As discussed in connection with the background of the letter to the Thessalonians, the exact time when the Parousia will take place and the fate of those who have already deceased in the Lord, before the return of Christ, caused a significant amount of confusion within the community. The prevailing situation required an urgent response from the apostle. Undoubtedly, Paul had already taught them about the second coming of Christ and the related eschatological events (2 Thess 2:5). But some others, obviously, entered into the community at a later stage and began to give a different type of teaching (2 Thess 2:2–3), which caused fatal confusion among Paul's converts. Although Paul leaves the question about the exact time of the Parousia in future open-ended, he categorically warns them not to let "anyone deceive you [Thessalonians] in any way, for that day will not come until the rebellion occurs and the man of lawlessness is revealed" (2 Thess 2:3, emphasis added). The only thing Paul is certain about is that the Lord Jesus had not returned at least till the time he was writing the letter to them. Hence, in 1 Thessalonians 5:2, Paul speaks of the coming of the Messiah on the Day of the Lord "like a thief in the night."

The use of the word *Parousia*, rather an interesting one, is "rich in connotative meaning, having a history in both Hellenistic Greek and

[25] Johnson, *1 and 2 Thessalonians*, 204.

[26] Witherington, *1 and 2 Thessalonians*, 233.

[27] Hafemann, "Divine Judgement," 193.

Judaistic Greek (LXX)."[28] Therefore, when Paul uses it in the Hellenistic or Judaistic context, the term refers either to political or religious reality. Ware says that, in the Hellenistic context, "it referred to the arrival of a ruler, a king, a god, an emperor, an angel, or even troops, with the connotation of help or assistance at this arrival."[29] However, in a Judaistic context, the term "was associated with the coming of God in revelation, the coming of God in history to redeem his faithful and punish the tyrannical and unrighteous who oppress his people, and (in later Judaism) the coming of the Messiah."[30] Many have understood the term against the Hellenistic background in order to explain the royal return of the Messiah. In 1 Thessalonians 4:16, Paul lays strong emphasis upon the personal return of the Lord, saying "the Lord *himself* will come down from heaven" (emphasis added), and enumerates three simultaneously occurring events: (i) he will return "with a loud command"; (ii) he will come "with the voice of the archangel"; and (iii) when he will appear, it will be accompanied "with the trumpet call of God." For our discussion, it is irrelevant to debate if these three together make one loud voice or more than that. It suffices to know that the three different voices are mentioned separately to underline the grand reality of the mighty, authoritative, and victorious appearance of the Lord.

The Parousia or the Second Coming of the Lord is like a victory parade of which Thessalonians must have been well-aware. In the Old Testament, as Morris mentions, the "trumpet" is attached with religious festivals. Particularly, when the mighty work of God takes place, the trumpet is mentioned (Exod 19:6; Isa 27:13; Joel 2:10).[31] In the context of Thessalonians 4:16, the sound of the trumpet might refer to the divine act of raising the dead ones in Christ, at first. Paul, explaining the order of events at the Parousia, teaches them that their grief for the dead is unfounded and the hope of the resurrection will be a reality. God will raise the dead in Christ, which will be followed by the catching up of those living at the time of the Parousia. The living ones will be together with the resurrected believers in Christ "in the clouds to meet the Lord in the air." Thereafter, they will live with the Lord in eternity (1 Thess 4:17). Undoubtedly, "the Parousia is not only about the coming of the exalted, cruciform Lord but also about the exaltation of his cruciform disciples."[32] Such a verbal depiction of the eschatological future in the hearing of the

---

28 Phil Ware, "The Coming of the Lord: Eschatology and 1 Thessalonians," *Restoration Quarterly* 22, no. 1–2 (1979): 110.

29 Ware, "The Coming of the Lord," 110.

30 Ware, "The Coming of the Lord," 111.

31 Leon Morris, *1, 2 Thessalonians*, Word Biblical Themes (Dallas, TX: Word Publishing, 1989), 47–48.

32 Johnson, *1 and 2 Thessalonians*, 259.

persecuted minority community of Christians in Thessalonica is sure to capture their imaginations to nurture hope against hope in a depressing existential context. They who suffer humiliation, shame, and physical violence, will at the Parousia be raised from resurrection as their divine vindication to be exalted with the Lord before their opponents and persecutors.[33]

In 2 Thessalonians 2:8, for Paul, Jesus, the Lord, is an irresistible mighty warrior who will gather his people with him to finally serve a devastating blow to the archrival, the man of lawlessness. Paul says that in the end, "the lawless one will be revealed, whom the Lord Jesus will overthrow with the breath of his mouth and destroy by the splendour of his coming." Such a strong portrayal of the Lord's might in defeating the archrival signifies his unparalleled authority and strength. The one who himself suffered unjustly and died like a weak victim is the one who comes in incomparable power. According to Marshall, the two parallel clauses describing the Lord's dramatic destruction of the man of lawlessness shows the Isaiahnic influence upon Paul (Isa 11:4 LXX),[34] while the trace of a similar thought is also found in 1 Enoch 62:2 and Wisdom of Solomon 11:19–20.[35] For him, "Paul merely uses appropriate OT phraseology to emphasise the sovereign power of annihilation demonstrated by the Lord."[36] Similarly, according to Johnson, Paul's language speaking about Jesus as the one "who rescues us from the coming wrath" in 1 Thessalonians 1:10 alludes to the Old Testament depiction of the divine warrior who comes to "rescue" some in Israel from wrath (Isa 59).[37] In the Thessalonian context, Paul is reminding them of their moral depravity and desperate need for God's grace in order to escape the destruction by teaching about the wrath of God.[38] Thereby, the missional intent of Paul is closely ingrained within the eschatological language.

3.3.2. Present suffering and the judgment

The judgment of all at the return of Christ is another important aspect of Paul's eschatology. In his two letters to the Thessalonians, Paul employs judgment to encourage his readers who were undergoing intense suffering for the sake of their newfound faith. The apostle uses the judgment idea: (i) to encourage them to stand firm amidst suffering, (ii) to warn

33 Johnson, *1 and 2 Thessalonians*, 258–59.

34 I. Howard Marshall, *1 and 2 Thessalonians*, New Century Bible Commentary (Grand Rapids, MI: William B. Eerdmans Publishing, 1983), 201.

35 Witherington, *1 and 2 Thessalonians*, 223.

36 Marshall, *1 and 2 Thessalonians*, 201.

37 Johnson, *1 and 2 Thessalonians*, 263.

38 Charles A. Gieschen, "Christ's Coming and the Church's Mission in 1 Thessalonians," *Concordia Theological Quarterly* 76, nos. 1–2 (2012): 42–43.

them of the possible destruction if they do not remain loyal to Christ at the Parousia (2 Thess 1:9), and (iii) to speak about God's retributive justice upon those who oppose him and his people in Thessalonica (1 Thess 2:13–16; 2 Thess 2:12). In Thessalonian correspondence, Paul does not speak of God's judgment as a futuristic event alone, but it is also something that is implicitly evident in his present faithfulness toward his people. In 2 Thessalonians 1:6, Morris says that the manner in which the Thessalonian believers "bear up under the opposition of evil is a manifest token of God's righteous judgement (v 5), and they should never forget that God's enabling of his people to endure persecution is part of his 'righteous judgment.'"[39] It proves that God will, as per his justice, punish the persecutors and reward the suffering community of God in future. They have a choice to make now, which will define their destiny because unrighteousness cannot go unpunished forever in God's moral economy.[40]

Paul is clear that God's judgment will coincide with his revelation from heaven. Paul has already taught in 1 Thessalonians 4:16 that the Lord will return from heaven to where he ascended earlier after the resurrection. However, here, it is not merely a return, but it involves revelation of something about which they are ignorant. Marshall and Morris are particularly on point explaining the word *revelation* (2 Thess 1:7) in relation to God's judgment as "the unveiling of that which is at present hidden"[41] that is, the hidden face of Jesus Christ as the Lord who is the judge of all. Unlike the Jesus who walked like a normal human in the world, whom some could even abuse and kill, the Lord who will be revealed from heaven will come just as he is. All will see him as the one who has authority to punish the evil and reward the faithful ones.[42] Moreover, Paul is clear that God's judgment is to "pay back" those who trouble the believers in Thessalonica (2 Thess 1:6). This is God's wrath that burns against them in judgment. According to Johnson, although the exact source of wrath is unknown in 1 Thessalonians 1:10 and 5:9, it is clear that "in both places God's eschatological judgment is in view."[43] For him, it is God's temporal refusal to bear human failure to honor God. Hence, God delivers them as part of his divine justice to experience the immediate consequence of their sins to which they will have to suffer also in final judgment.[44] Moreover, "through the use of the aorist (in 1 Thess 1:10), Paul is stressing that these

39 Morris, *1, 2 Thessalonians*, 53.

40 Morris, *1, 2 Thessalonians*, 53.

41 Marshall, *1 and 2 Thessalonians*, 176.

42 Morris, *1, 2 Thessalonians*, 54.

43 Johnson, *1 and 2 Thessalonians*, 265.

44 Johnson, *1 and 2 Thessalonians*, 265–66.

unbelieving Jews already stand under God's judgment as those who will experience his end-time wrath."[45]

Similarly, in 2 Thessalonians 2:7, Paul teaches that "the secret power of lawlessness is already at work, but the one who now holds it back will continue to do so till he is taken out of the way." The expression that the lawless one is "already at work" refers to his twin activity in the present, that is, persecution and deception. The false teachings spread through some in Thessalonica are ultimately his activity along with self-exaltation above all others and placing himself in "God's temple, proclaiming himself to be God" (2 Thess 2:4). The Christians are to be cautious of the deception in the present (2 Thess 2:3). But, finally, when he will come, he will perform all sorts of "signs and wonders that serve the lie" inspired by Satan and God will allow them to believe it by sending "a powerful delusion" (2 Thess 2:9–11). The divine act of allowing some to be deceived, both who are not in the church and some who are in the church but are inclined to believe the lies, does not dilute God's justice because it is simply God's permissive will toward those who desist intentionally "to love the truth and so be saved" (2 Thess 2:10). They refuse to believe in the gospel and on the contrary "have delighted in wickedness" (2 Thess 2:11). According to Beale, "God righteously sends delusion because it is a beginning part of his just judgment."[46] God allowing those wilfully continuing in sin and refusing to give glory to God and to believe in him is his ultimate response of condemnation. In Romans 1:24, stating God's response toward the wilful sin of human ingratitude toward God, Paul says that "God *gave them over* in the sinful desires of their hearts" (emphasis added). Similarly, in Deuteronomy 29:3–4 God's response toward human insistence to sin is said as: "With your own eyes you saw those great trials, those signs and great wonders. But this day the LORD has not given you a mind that understands or eyes that see or ears that hear."

According to Beale, for Paul, the second part of the divine condemnation of "the unbelievers is that *all will be condemned.* The nature of this condemnation is best understood in conjunction with Christ's *overthrow* (or 'slaying) of the lawless one *with the breath of his mouth* (2:8; an allusion to Isa 11:4)."[47] Paul's words about the judgment of the lawless one in the future is inspired by the messianic warrior image from the Jewish tradition. Isaiah describes the Davidic Messiah's judgment with justice of the righteous and the wicked in contradictory terms: "but with righteousness he will judge the needy, with justice he will give decisions for the poor of the earth. He will strike the earth with the rod of his mouth;

45 Gieschen, "Christ's Coming," 44 (parenthesis added).

46 Beale, *1–2 Thessalonians*, 222.

47 Beale, *1–2 Thessalonians*, 223 (emphasis original).

with the breath of his lips he will slay the wicked" (Isa 11:4). According to Bruce, "there 'the wicked one' is generic; here he is the particular individual," through whom the secret of lawlessness becomes public.[48] For Paul, the destruction of the lawless one is just a matter of time in the future. As soon as the restrainer is "taken out of the way," the lawless one will be revealed in public with his secret power operational already in the world. At that time, the Lord Jesus will condemn him and put an end to his secret power operational already in the world (2 Thess 2:3, 8). However, what does the condemnation of the antigod figure like the lawless one by the Lord Jesus signify? The combination of the titular use of the high imperial title for Jesus, the "Lord," along with the Old Testament messianic language, proves the "sovereign power of annihilation" of the Lord Jesus. Importantly, at his Parousia, Jesus is not the same vulnerable human who could be judged and killed by human beings, but he now appears like the sovereign Lord and judge who has the absolute power to destroy every power of wickedness arising against him and his people.

If so, what is its implication to the life of believers in Thessalonica? The primary purpose of Paul appears to strengthen the believers amidst suffering and persecution to stand firm in their faith in Christ. He wants them to rationalize their present suffering in the light of the eschatology when the Messiah shall come in the air to receive them after those who have already died in Christ rise up from the dead. Then, the Messiah who died to rescue them from the coming wrath shall judge those who persecute them at present and destroy the power of wickedness that is working against him and his people including the Thessalonian believers. Paul does not want them to fall away from their faith. Hence, with a missional purpose, Paul addresses them through the eschatological lens, explaining their elect status in Christ and the necessity of living a life that is holy and blameless. In fact, Kaye has strongly underlined, approximately five decades ago, the positive ethical significance of Paul's eschatology in his letters to the Thessalonians. He concludes his study of the three vital eschatological literary blocks in the letters (1 Thess 4:13–18; 5:1–11; 2 Thess 2:1–12) stating that while the eschatological material "in 2 Thessalonians does not have any implications which might lead to a loss of moral earnestness," we find that "in 1 Thessalonians positive ethical implications are actually drawn from the eschatological material."[49] To realize their higher calling as the elect community, Paul wants them to envision themselves and their existential reality through the eschatological lens. Thus, they ought to nurture their eternal hope of resurrection at the time of the

---

48 Bruce, *1 and 2 Thessalonians*, 172.

49 Bruce N. Kaye, "Eschatology and Ethics in 1 and 2 Thessalonians," *Novum Testamentum* 17, no. 1 (1975): 57.

Parousia and live lives faithful to the gospel of the Lord Jesus who is to return as the judge and the sovereign Lord. Rightly, Gieschen studying the significance of eschatology for Paul's mission in his two letters to the Thessalonians concludes that eschatology "was central to Paul's apostolic missionary preaching and remains a vital foundation of the church's ongoing faith, daily living in hope, and mission of proclaiming salvation from the wrath to come."[50]

3.4.1. Eschatology and missional praxis for today

Underlining the significance of the eschatological thought for the Thessalonians who were waiting for the Parousia to happen, Marshall states that "the present existence of the Thessalonian Christians was determined by their expectations regarding the future."[51] In a sense, Marshall's words highlight the inner reality of every practicing Christian's daily experience in the world through the centuries. The gospel we preach ought to be rooted in the past salvific event for all in Christ. However, it must be nourished by the eschatological hope of salvation, victory over death and corruption through resurrection, and a lifestyle controlled by the reality of divine judgment at the end. An individual or ecclesial existence oblivious of the promised future in Christ runs the risk of subscribing to a confession of dry faith that does not strengthen a believer to live today facing the challenges with a robust conscience. As a result, moral slackness, spiritual cynicism, and religious nominalism characterize a community that is called, destined, and equipped through the Holy Spirit to enthusiastically fulfill its missional call and purpose today. Probably, a missional reading of Paul's letters to the Thessalonians gives us ample reasons to recognize the value of the eschatological lens in interpreting our corporate existence in Christ for the rest of humanity.

Eschatology provides an important conceptual framework as it enables us to view ourselves not only from a futuristic point of view but also to comprehend our existence, its nature, goal, and purpose from a theological point of view. Despite several problems rightly or wrongly associated with the pentecostal-charismatic movements, which cause many other Christians to distance themselves from them at times, a glance at the exponential growth of pentecostal-charismatic churches in the past century enables us to appreciate the significance of Paul's eschatology colored worldview for mission and church growth in India today. Tennent, an eminent contemporary missiologist, studying the role of the Holy Spirit in Christian mission within a pluralistic context highlights the eschatological emphasis of the Pentecostals as a key reason for its missionary

50 Gieschen, "Christ's Coming and the Church's Mission in 1 Thessalonians," 55.

51 Marshall, *1 and 2 Thessalonians*, 58.

zeal and growth of the churches in the world. He maintains that "because Pentecostals believe that they are living in the last days before the return of Christ, they are marked by a special urgency to evangelize the world."[52] Tyra reaffirms the same truth emphasizing the vitality of eschatological urgency in pentecostal mission. He states that "because of their embrace of the ideas that the return of Christ is imminent and that eternal punishment awaits those who fail to confess Christ as Lord in this life, pentecostal-charismatic believers have historically felt compelled by a sense of eschatological urgency to become involved in missional activities."[53] The churches, in general, in India capturing such a vision of the time and history coming to an end in the indefinite future must raise a sense of urgency in them. Their missional existence in the eternal divine purpose must occupy central stage in their missional existence with all the aspects of life.

In the context of suffering opposition and persecution, as discussed in the earlier chapter, capturing the gospel of hope for the churches in India is vital for their continued survival. As Paul rightly responds to the existential crisis emerging out of violent opposition through the eschatological vision, Christians in India at times should find rest in Christ realizing that persecution proves the secret power of the evil force that is opposed to God and his subjects in the kingdom of God. However, it is not an eternal phenomenon but will be abolished and destroyed by the judge of all, the Messiah, at his return. At the Last Judgment, God will justly recompense the forces of opposition represented in human agencies. Hence, both the content of proclamation and missional self-consciousness of the church in India must begin with Paul's missional-theological pattern, that is, "Christ's past work and then proclaim this as the sure basis for Christ's future work at his coming on the last day."[54] Such a pattern of missional engagement both in being and preaching is bound to impart hope amidst hopelessness and suffering in India.

The danger associated with the eschatological understanding of the historical reality without conscious efforts on the part of the churches to stay relevant within the local historical context is that they could become pessimistic and overly other-world oriented. The church can suffer from a victim syndrome absolving herself of the responsibility to make conscious efforts to stay relevant to the communities around as God's elect representatives amidst all sorts of oppressive social structures. However,

52 Timothy C. Tennent, "Holy Spirit and Christian Mission in a Religious Pluralistic Context," in *The Holy Spirit and Christian Mission in a Pluralistic Context*, ed. Roji T. George (Bangalore: SAIACS Press, 2017), 73.

53 Gary Tyra, *The Holy Spirit in Mission: Prophetic Speech and Action in Christian Witness* (Downers Grove, IL: IVP Academic, 2011), 116.

54 Gieschen, "Christ's Coming," 52.

if the missional consciousness of the church as God's agent of transformation informs the church's eschatological understanding of the historical reality, then social engagements for liberation to the church becoming the light of the earth will be intentional. The fight against every oppressive social structure, religious systems that perpetuate human exploitation and spread communal hatred will not be seen merely as human engagement in the name of God but as intervention in the human arena as God's partners. The ethical implication of the eschatological vision would not be merely guided by an individual's otherworldly oriented goal, but in truly becoming the community of God; will be the agent of transformation in the eschatological times.

In short, eschatology inspired by the apocalyptic categories has played a vital role in Paul's theology. The teachings on the last days occasioned by the unique situation that arose among the Thessalonian Christians necessitated a response from Paul explaining it with more details. However, Paul employed eschatology as a framework to interpret, explain, and exhort his readers in order to strengthen them in their faith amidst suffering persecution and disillusionment. Eschatology provides him a strong structure that can hold together his other theological content within the letters. Eschatology equipped him with the vision of universality, which further encouraged Paul to move out in mission with urgency. Paul envisions God as active in history in the last days through his Son for whom the Christians in Thessalonica await eagerly. However, the interim period is to be saved by turning toward the living God and to save others, knowing that along with the ultimate power of wickedness those who express allegiance to him by refusing to believe the gospel will be condemned forever. The ethics of Paul is closely connected with his eschatological understanding because God sanctifies them in the present so that they will seek to walk worthy of the gospel they received. Even for his mission, the perseverance of the Thessalonian believers in faith is detrimental for eternal reward. In fact, for him their salvation is his reward in the last days. While the divine judgment passed implicitly in the present and to be done publicly on the last day must warn each one to live according to the divine missional plan and purpose, it must encourage the persecuted minority of Christians that at the return of the Messiah they will receive rest. Their suffering due to their faith in Christ is temporal, and by believing in Christ they will escape the wrath of God. Hence, as the elect ones of God, they must live, preach, and become as per God's will for them from the eschatological perspective.

4

GOD AND HIS COMMUNITY IN THESSALONICA

Attempting to unravel the missional theology, nature, and purpose of Paul's two letters to the Thessalonians requires a careful reconstruction of his understanding of God and the Christian community in Thessalonica. I presuppose that his understanding of God and his relation to the newly founded community of believers is intentionally missional in nature because Paul had a missional interest in sending the letters to the believers in Thessalonica. He intended to teach them to recognize and fulfill their missional call, and thereby fulfill the very purpose of God in bringing them into existence as his elect community. It requires us to understand the theological significance, background, and missional thrust of the words and phrases he used to speak about God. Similarly, one also needs to undertake a comprehensive presentation of Paul's understanding of church, her identity, and responsibility to witness within the local historical context through a missional lens.

In this chapter, an attempt is made, at first, to portray Paul's understanding of God and his missional activity in the world. Second, the role of God in the life and origin of the church in Thessalonica appears to hold the key to open the door to a missional reading of the letters. Hence, we ask: How does Paul speak of God and church in the letters? What are the key terms and expressions he uses to encourage his audience to understand their participation in the universal mission of God? How do his ideas translate within the missional context of Thessalonica?

4.1. God in 1 and 2 Thessalonians

"Paul is a God-intoxicated man," says Morris, because of the centrality of God in the thoughts of the apostle and the excessive use of the word *Theos*,

"God," in all his letters. Statistically, roughly forty percent of the appearances of the term within the New Testament may be credited to Paul (528 of 1314 occurrences). Of them all, he uses the word *God* fifty-four times in his Thessalonian correspondence alone.[1] In his letter to the Thessalonians, we find the earliest evidence of his theological understanding, which is developed and elaborately discussed in his other letters. Paul's understanding of God in the Thessalonian Correspondence is found in relation to the divine activity in the life of the believers. It must not surprise us that Paul does not systematically talk about God in his letters because the sole purpose of sending letters was determined by the real-life situation of his readers and their Christian spiritual formation. In other words, Paul is not a systematic theologian but a missionary-theologian whose sole aim is to nurture, care for, and equip the new found community of believers in Thessalonica to comprehend and act within their context in line with the universal missional purpose of God. Hence, he speaks about God in the letters as much as it enabled him to teach, encourage, and exhort his readers to grow in their work of faith, love of God, and hope of salvation.

To gain the missional emphasis of Paul's understanding of God in the Thessalonian correspondence, we should recognize: (i) the theological-missional roots (the OT traditions) informing his understanding of God, (ii) the unique reuse of those traditions for a specific purpose, and (iii) we also need to unravel the possible binding together of different cultural traditions by the apostle to illuminate the missional role and meaning of the ecclesial existence in the then context. It would enable us to recognize the missional thrust of Paul's understanding of God as translating into our ecclesial context today. The ensuing sections below would seek to discuss the key elements of Paul's theology concerning the newly formed missional community of God in Thessalonica.

4.1.1. God the Father, the Son and the Holy Spirit and the Thessalonian Church

In the Thessalonian correspondence, though there is no explicit mention of the Triune God as the church came to confess and profess her faith in the later centuries, it is evident that in these letters the seed of such a developed articulation of faith is not absent from Paul's mind. Strandenaes observes that "without developing a systematic Trinitarian teaching about God, Jesus Christ, and the Holy Spirit, Paul's letters to the Thessalonians certainly reflect his theology on each of them."[2] For Paul, God is the one "living and true God" (firmly monotheistic) which in a polemical sense

1 Morris, *1, 2 Thessalonians*, 11–12, cited from 11.

2 Thor Strandenaes, "Completing the Mission: Paul's Application of the Gospel to the Faith and Life of the Thessalonian Converts in 1 and 2 Thessalonians," *Svensk Missionstidskrift* 98, no. 1 (2010): 89.

denies the existence of all other gods (1 Thess 1:9). He is "the Father" (1 Thess 1:1) of "the Lord Jesus Christ" (cf. "his Son" 1 Thess 1:10) and of Paul and the Thessalonians believers (1 Thess 1:3; 3:11, 13;2 Thess 1:1–2; 2:16). He is the "God of peace" (1 Thess 5:23; 2 Thess 3:16) and is "just" (2 Thess 1:6–10). He is the God who elects people, like the Thessalonian believers, for his special universal purpose. He sanctifies them (1 Thess 5:23 cf. 2 Thess 2:13) and makes them "worthy of his calling" (2 Thess 1:11).

Referring to the core content of the gospel about "his Son," Jesus, Paul states that "he raised [Jesus] from the dead" (1 Thess 1:10). He mentions the Son, Jesus "the Lord," in the same breath along with God, the Father, "as the source of the Thessalonian church's existence (1 Thess 1:1; 2 Thess 1:1), as the guide to the apostolic mission (1 Thess 3:11) and as the giver of Christian comfort and hope (2 Thess 2:16)."[3] Moreover, Jesus Christ is the mystical space along with God, the Father, where the Thessalonian believers are grounded. In both the letters he says, "the church of the Thessalonians *in* God the Father and the Lord Jesus Christ" (1 Thess 1:1; 2 Thess 1:1, emphasis added). Even the source of grace and peace to the believers in Thessalonica is jointly God and the Lord Jesus Christ (2 Thess 1:2). It proves the intimate relationship shared between God and Jesus with the gentile Christian believers in Thessalonica. In the same way, the role of the Holy Spirit overlaps the special function of God in the life of the believers. For example, the empowering and joy imparting role of the Holy Spirit mediates their divine election through the gospel (1 Thess 1:5–6 cf. 4:8). The Spirit does the sanctifying work of God in the life of the Thessalonians (2 Thess 2:13).

In short, the eternal God has entered into a new relationship through the Son with the recent converts in Thessalonica. God, the Father, and the Son are at work in their lives with the single purpose of universal salvation. In the process, the Holy Spirit functions along with God the Father to usher, nurture, and prepare the believers through his role of sanctification.

4.1.2. The living and true God

Relating to the instances of their conversion in the past, Paul reminds his Christian believers in Thessalonica that their conversion means turning "to God from idols to serve the living and true God" (1 Thess 1:9). It marks a decisive event of reversal in their lives. His assertion about God as "living and true" forms the foundational truth about the God whom he preached relentlessly and boldly. True to his Jewish heritage and scriptural understanding, Paul cannot resist from pitching the God, whom the

3 J. W. Simpson, "Thessalonians, Letters to The," in *Dictionary of Paul and His Letters* (Downers Grove, IL: IVP, 1993), 938.

Thessalonian believers serve now, opposite to the gods in whom they believed earlier. From Paul, it is an unapologetic monotheistic assertion in a multicultural and polytheistic religious context with a clear message of radical shift their lives have already taken and its missional implications. Their "turned to God" (1 Thess 1:9), within an imperial context, implies not just their rejection of the past life in native religious traditions, but also their separation from the imperial cult.[4] Otherwise, they violate the purpose of their calling and defy their difference from the gentile lifestyle (1 Thess 4:3–7).

In the Old Testament, idolatry is viewed negatively; so, it is prohibited. In Deuteronomy 4:23, Moses warns the Israelites against making images of any form and worshipping them. He says, "Be careful not to forget the covenant of the LORD your God that he made with you; do not make for yourselves an idol in the form of anything the LORD your God has forbidden." The reasons for the absolute prohibition of worshipping idols are in Deuteronomy 4:12–24: First, they "saw no form of any kind the day the LORD spoke" to them but only heard a voice at Mt. Horeb (4:15). Second, Moses reminds them that "the LORD took you and brought you out of the iron-smelting furnace, out of Egypt, to be a people of his own inheritance, as you now are" (4:20). Third, Israel must remember that "the LORD your God is a consuming fire, a jealous God" (4:24). Later in the prophetic tradition, too, idols were ridiculed for they are not alive and are impotent to do any harm (Jer 10:3–5). Jeremiah says they are "fraud," "have no breath," and are "worthless" (Jer 10:14–15). Isaiah reminds his readers that the LORD is incomparable for he is seated above all, his mighty deeds include the entire creation, and He is the One who determines the destiny of the rulers of the earth (Isa 40:18–25). Idols are mere works of craftsmen, but the LORD is "great" and his "name is mighty in power" (Jer 10:6). Yahweh is "the true God; he is the living God and eternal King" (Jer 10:10). However, the sin of Israel was to imitate the neighboring gentile nations by making images to worship. But, God condemned and punished them. The event of making the golden calf in Exodus 32–34 and God's wrath burning against the sin of Israel in the wilderness epitomize God's displeasure. However, Israel fell repeatedly into the sin of idolatry (Judg 17–18; 1 Kgs 12:28–33). According to Gaventa, "here Paul echoes a well-established Jewish polemic against the religious practices of gentiles whose gods, from the perspective of Jews, were neither living nor true (see, for example, Isa. 44:9–20; Wisd. Sol. 13–15; Philo, *Decalogue* 52–81; *Special Laws* 1:13–31)."[5]

---

4 Boring, *I & II Thessalonians*, 68–69.

5 Beverly Roberts Gaventa, *First and Second Thessalonians*, 19.

However, the apostle modified the Jewish faith and worldview to reuse them in the context of the Thessalonians. Paul, as a Jewish Christian, tweaks it with christological material in 1 Thessalonians 1:10. God, the Father, is active in and through Jesus, his Son, to rescue the Thessalonians from the day of wrath. He is the God of Israel, who has now become their Father (1 Thess 1:3). In the words of Morris, it is "a typically Christian way of speaking. Jews might well use Paul's words about the 'living and true' God (1 Thess 1:9), but they did not emphasise God as Father to the extent that Paul and other Christians did."[6]

It is to this true and living God that the Thessalonian believers have turned now. The missional significance of Paul's reference to their conversion experience is evident. Paul uses the term *turning* three times (Gal 4:9; 2 Cor 3:16; 1 Thess 1:9), always referring to "some form of conversion either to or away from God."[7] Paul teaches the Thessalonian believers that they have already made a shift away from the false gods to the true and living God who has acted in "his Son" to rescue them from the coming wrath (1 Thess 1:10). Their turning toward the living and true God is complete and decisive, once and for all by burning the bridge they have crossed by faith. If Wanamaker's interpretation of the term *idols* as a symbolic reference to the "totality of the religious experience of his readers (and by implication their social existence) before their conversion" is acceptable, then they do not have a choice to return to their past faith and practices. The reason is that their turn to God "embraces the totality of their Christian religious (and social) experience."[8] Hence, they are no more to live and behave like their non-Christian neighbors because the "living and true God" is the one who has called them. They ought to live as the people of God.

4.1.3. The God who elects

In 1 and 2 Thessalonians, Paul touches an important theme, "election," that runs through both the Old and the New Testament. Though the theme assumes greater importance in the later writings of Paul, it is interesting that the initial thought on the theme is present in Thessalonians, one of his earliest letters. In the Bible, the significance of "election" is not only underlined by the uniqueness and the privilege of the God's elect people, like Israel, but it also highlights their role, responsibility, and purpose of existence in God's plan. By employing the theme in his writing, Paul wants the Thessalonians to understand that their turn to the living God is not an accident, but the result of God's definite act. As a result,

6 Morris, *1, 2 Thessalonians*, 13.

7 Wanamaker, *Epistles to the Thessalonians*, 85.

8 Wanamaker, *Epistles to the Thessalonians*, 86.

they stand in the eternal plan of God to which the Old Testament bears strong testimony. Even in 1 and 2 Thessalonians, the theme resonates with teaching God's role in the believers' life, his purpose for their new existence, and their status in God's economy. Thus, the Thessalonians need to see, understand, and act in the light of their call, the decisive act of God in their personal and corporate lives.

Stating the importance of the election motif in the Thessalonian correspondence, Witherington observes that "the language of election is one thing that binds these two letters together and distinguishes them from other Pauline documents."[9] In the Thessalonian correspondence, Paul employs different words connected to the idea of God's call to teach the believers. He employs the words connected to *kaleō* (meaning "I call" in 1 Thess 1:1; 2:12; 4:7: 5:24; 2 Thess 1:11; 2:14), *eklogō* (meaning "I choose" in 1 Thess 1:4), *etheto* (meaning "I appoint or destine" in 1 Thess 5:9), and *haireomai* (meaning "I choose" in 2 Thess 2:13). The significance of the meaning of the two terms *eklogō* and *kaleō* is that while the former means "God's choice, election and selection," the latter "marks the act of realising and actualising this prior divine choice."[10] Interestingly, in their election, God is always the sole active agent. Paul can thank God (cf. 1 Thess 1:2–5) for the particular event of conversion in the lives of the Thessalonians. It proves God's sole initiative in their election. Human beings have no role in it except to respond to God, either accepting or rejecting it. The Thessalonians need to live their daily lives among the non-Christian Thessalonians according to their election by God. They ought to know their privileged status in Christ as a result of the divine act of election. Thereby, they bear the responsibility to fulfill God's purpose in the world.

Hence, in 1 Thessalonians 1:4, Paul says that God "has chosen you." The idea of election is dominant in the Old Testament. God chose Abraham out of Ur of Chaldeans and promised to bless him and make him a great nation and bless all people on earth through him (Gen 12:1–3; Neh 9:7). Later, God out of his love for the ancestors of Israel "chose their descendants after them" (Deut 4:37) and made covenant with Israel on Mt. Sinai saying if they keep the covenant, he will make them his "treasured possession" from among all the peoples of the earth (Exod 19:5). God loved them and made them his own in a unique way. So, Paul redefines the Christian identity by reapplying the election words for the Thessalonian community, primarily composed of gentile Christians. It is no more just the ethnic Israel that is the community of God's elect, but the real God's chosen possession in Christ are those called through the gospel that Paul preached. They are no longer just one more group of people

9 Witherington, *1 and 2 Thessalonians*, 64.

10 Donfried, "Theology of 1 Thessalonians," 29.

believing in a different god but they have become the elect people of the true and living God. God is at work in and through them to accomplish his universal salvific plan for the nations. So, Paul's effort to redefine their identity in the Old Testament terms continues in 1 Thessalonians 1:4 and 5:24 by employing two important words defining God's character—love and faithfulness. They both are borrowed from the Old Testament and re-applied to the Thessalonians affirming their new identity as the elect ones of God.

First, Paul addresses them as "loved by God" (1 Thess 1:4). Jeffery A. D. Weima observes that it is an instance in Paul's letter when he re-applies a term to the Thessalonians that was "originally applied to Israel (Deut. 32:25; 33:12; Ps. 60:5; 108:6; Isa. 44:2; Jer. 11:15; 12:7; Sir. 45:1; Bar. 3:36; etc.)."[11] It proves that Paul considered the church as a body made up of the Jews and gentiles but standing in continuity with the Israel of the Old Testament through whom God is faithful to fulfill his promise to Abraham to bless the nations. The love of God is no more limited to ethnic Israel, but it is graciously extended to include the gentile believers in Christ in Thessalonica. The idea gets developed later in Romans 9–11, but it is interesting to notice that the vital seed of the thought had already started germinating in his mind as early as 50/51 C.E. The believers in Thessalonica are "now incorporated into the ongoing history of God's people."[12]

Second, Paul reminds them that "the one who calls you *is faithful*" (1 Thess 5:24). The term *pistos*, translated as "faithful" actually implies God's trustworthiness. Paul intends to tell the Thessalonians that the God who saves them from the day of wrath is faithful to save them ultimately. The purpose is not merely rescuing them from the impending destruction but to save the Thessalonians through his Son, the Lord Jesus Christ (1 Thess 5:9). Their salvation is important because "already now, in the present, God acts decisively in the revelation, death and resurrection of his Son, but the imminent consummation, the approaching deliverance of 'the wrath to come' and the fulfillment of the promise of salvation is yet to occur."[13] Paul assures the believers that they have no reason to be intimidated or skeptical about their future by emphasizing the divine activity; "he will do it" (1 Thess 5:24). Paul prays the same for his Thessalonian believers in 1 Thessalonians 5:23: "May God himself, the God of peace, *sanctify* you through and through. May your whole spirit, soul and body be *kept blameless* at the coming of our Lord Jesus Christ" (emphasis added).

11 Jeffrey A. D. Weima, *1-2 Thessalonians*, Baker Exegetical Commentary on the New Testament (Grand Rapids, MI: Baker Academic, 2014), 90.

12 Boring, *I & II Thessalonians*, 62.

13 Donfried, "Theology of 1 Thessalonians," 29.

4.1.4. The just God

An important idea that connects the relevance of God to the Thessalonian believers' current state of suffering persecution is God's justice. How does God deal with those who persecute them because of their new found faith? How does God who involves them in his universal mission according to his own plans protect and reward them against their unjust persecutors? In 2 Thessalonians 1:6, Paul says, "God is just." The righteous character of God is beyond dispute because "God's judgment is right" (2 Thess 1:5). He repays those who trouble the Thessalonian believers because they persevere amidst suffering extreme persecution. They also possess a faith that "enables them to remain steadfast under persecution and other forms of trials (cf. 1 Thess 3:7)."[14] Hence, the Thessalonian believers' perseverance and faith that enables them to endure hardship, on the one hand, function as the evidence (*endeigma*) of the coming judgment of God upon their persecutors and, on the other hand, as evidence of their divine vindication at the return of Christ. Bruce connects this unique term within the New Testament with *endeixis* in Philippians 1:28, due to the similarity of the context in which they are used. The Philippians believers' refusal to be intimidated by the physical and subtle attacks parallels the Thessalonian believers' perseverance and faith that enables them to endure hardship. Thereby, they prove God's righteous judgment at the end.[15]

In 2 Thessalonians 1:4–10, Paul draws two sets of contradictory responses of God toward the persecutors and the believers in Thessalonica. The divine response is not arbitrary but determined by the kind of human response to God's offer of eternal life. The former group is mentioned as "those who trouble" them (2 Thess 1:6). In 1 Thessalonians 2:15–16, according to Paul, their persecuting act and opposition to his gospel preaching mission not only makes them displeasing to God but they "heap up their sins" by which they invite the wrath of God. They indulge in such activities because they "do not know God and do not obey the gospel of our Lord Jesus Christ" (2 Thess 1:8). It is not just their ignorance about God that is implied here, because their refusal to obey the gospel of Christ underlines their responsibility in choosing to respond negatively to God and the offer of equal opportunity to all (like the Thessalonian believers) to hear the gospel of Christ. Undoubtedly, Paul is, in particular, referring here to those who despite hearing the gospel chose not just to reject it, but have also turned violent against the believers. They are sure to be punished "with eternal destruction" by God and by shutting them "out of the presence of the Lord and from the glory of his might" (2 Thess 1:9). Paul here appears to depend upon the Old Testament tradition on God's

14 Bruce, *1 and 2 Thessalonians*, 146.

15 Bruce, *1 and 2 Thessalonians*, 149.

recompense, which appears to have continued even during the intertestamental period. Beale points out that both in Isaiah 66:24 and the intertestamental writing, 4 Maccabees 9:9, 10:11 and 15, 12:12 and 18, and 13:15, we find the evidence that eternal destruction was understood as unending destruction in the fire where the worms won't die.[16] Such an unending experience of destruction also implies being "shut out" of God's presence as they have chosen not to remain faithful (contra. *pisteōs* in 2 Thess 1:4) to God in this life. They have rejected the gospel by which they had the opportunity to be found in Christ and declare their loyalty to God by faith just as the Thessalonian believers have done, at present.

The latter group, that is, those who have believed in the gospel, will gain entry into God's kingdom (2 Thess 1:5) because they have expressed their loyalty to the king (God) by persevering and enduring in faith. God's righteous judgment will ensure their participation in the kingdom of God. So, they will experience the eschatological "relief" (*anesis* in 2 Thess 1:7), meaning "relief from suffering, as in 2 Cor. 2:13; 7:5; 8:13 (cf. Josephus, *Antiquities* 12.112; 16:22)."[17] Also, Paul as a fellow sufferer with them in Thessalonica and elsewhere during his apostolic mission shares the same hope of participating in eschatological relief with them ("and to us as well"—2 Thess 1:7). In other words, there is no immediate relief promised to believers from the present persecution and trials. Unlike their persecutors in Thessalonica who await their eternal destruction, Paul's believers have a hope of ending their suffering at the Parousia and entering into the eternal rest. Paul says, "this will happen when the Lord Jesus is revealed from heaven in blazing fire with his powerful angels" (2 Thess 1:7).

Does it mean that perpetual suffering in this life for the sake of their faith is essential to be counted worthy of the kingdom of God in the eschatological time? Surely not! Their allegiance to the gospel of Christ would invite persecution from those who do not know God and intentionally pitch themselves against him because they are deceived by the satanic works (2 Thess 2:10). But the Thessalonian believers' endurance amidst the present suffering ensures them to be worthy of receiving the eternal inheritance of salvation. God is at work in them to make them worthy of his call (1:11 cf. 1 Thess 2:12). Thus, Paul prays for them that "by his power he may bring to fruition your [Thessalonian believers'] every desire for goodness and your [Thessalonian believers'] every deed prompted by faith" (2 Thess 1:11 parenthesis added). Their salvation and rescue from the impending disaster is the work of God beginning at their election, which brings their desires and deeds to fruition at last.

---

16 Witherington, *1 and 2 Thessalonians*, 196.

17 Witherington, *1 and 2 Thessalonians*, 194.

Finally, the day of the Parousia is the appointed day of culminating their journey of faith in serving to fulfill God's plan in this world. Those who believe in the testimony of the apostle will experience the culmination of their election when the Lord will be glorified in "his holy people," including the believers in Thessalonica. Their enduring journey in faith amidst suffering and identity as a missional tool in the hand of God is moving toward the destined end of glorifying God. The greatness of God's power and character will be acknowledged and demonstrated in the believers' transformed lives (notice "be glorified *in* his holy people"—2 Thess 1:10) on that day. Their seemingly defeated present state will be turned into a victory in every sense when the crucified Lord shall appear as the victor (cf. 1 Thess 1:10; 4:14). They will marvel at his magnificent glory on that day.

In short, Paul speaks about the living and true God who has elected them for his purpose to fulfill his plan of universal salvation. Paul leans back on the Abrahamic election tradition to teach that the Thessalonians are co-opted into the universal salvific mission of God. He modifies the tradition through his christological lens to say that they participate in God's continuing universal mission by divine election. Thus, they have become a unique object of God's love and faithfulness. Paul assures them that their present suffering does not break God's trustworthiness. God, in his justice, not only rescues them from the coming wrath but has destined them in Christ by faith to be saved. Their evil persecutors will not go scot-free, for God will repay them in full measure on the last day. However, a better understanding of the missional thrust of who God is for Paul and his missional activity in the world can be fully known only by learning the nature, identity, and function of the church within the Thessalonian correspondence.

4.2. God and the Missional Community in Thessalonica

The church in Thessalonica was formed as a result of Paul and his team members' missionary activity in the city. However, Paul wants them to have a greater vision of themselves as vital instruments in the hands of God. For Paul, it is important because it not only grants them a true vision of themselves in the light of God's plan and purpose, but it also insulates them from being disillusioned amidst problems and wavering away from the truth. Based on the two letters, there are three vital areas relevant to our interest in Paul's ecclesiology: (i) Paul, speaking about the Thessalonian believers' specific context of internal and external problems, exhorts and instructs them about their mystical union with the living and true God who is at work in them. (ii) Paul defines their identity with an implicit missional promise by borrowing an idea from the Old Testament cultic context. (iii) Paul appreciates the Thessalonian church for three vital Christian virtues, which in essence are missional. Within Paul's rhetoric, such appreciations of positive characteristics in someone could be viewed as functioning as an encouragement to his audience to continue doing the same. In the discussion below, Paul's missional understanding of the church shall be elaborated further.

4.2.1. Church founded in God and Christ

The consequence of Paul's mission in Thessalonica, despite intense violent opposition from the non-Christian folks in the city, was the formation of a minority community of Jewish and native believers in the gospel of Jesus Christ. Having taught them that God has elected them according to his eternal plan, Paul affirms their new relationship with the living and true God by calling them to join the *ekklesia*, a local assembly of the called out ones in Thessalonica (1 Thess 1:1). Although some have argued for the etymological root of the word *ekklesia* meaning "that which is called forth, an assembly,"[18] within the context of Paul's Thessalonian correspondence the significance of election and call ideas would require us to view the church as a community for the called out ones for a particular purpose. If 1 Thessalonians is the earliest extant letter of Paul to us, we find in it the earliest use of *ekklesia* by him. He greets the church in Thessalonica as "*in* God the Father and the Lord Jesus Christ" (1 Thess 1:1; 2 Thess 1:1). Paul uses two variant expressions "in Christ" (1 Thess 2:14; 4:16) and "in the Lord" (1 Thess 3:8; 5:12), interchangeably referring to the same truth. The preposition "in" though shows primarily the location of their new spiritual existence, it also implicitly highlights that God and Jesus Christ together form the inevitable foundation of their new found status. It is consistent with the fact that they are called purely by the grace of God and not by their merit. According to Marshall,

> This phrase means not only that the Christian community was brought into existence by God the Father and the Lord Jesus Christ through the preached word, but that there also exists a mystical and spiritual union with the Father and the Son made real through participation in the church as the eschatological 'called out' community which waits for the last day.[19]

We do not find in 1 Thessalonians a bold, direct statement of Paul on Christian mystical union "in Christ" like in Galatians 3:28 and 2 Corinthians 5:17. But the mystical union idea is not absent from these letters.[20] Paul envisions the participation of all people, including the Jews

---

18 Roy Bowen Ward, "Ekklesia: A Word Study," *Restoration Quarterly* 2, no. 4 (1958): 165.

19 Donfried, "Theology of 1 Thessalonians," 59.

20 Cf. Donfried, "Assembly of the Thessalonians," 151–53.

and Greek Thessalonians, in Christ. Apart from his reference to it in formal greetings (1 Thess 1:1; 2 Thess 1:1), he and his companions live by the standing firm of the Thessalonians "in the Lord" (1 Thess 3:8 cf. 3:12). Here, in this locale, they in the Lord Jesus and the Lord Jesus in them are mutually glorified (2 Thess 1:12). In fact, to Paul, one enters into this space by faith and is saved by the vicarious death of Jesus Christ (1 Thess 1:8; 2:13; 5:5, 9–10). Even God's will for the Thessalonians is known only in Christ Jesus (1 Thess 5:18). Further, Paul's apostolic mission of preaching and exhortation is carried out "in the Lord Jesus" (1 Thess 4:1; 2 Thess 3:12). In short, according to Paul, it is the sphere where both individual and corporate ecclesial life of the Thessalonians is located.

4.2.2. Local church as elect "firstfruits" and its missional function

In 2 Thessalonians 2:13, Paul reminds the audience that they are the "firstfruits" of God's chosen ones. The term *firstfruit* (*aparchēn*)[21] is an important term in the Old Testament cultic system. The Lord demanded the firstfruit of the harvest to be brought to the priest for the offering. It sanctified the whole remaining lot of harvest (Lev 23:9–20). For Paul, the believers in Thessalonica are the firstfruit of his labor in the city and the evidence of God's pleasure in gathering people from the gentiles to himself. Their experience of salvation as firstfruits is a pleasing offering to God, which symbolically stands for the greater number of converts to follow. Despite persecution and opposition of the minority community of primarily native believers in Thessalonica, Paul's audience has reason to rejoice by looking at themselves. The God who called and incorporated them into himself will save many more. Probably, they can hope that even those who persecute them at present might join them in Christ.[22] Their very identity as elect "firstfruits" holds the encouraging promise of God to all that many more are sure to join the community of the elect of God. According to Johnson, this should be the natural meaning for the original

[21] Some others have accepted another variant reading mentioning *ap' archēs* meaning "from the beginning" instead of *aparchēn* translated as "firstfruits." The latter meaning is accepted here because of the stronger support of manuscripts. Scholars like Boring, Johnson, and Bruce have accepted the latter term against some like Beale and Marshall who argue for the former reading. Boring, *I & II Thessalonians*, 285; Johnson, *1 and 2 Thessalonians*, 202; F. F. Bruce, *1 and 2 Thessalonians*, 190; G. K. Beale, *1–2 Thessalonians*, The IVP New Testament Commentary Series (Downer Grove, IL: IVP Academic, 2003), 225–26; I. Howard Marshall, *1 and 2 Thessalonians: Based on the Revised Standard Version*, New Century Bible Commentary (Grand Rapids, MI: William B. Eerdmans Publishing, 1983), 207.

[22] Gordon D. Fee, *The First and the Second Letters to the Thessalonians*, The New International Commentary on the New Testament (Grand Rapids, MI: William B. Eerdmans Publishing, 2009), 301–2.

audience because "Paul had mentioned earlier in the letter the expectation of others coming to faith because he had entrusted his testimony to the Thessalonian church (2 Thess 1:10)."[23]

Hence, in 2 Thessalonians 3:1–2, Paul requests the church in Thessalonica to pray, first, for him and his missionary team that through their activities "the message of the Lord may spread rapidly and be honored." The prayer request is grounded upon what has transpired among them recently: "just as it was with you." By this, Paul reminds the elect community of God that they ought to pray for evangelistic activities for it is by the same activities of the apostle and his team in Thessalonica that they are saved. Beale, going further, observes that "prayer and evangelism are two marks of God's elect people"[24] because "while it is true that God elects people, saints are to pray for the evangelization of lost humanity because Scripture tells them to do so."[25] The motivation behind the elect community's missional prayer is that the Lord "be honored" at last (2 Thess 3:1). Connecting the glorification of God at the end with the athletic image employed in the same sentence ("the message...may *spread rapidly*" he translates as "running" in 2 Thess 3:1), Beale contends that Paul is speaking here about the victorious march of the gospel in the present. The glorification of God is happening among them at present through the victorious march of the gospel. It will continue until the eschatological time for the glory of God, just as an athlete in the Olympics runs fast to win an honor at the end. For Beale, Paul also alludes to the Old Testament tradition about God's word running swiftly from one end of the earth to the other to fulfill God's purpose for creation (Ps 147:15 cf. 19:5). Similarly, the gospel will be the ultimate winner against every philosophy, worldview, and religious idea that appears to contend against it.[26] Paul encourages them that their missional prayer for the rapid spread of the gospel through him and his team's ministry in the present is based on the visible evidence of the gospel's victorious course of the race that is resulting in the glorification of the Lord among them. So also, their prayers as the elect missional community of God must be for the glorification of the Lord by the rapid spread of the gospel among others who have not yet heard the gospel.

Second, Paul asks them to pray for their deliverance from the hands of the unbelieving evil folks who oppose them. While the request is to pray for the apostolic team, he assures them that the Lord is faithful (2 Thess 3:3; cf. 1 Thess 5:24) to them. It is he who strengthens and protects them.

---

23 Johnson, *1 and 2 Thessalonians*, 202.

24 Beale, *1–2 Thessalonians*, 235.

25 Beale, *1–2 Thessalonians*, 236.

26 Beale, *1–2 Thessalonians*, 237–38.

Opposition to the gospel by the "evil one" (cf. Matt 6:13—"evil one" refers to Satan) through his human agents is not going to defeat the believers in Thessalonica because the Lord is faithful to his promise to save them (cf. 2 Thess 2:13). As Witherington maintains, "the verbs ('strengthen' and 'protect') here should be seen as having ongoing force: the Lord will continue to strengthen and continue to guard."[27] As discussed earlier, God's continued role in the lives of his elect people is further underlined here. There is no promise to end their present suffering, but a divinely inspired confidence by being "in the Lord" (2 Thess 3:4). Thus, God exhibits his faithfulness toward them by protecting them in their present suffering.

Paul's confidence in the continuing and unending faithfulness of God toward his elect ones also gives him confidence "in the Lord" that they are "doing and will continue to do the things" the apostolic team has commanded (2 Thess 3:4). As Witherington points out, it is also a rhetorical technique of the apostle to encourage his audience to do and continue to do something that he has already commanded and is about to state in 2 Thessalonians 3:6–15.[28] In other words, within the immediate context, it refers to the command to pray for divine protection upon the apostolic team and the spread of the gospel for the salvation of the unbelievers. It includes every other command Paul has given them through teaching, preaching, and the letters that pertain to their ethical living for the glory of God in Thessalonica.

Finally, his request in 2 Thessalonians 3:1–4 ends with a short prayer for them in 3:5: "May the Lord direct your hearts into God's love and Christ's perseverance." It is unclear if "God's love" and "Christ's perseverance" should be understood as an objective or subjective genitive. However, the former expression refers to God's love for humanity and in particular toward them, since Paul has made repeated references to God's love within the two letters. But, as Witherington points out, this divine love is located in their hearts that God now requires to be directed toward himself.[29] If God's love is reflected toward the sinful humanity in the sacrificial death of his Son, then the missional prayer for the Thessalonians is that they reflect God's *agapē* toward others.

Similarly, the second expression, "Christ's perseverance," appears to deepen the same idea further. Paul prays that they would not fall away from their faith but persevere in faith amidst violent opposition like Christ persevered in suffering for the sake of others.[30] The church in Thessalonica, as a called out community of God living "in God the Father

27 Witherington, *1 and 2 Thessalonians*, 242 (parenthesis added).

28 Witherington, *1 and 2 Thessalonians*, 243.

29 Witherington, *1 and 2 Thessalonians*, 243.

30 Witherington, *1 and 2 Thessalonians*, 243.

and the Lord Jesus Christ" must not only possess the love of God, but they must also reflect the same toward others and persevere in faith.

4.2.3. Missional consequence of the Thessalonians' faith, love, and hope

Paul mentions three specific reasons for remembering the church in his prayers: (i) their "work produced by faith," (ii) their "labor prompted by love," and (iii) their "endurance inspired by hope" (1 Thess 1:3). It is interesting to notice that the triad—"work," "labor," and "endurance"—for which Paul remembers them in prayer is the consequences of another important triad of Christian realities to which he repeatedly returns in the letters—"faith," "love," and "hope." They are the defining characteristics of the community in Thessalonica. Scholars have generally consented that each of the second nouns is a subjective genitive that "expresses the source or origin of the former."[31] First, although the term *faith* can be understood traditionally to mean "someone's trust in God,"[32] the context requires us to translate the term as *faithfulness*, a subjective genitive.[33] Then, the term *work* (*ergon*) may refer to their deeds that demonstrate their loyalty/faithfulness to God amidst violent opposition. For example, it could refer to works done in service to God like their evangelistic activities by which their faithfulness is made known everywhere (1 Thess 1:8).[34] In other words, their work producing faithfulness is not only commendable and famous, but it is also a concrete evidence of their self-recognition as a missional community of God by nature.

Second, the word *labor* (*kopos*) is not very different from the word *work* (*ergon*) mentioned in 1 Thessalonians 1:3. It may not have a unique meaning always but its use with *agapē* (1 Thess 1:3) might require a contextual understanding of the term. Witherington maintains that these two terms together refer to works that the Thessalonian believers have done for those who are within or outside the church (cf. 1 Thess 3:12).[35] In 1 Thessalonians 4:9–10, Paul appreciates their love, taught by God, for one another and the larger community of Christians in Macedonia. As Johnson maintains, the "labor of love" could refer to hard physical labor that would reflect a cruciform character visibly embodying the gospel before others. He states, "it is embodied in the kind of self-giving practices Paul narrates in 2:6–12, practices that exhibit a cruciform structure

31 Marshall, *1 and 2 Thessalonians*, 51.

32 Cf. Leon Morris, *The First and Second Epistles to the Thessalonians*, The New International Commentary on the New Testament (Grand Rapids, MI: William B. Eerdmans Publishing, 1959), 51.

33 Witherington, *1 and 2 Thessalonians*, 58; Johnson, *1 and 2 Thessalonians*, 38.

34 Beale, *1-2 Thessalonians*, 46.

35 Witherington, *1 and 2 Thessalonians*, 59.

paralleling the actions of Christ in Philippians 2:6–8."[36] In other words, it is a self-sacrificial act of care done for the well-being of others. The internal evidence of such self-sacrificial acts of benefaction by at least some Christians is evident in 2 Thessalonians 3:13. Paul exhorts his believers in Thessalonica to "never tire of doing what is good." According to Bruce Winter, "the over-arching consideration which stood at the centre of Christian reflection and activity" is "the doing of good which benefited the lives of others"[37] He continues to argue that here, Paul is encouraging Christian benefactors who must have been becoming weary of doing good and were beginning to question the validity of Christians involving in doing good. Despite the problem of idleness (against which he gives firm directives in 2 Thess 3:11–12) and hostility from the non-Christian population in the city, Paul encourages Christian benefactors to continue their acts of benefaction in private and public.[38]

Third, the word *endurance* (*hupamonē*) originating from their hope founded upon their faith in the gospel of Christ preached to them is vital (1 Thess 4:13–14). Amidst utter suffering, it stands for their perseverance in faith (cf. 1 Thess 3:7), which is founded upon the hope of resurrection at the Parousia (1 Thess 4:15–18; 5:10). Repeating the triad—"faith," "love," and "hope"—in 1 Thessalonians 5:8, Paul continues to teach the hope that when the Lord Jesus returns they will be rescued from the coming wrath. Undoubtedly, their "endurance" is the concrete evidence of the invisible hope treasured in their hearts. Paul, remembering this quality of the Thessalonian church with gratitude before God, is not unusual as he was worried about their well-being in faith during the persecution. Paul goes to a great extent to express his great joy upon hearing (1 Thess 3:6) about their steadfastness in faith. He says, "now we really live, since you are standing firm in the Lord. How can we thank God enough for you in return for all the joy we have in the presence of our God because of you?" (1 Thess 3:8–9).

Thus, the *ekklesia* "in God the Father and the Lord Jesus Christ" explains their status as a community located and nurtured mystically. The believers are sustained amidst violent persecution and internal problems by the grace and peace available in the mystical union (2 Thess 1:2). Their election from among the rest of the non-believing population as "first-fruits" explains their current identity and the promise for the salvation of

---

36 Johnson, *1 and 2 Thessalonians*, 40.

37 Bruce W. Winter, "From Secular Clients to Christian Benefactors: 1 Thessalonians 4:11-12 and 2 Thessalonians 3:6-13," in *Seeking the Welfare of the City: Christians as Benefactors and Citizens*, First Century Christians In the Graeco-Roman World (Grand Rapids, MI: William B. Eerdmans Publishing, 1994), 58.

38 Winter, "From Secular Clients to Christian Benefactors," 58–59.

others. Hence, they are exhorted to pray for the speedy evangelization of others and the divine protection of the apostolic team. Meanwhile, the good results of their faithfulness, love, and hope are appreciated, and they must continue the works of evangelism as the expression of faithfulness, hard and self-sacrificial labor of benefaction reflecting their cruciformity, and endurance in faith as Christ has persevered as a mark of eternal hope treasured in their hearts.

4.3. The Church as a Risk-Taking Missional Community

An important characteristic of a missional church is its countercultural dynamism founded upon absolute obedience to the truth of the gospel. The observable pattern of a missional church is that it learns "to take risks for the sake of the gospel. It understands itself as different from the world because of its participation in the life, death, and resurrection of its Lord. It is raising questions, often threatening, about the church's cultural captivity and grappling with the ethical and structural implications of its missional vocation."[39] The subversive and risk-taking nature of the church in Thessalonica is evident in the message, content, and the language of the gospel through which they were incorporated into the community of God. Within the Roman imperial context, the gospel message that the Thessalonian believers received is the story of Jesus, scripted by God for human salvation. Their expression of allegiance through faith in it is dangerously subversive. According to Todd D. Still, the key component of the gospel that Paul preached in Thessalonica, based on 1 Thessalonians, is the story of Jesus' death and resurrection.[40] It is a countercultural narrative of Paul, an apocalyptically minded Jew, who envisions the whole Jesus event as the divine intervention in human history. For him, it signified the overthrow of the ideology-ridden imperial narrative of history. A closer look at Paul's understanding of the gospel, in the language of Bhabha, mimics-mocks the Roman colonial discourse, simultaneously.

The language of the gospel borrows and reuses terms from the Roman imperial vocabulary with a twist. It redraws a new map of the universe in which Rome is decentered by Jesus, the Lord.[41] Unlike parroting Caesar's

---

39 Lois Y. Barrett, "Taking Risks as a Contrast Community," in *Treasure in Clay Jars: Patterns in Missional Faithfulness*, ed. Lois Y. Barrett, The Gospel and Our Culture Series (Grand Rapids, MI: William B. Eerdmans Publishing, 2004), 74.

40 Todd D. Still, "'Since We Believe That Jesus Died and Rose Again': The Gospel Paul Preached in Thessalonica as Evidenced by 1 Thessalonians," *Restoration Quarterly* 54, no. 1 (2012): 7–18.

41 Peter Oakes, "Re-Mapping the Universe: Paul and the Emperor in 1 Thessalonians and Philippians," *Journal for the Study of the New Testament* 27, no. 3 (2005): 315–18. Oakes maintains that the act of decentring Rome does not seem to be Paul

gospel as the victory of Rome over his enemy (e.g., Josephus, *J.W.* 4.10.6), the representation of the emperor as divine,[42] or the news of the birth of Augustus,[43] "the gospel" is God the Father's (1 Thess 1:1) offer of salvation to all through "Jesus" (1 Thess 1:10; 4:14 cf. 3:11) who suffered unjustly the colonial punishment (crucifixion). Ambivalence defines the character of the gospel they believed and preached in which "Jesus"—a humiliated, defeated, and colonized subject—stands in opposition to Caesar—the proud, victorious, and colonizing subject. Contrary to the offer of salvation through bloodshed and silencing of the other, God in Christ Jesus offers the true salvation, eschatological hope, and peace and security through his death on the cross (cf. 1 Thess 5:10).

The depth of subversive and countercultural dynamism of the gospel is further articulated by the deliberate use of the high Roman imperial titles of Caesar for Jesus (for example, *kyrios*, and *sōtēria*, while also other terms that formed the Roman imperial propaganda like *eirēnē*, *asphaleia*, *ekklēsia*, *parousia*, and *apostolos*).[44] The use of titles and terms with politically charged meanings for Jesus is neither unintentional nor unnoticed. Luke mentions that Paul preached Jesus, "the Christ," which was heard with strong political subversive tone (Acts 17:3, 5–9). Within a culturally hybrid context, the messianic title "Christ" evoked multiple meanings. The use of the title "Christ" implying a rival "King" seemingly robs Caesar of his imperial claim. It was deciphered clearly by his Jewish auditors because they must have known it as "a title for the eschatological king."[45] Similarly, while the title "Lord" was used exclusively for the Roman emperors in the Roman imperial discourse,[46] in the Jewish religio-cultural discourse it was used for YHWH.[47] It formed the primary basis for the Jewish nationalists like the Zealots, who refused to address their Roman imperial masters as "Lord" (Josephus, *J.W.* 2.8.1; 7.10.1). However, for Paul, Jesus, the kingly Jewish figure, died under the Roman law, but he resurrected from the dead transcending and challenging the imperial order of power. Unlike the imperial eschatological and apotheosis

intent. However, "it has already gone in any case along with all the other 'idols' from which the Thessalonians had turned" (321).

42 G. Friedrich, "Ευαγγελιζομαι Κτλ," *Theological Dictionary of the New Testament*, 2: 724–26.

43 Friedrich, "Ευαγγελιζομαι Κτλ," 2: 724; Michael J. Gorman, *Apostle of the Crucified Lord: A Theological Introduction to Paul and His Letters* (Grand Rapids, MI/Cambridge: William B. Eerdmans Publishing, 2004), 107; Harrison, "Paul and the Imperial Gospel," 90.

44 See J. R. Harrison, "Paul and the Imperial Gospel," 82–88.

45 Boring, *I & II Thessalonians*, 52. See also, George, *Paul's Identity in Galatians*, 142–43.

46 Harrison, "Paul and the Imperial Gospel," 78–79.

47 George, *Paul's Identity in Galatians*, 143–45.

traditions that depicted Augustus as seated in heaven and ruling over the world, Paul mimicking-mocking the imperial discourse states that Jesus, our Lord, will return from heaven at the Parousia (1 Thess 1:10; 4:16) with a great sound of trumpet in victory of whom he is an apostle (1 Thess 2:7; cf. 2:19; 3:13).[48] The term *Parousia* is a borrowed term for Paul, but it has multiple nuances. While, as Malherbe states, in the Greek setting it referred to "the ceremonial arrival of a king or ruler with honors or of the coming of a god to help people in need,"[49] for Weima despite its Jewish (OT) roots, "the predominately gentile church of Thessalonica would naturally have understood the Parousia in terms of the royal visit of the Roman emperors and officials."[50] In fact, the identity of Jesus articulated in ambivalent terms within the lucid culturally hybridized space subverts the oppressor-oppressed relationship structure established by Rome.

If so, how could such a sly subversive claim be lived out by a missional community in a colonial context? In a hostile environment, the Christian response is not articulated in unilateral terms but ambivalently. On the one hand, Paul exhorts the Thessalonian believers "to lead a quiet life and attend to your own business and work with your hands" (1 Thess 4:11), and on the other hand, to him, they are called into God's "kingdom and glory" (1 Thess 2:12 cf. 2 Thess 1:5) that requires them to lead a life worthy of it. Paul's appeal "to lead a quiet life" in the context of conflict triggered by the politically charged gospel preached in the city is to "maintain a low profile and seek to be respected by society at large."[51] However, it is not retiring from the society; rather the term *Philotimeisthai* means to "aspire," or "avoidance of conflict and doing purposeful work and community-building."[52] In other words, for Paul, even manual labor must not be out of the scope of proper Christian conduct. They ought not to depend upon their previous patrons.[53] Within a hostile and politically repressive context, it is a strategic posture of the missional community to ensure fulfilling the purpose of its election, while avoiding imperial censure.[54]

---

48 Harrison, "Paul and the Imperial Gospel," 88–96 especially 95; Wanamaker, *Epistles to the Thessalonians*, 86. According to Wanamaker, the infinitive term, "to await," in 1:10, "is a hapax legomenon not only in Paul but also in the NT as a whole…for the coming of Christ.""

49 Malherbe, *Paul and the Thessalonians*, 272.

50 Weima, *1–2 Thessalonians*, 205.

51 Boring, *I & II Thessalonians*, 153.

52 Witherington, *1 and 2 Thessalonians*, 121. See Weima, *1-2 Thessalonians*, 294–95 for a summary discussion on various views on the meaning of Paul's words "live a quiet life."

53 Cf. Witherington, *1 and 2 Thessalonians*, 124.

54 Witherington, *1 and 2 Thessalonians*, 122.

A missional community, for Paul, anticipates the imminent doom of the Roman Empire at the return of "the Lord" (1 Thess 5:2–4). According to Paul, while in the present the Roman imperial discourse propagates the establishment of Roman peace and security (Josephus, *Ant.* 14.9.2, 14.10.22; cf. "they" used by Paul in 1 Thess 5:3),[55] the eschatological liberation for him and the persecuted believers in Thessalonica is sure to happen. He anticipates God's impending judgment in 1 Thessalonians 1:10 upon all who refuse allegiance to him. However, the missional community must respond in assimilative-abrogative terms. It means, seemingly, an assimilative lifestyle ("to lead a quiet life") is informed by the extra vision[56] of doom of every dominant power structure that stands against God and his eternal missional agenda. Hence, Paul articulated the hope of vindication of his readers in Isaiahnic words (Isa 59:17), exhorting them to live a life that is worthy of God: "sober, putting on faith and love as breastplate, and the hope of salvation as a helmet" (1 Thess 5:8 cf. 1:3).[57]

4.4. Church in India: A missional call

A vital self-realization that constantly needs to happen to the church in India is the unique relationship the community shares with God. They are the elect ones of God for God loves them and they enjoy God's unflinching faithfulness. Paul reminds the Thessalonian believers about their conversion as their decisive and conscious turn toward the true and living God from the idols. Within the missional pluralistic context of India, it is important for the modern readers of Paul's letters to acknowledge for the sake of Christian witness that they enter into the community of God by their own conscious choice. Their faith in the gospel of Christ is a decisive reversal from their former lifestyle that radically alters their life. As an elect community of God, they stand in the Abrahamic election to fulfill the divine plan to save humanity. In fact, by virtue of election, the church is a partner in the mission of God. Hence, as mentioned earlier, despite suffering persecution and murder, the church can rely upon God's justice that he will retribute the wrongdoers justly on the last day while he will rescue the faithful ones from the wrath of God. It is also the exhibition of God's faithfulness toward the persecuted minority in India to ensure their entry into God's kingdom.

55 See Klaus Wengst, *PAX ROMANA and the Peace of Jesus Christ*, trans. John Bowden (Philadelphia, PA: Fortress Press, 1987), 19–26, 77–78.

56 Homi K. Bhabha, "Of Mimicry and Man: The Ambivalence of Colonial Discourse," in *The Location of Culture* (London: Routledge, 1994), 126. In Bhabha's terms, it is the double vision of a postcolonial subject.

57 Cf. Sylvia C. Keesmaat, "Crucified Lord of Conquering Savior: Whose Story of Salvation?," *Horizons in Biblical Theology* 26, no. 2 (2004): 91.

Another foundational truth that the church should hold fast to is that they are not only mystically founded in Christ, but they are also God's elect "firstfruits" in their local social situation. Although Christians form a minority community in India, their election from different castes, tribes, and people groups is God's promise both to them and to the rest of the nation that many more, perhaps including their present persecutors, are to join the body of Christ. In other words, those who are already saved not only symbolize the divine promise of salvation for others in and through their election, but they also have the responsibility of functioning as a missional community participating in the ongoing eternal salvific act of God. There is a moral obligation upon them to recognize, actualize, and creatively engage in living as a worthy people of God before others through prayers offered on behalf of other saints and engaging in actual evangelization. Though evangelization is only a part of the larger missional activity of God through his community in the present world, it is a vital act of testifying the gospel before others.

Thus, the three reasons of Paul's thanksgiving to God on behalf of the believers in Thessalonica—"work produced by faith," "labor prompted by love," and "endurance inspired by hope"—ought to characterize the missional existence of the church in India too. They ought to engage in missional activities too out of their faithfulness to God and his mission, although Christians in India have been violently attacked and persecuted for doing so. However, the primary engagement within the pluralistic community of bearing witness in words before others is the church's temporal reciprocation to God's eternal faithfulness toward them. Every local congregation ought to become famous and exemplary to other congregations for them to emulate the visible model. Further, the repeated violent response from outsiders must not stop or discourage the church from restricting the scope of benefaction, that is, the "labor of love" for which the church in India is well-known. Although such acts of Christian love have been misconstrued as the Christian missionary's allurement of the illiterate poor and vulnerable people of the lower social segment, the community of the living God cannot afford to restrict the sphere of its missional influence. The numerous educational institutions, hospitals, orphanages, homes for the poor and destitute, care centers for the terminally ill individuals, old age homes serving the disowned elderly individuals, etc., must continue unrestricted from our side as part of our mission. Even the effort to endure in hope amidst hopelessness, in general, must be practically lived out by the church. In fact, the suffering that the church undergoes under the political dispensation is its cruciform identity. But, the church must remember that along with them for different unjust reasons, including seeking the truth in Christ, even other members of the society outside the church suffers. The Christians suffering joyously is a testimony to others about the value and truthfulness of what they believe.

However, the church must become the mouthpiece of the silenced community of the marginalized by taking the risk of confronting the unjust structures and evil propagandas. As a community of God in India, the Christians must willingly take on the oppressive structures and agents of exploitation, thus proving to be true to the subversive nature of the gospel. The church cannot afford to be coopted by the dominant oppressive powers against the poor and the exploited, for it contradicts the very gospel of the crucified Messiah who died upon the colonial cross under the Roman imperial power. The mission of the church needs to persist in enthroning Jesus as the Lord of the whole cosmos ruled by the principles of justice, love, and fraternity. Hence, our mission is to participate voluntarily in the sufferings of the poor. The agenda of risking the self is to establish a just society permeated by love and equality of all. The marginalized communities like the dalits and outcasts of the society must be enabled through the critical engagement of the church to voice their demands, seek justice, and restore their human rights. Interestingly, in things apart from these, a Christian has no other focus but to lead a quiet life.

To sum up, in his two letters to the Thessalonian community, Paul speaks of a Triune God who is engaged in restoring the lost world to him. In other words, the mission of God originates from the Triune God who, for Paul, is involved in the mission of saving the world out of love, from eschatological destruction. God, the Father, is the living and true God who acts justly with humans. He sent his Son, the second person of the Trinity, to die for human salvation. However, God vindicated him by raising him from the dead and thereby guaranteeing his people of future resurrection from the dead. He sanctifies the believers as also the Holy Spirit is equally performing the same function within the church. Amidst the prevailing persecution in Thessalonica, Paul encourages them with the intention to keep them steadfast in their faith in Christ. Founded in Christ together as a community of God, the church ought to be spiritually nourished through the mystical union as now they belong to God. Their election gives them a unique status as the "firstfruits" of the community to which they belong. By this, Paul wants the church in Thessalonica to recognize its missional role in leading others into salvation in Christ and their missional significance as the living symbols of God's eternal promise to save those who turn toward him from an idolatrous pattern of lifestyle. The church as a community produces the "work" through faith, "labor" inspired by love, and "endurance" born out of hope in Christ. For Paul, the Thessalonian believers live out their missional purpose of God in and through these three modes of witnessing to God by living out the core of the gospel before others.

However, it also implies that living true to the essence of the gospel of Christ means they willingly risk being violently eliminated for opposing the evil social structures of darkness.

5

THE GOSPEL AND MISSIONAL PNEUMATOLOGY

The two important interrelated aspects in the formation of an effective missional community are the content of the gospel it preaches along with its significance in a particular sociocultural context and the way the significance of the Holy Spirit is recognized in fulfilling its missional call and purpose of existence in the world. The question of the content, nature, and significance of the gospel may be perceived variedly, but the key to successful existence as a missional community in a given context lies in the ability of the community to become a hermeneutic of the gospel before others. In doing that, the role of the Holy Spirit is vital to effectively concretize the gospel visibly before others, attracting them to join the cruciform community of God, and imparting the hope of the gospel amidst the rampant negativity around. In the Thessalonian correspondence, Paul speaks about "the gospel" as something that the local community embodies in critical engagement with the culture outside the church. Moreover, the apostle reminds the believers of the significance of their dependence upon the Holy Spirit in becoming a missional community.

If so, what is the core content of the gospel Paul and others preached in Thessalonica? How does it establish, enable, and enrich the community of believers amidst violent opposition from outside and the question of the death of the members of the community causing disenchantment among them? What is the role of the Holy Spirit in strengthening and nurturing the community of God in Thessalonica? Should the believers in Thessalonica desire and depend upon the Holy Spirit and the charismatic gifts to become a more effective missional community? In the discussion that ensues below, first, an attempt shall be made to explain the content of the gospel that the missionary team preached in the city, its importance in the local context and its creative role in the individual lives of the believers in God. Second, the powerful presence and role of the Holy Spirit within the Thessalonian correspondence shall be discussed.

5.1. The gospel in Thessalonica

Paul's apostolic consciousness and dedication to always conduct himself responsibly before others, according to the divine vocation he received at the gate of Damascus (Acts 9), hinges upon the purity of the gospel he claimed to preach before his audience. His encounter with Christ coincided with the divine revelation, the gospel that he received. Hence, he defended "the gospel" he preached and was undeterred by the circumstances while preaching the same to others. He did not doubt in his mind that by his preaching, he is actualizing God's promise to Abraham to bless the nations. He saw it happening before his eyes through the gospel of Christ that was equipping the community of the newly converted believers to behave as the missional community of God intentionally.

5.1.1. Paul and the gospel

Paul arrived in Thessalonica as a messenger of God preaching the "gospel" to the people there. Paul calls "the gospel" he preached along with his companions in Thessalonica, in personalized terms, "our gospel" (1 Thess 1:5; 2 Thess 2:14). The personalized reference to the gospel that he and his companions preached, is vital because it attests the genuineness of their preaching ministry. He says that "we speak as those *approved* by God to be *entrusted* with the gospel" (1 Thess 2:4, emphasis added). Turning away from enlisting their humanly credentials to contrast themselves against the others who preach with "impure motives" (1 Thess 2:3), Paul appeals to God's approval to validate: (i) at the primary level, their reliability and trustworthiness as ideal preachers, and (ii) at the secondary level, the unique authenticity and purity of the gospel they have preached fearlessly (cf. 1 Thess 2:2).

First, owing to Paul's familiarity with prophet Jeremiah (cf. Jer 1:5; Gal 1:15), as Johnson maintains, it is probable that Paul is staking claim for his loyalty toward God just as prophet Jeremiah does before God (cf. Jer 9:7; 11:20; 17:10). Especially, by using the term *heart*, that is also used in the LXX referring to the inner-self of a person, "Paul, like Jeremiah, affirms that God plumbs the very depths of human beings, testing the motives that lie behind their public practices, especially the practices of those who profess to be engaged in the *missio Dei*."[1] Second, as a result, God approved their sincerity toward him and trusted them with the gospel. God is the

[1] Johnson, *1 and 2 Thessalonians*, 62.

subject who trusted (*pisteuō*) Paul with something, that is, the gospel. Later, in Galatians 2:7, Paul employs the same term, *pisteuō*, in his defence to say that even the pillars in Jerusalem have recognized that he has been given the gospel to the gentiles. Interestingly, in Galatians 1:6–12, Paul defends the gospel he has received from God, and not from any human. He pronounces curses upon anyone who preaches a gospel apart from that he has received from God. For him, the gospel he preached is pure and reliable. It is distinct from other perverted gospels. If Galatians helps us to identify rightly Paul's preoccupation with the gospel he received, then, the expression "our gospel" in 1 Thessalonians 1:5 would mean the gospel he received through revelation from God and has been preaching to them with a pure motive. Hence, the gospel he preached when identified as "our gospel" is a short form for a load of claim Paul might make otherwise for what he preached and that others ought to believe.

In his two letters to the Thessalonians, Paul interchangeably uses two genitive expressions "of God" (1 Thess 2:8); and "of Christ" (1 Thess 3:2 cf. 2 Thess 1:8) that qualify the term *gospel* (*euangelion* 1 Thess 1:5; 2:2, 4, 8–9; 3:2). They bear unique emphases, but they qualify the gospel they preached in the city. It is "the gospel of God" because God stands behind the gospel lending authority to the gospel he preaches, who entrusts it to the apostle. Paul is merely a recipient of that which is entrusted to him. At the same time, "the Christ" being the sole focus of the gospel handed over by God makes it "the gospel of Christ."[2]

If so, what is the content of the gospel they proclaimed in Thessalonica? In the letters, Paul does not state in explicit terms the content of their preaching in Thessalonica. However, Paul's regular reference to what he and the believers in the city have believed could be treated as the very content of his preaching. Collins argues that in Thessalonica "what is believed is that which has been preached" because in Thessalonians *kerussō*, *euangelion*, *pisteuō*, and the faith formula that includes Jesus's death and resurrection "belong to one and the same linguistic register."[3] In 1 Thessalonians 4:14, Paul mentions two basic tenets of faith that he shares in common with others in Thessalonica, that is, "Jesus died and rose again." According to F. F. Bruce, it is "the irreducible basis of the gospel" quoted from "the pre-Pauline creedal formula" because he uses *Iēsous* and not *Christos* contrary to his normal pattern and he also employs *anestē*

2 Raymond F. Collins, "'The Gospel of Our Lord Jesus' (2 Thess 1, 8): A Symbolic Shift of Paradigm," in *The Thessalonian Correspondence*, ed. Raymond F. Collins, *Bibliotheca Ephemeridum Theologicarum Lovaniensium*, vol. 87 (Leuven: Leuven University Press, 1990), 429.

3 Collins, "'Gospel of Our Lord Jesus' (2 Thess 1, 8)," 435.

instead of *ēgerthē*.[4] Unlike this in 1 Thessalonians 1:10, Paul using the term *egeirein* speaks of God as the one who raised Jesus from the dead. It is important to notice that such a confessional material became the basis of our hope that God will raise those who have already died in him (1 Thess 4:14).

If so, how does the gospel interact in a pluralistic cultural context? How did the people of Thessalonica experience the power of "the gospel of Christ" in their public space? What is the role of the congregation in interpreting the gospel of Christ to the people as part of its missional presence? In the following discussion, an attempt shall be made to recognize how the community of believers in Thessalonica were to interpret the gospel of Christ in and through its corporate being before others. Undoubtedly, the gospel as the story of Jesus retold in the city was intended to impact the newly founded community there, while visibly interpreting the gospel in the public space for transformation as part of its missional engagement.

5.1.2. The gospel interpreted in public through the congregation

Speaking about the possible ways in which the gospel could become credible to the people, Lesslie Newbigin maintains that "the only answer, the only hermeneutics of the gospel, is a congregation of men and women who believe it and live by it."[5] In order to do that, for Newbigin, the congregation must expand the scope of its missional presence from mere evangelism and a narrow vision of Christian discipleship limited to the private sphere of life to a larger and higher level of faithful embodiment of the "message which concerns the kingdom of God" in the public space.[6] Of the six characteristics he identifies to make the congregation become a key to the hermeneutic of the gospel, his view that the community must be "a community of hope" is relevant for our current discussion.[7] Newbigin states that "the gospel offers an understanding of the human situation which makes it possible to be filled with a hope which is both eager and patient even in the most hopeless situations." He continues saying, "as we are truly 'indwelling' the gospel story . . . we are able steadily and confidently to live in this attitude of eager hope."[8]

As discussed earlier, the direct consequence of the gospel of Christ preached by Paul and his companions in Thessalonica is the hope of resurrection for the new Thessalonian believer. Amidst the despair creeping

---

4 Bruce, *1 and 2 Thessalonians*, 97.

5 Lesslie Newbigin, *The Gospel in a Pluralist Society* (Grand Rapids, MI: William B. Eerdmans Publishing, 1989), 227.

6 Newbigin, *Gospel in a Pluralist Society*, 222.

7 Newbigin, *Gospel in a Pluralist Society*, 227–33, cited from 232.

8 Newbigin, *Gospel in a Pluralist Society*, 232.

into the community of disciples due to the death of those in Christ, the gospel imparting hope, according to Paul, is to "encourage one another with these words" (1 Thess 4:18). In the transcultural hybrid Thessalonian context, as Jewett mentions, Paul's description of Jesus as the one who is killed and has resurrected evokes the native Thessalonian hope of Cabirus' return for the oppressed class. In the original context, the Cabirus cult provided space for the poor native population to imagine a glorious future against the wealthy class's exploitative behavior by believing in the hope of the return of Cabirus from the dead. Later, it reincarnated in the Roman coopting of their religion into the imperial civil religion, thus shattering their real hope of liberation.[9] However, unlike Caesar's bloody imposition of peace within the empire, the gospel of Jesus's death and resurrection was effective in imparting the lost hope of liberation to the poor native population.

In 1 Thessalonians 5:8, Paul escalates the significance of hope in living out the Christian life in a hostile world by adopting Isaiah's prophecy about God who wears the "helmet of salvation" in bringing salvation to his people (Isa 59:17). Paul too mentions hope "as a helmet" (1 Thess 5:8) that protects a warrior's "most vulnerable part ('head') . . . in a life-threatening situation."[10] According to Johnson, for a community facing violent opposition from outside and facing challenge to sustain their fidelity toward God, "this communal hope for the consummation of their salvation that God will bring 'through our Lord Jesus Christ' (v. 9) sustains the audience in their fidelity towards God and love towards others as God continues his rectifying mission through them."[11] Thessalonians, as the children of light belonging to the day, ought to radiate their hope to others while guarding themselves against every contrary thought, ideas, and philosophies that disillusions people and spreads darkness. Paul, remembering and rehearsing the ministry of Timothy in Thessalonica, says that the purpose of partnering in *missio Dei* "spreading the gospel of Christ" is to "strengthen and encourage" the Thessalonians in their faith (1 Thess 3:2).

Underlining the significance of hope in modern culture that has turned it into mere "mindless optimism," Morris says "no movement has really gripped the hearts of any considerable number of people that has not given them hope. It is no gain, but a considerable loss, if we let go of this significant New Testament teaching."[12] In Newbigin's terms, when "plausibility structure"—the existing societal reality—contradicts our Christian hope saying "that it is absurd to believe that the true authority over all

9 Jewett, *Thessalonian Correspondence*, 131–32.

10 Witherington, *1 and 2 Thessalonians*, 150 (parenthesis added).

11 Johnson, *1 and 2 Thessalonians*, 143.

12 Morris, *1, 2 Thessalonians*, 97.

things is represented in a crucified man," there is an inevitable space for the reassertion of Christian hope visibly in the communal life of the body of Christ that comes through the gospel. Paul realizes that mere assertion of the salvific death of Jesus and his resurrection without concrete implications to the despairing question of the Thessalonians will do no good because "no amount of brilliant argument can make it sound reasonable to the inhabitants of the reigning plausibility structure."[13] Undoubtedly, such a goal is achievable only if the content of faith is capable of restoring hope both within the community and out in the society.

Thus, talking about the "gospel of Christ" that has quickly spread out from the Thessalonians to the surrounding regions of Macedonia and Achaia, Paul mentions it as "the Lord's message" (1 Thess 1:8). Identifying the gospel they preached with "the Lord" is important because it is "the Lord's words" of hope that both the dead in Christ will rise up at his coming and those alive on the day of the Parousia will "be caught up together with them in the clouds to meet the Lord in the air" (1 Thess 4:15–17). In short, the believers have no reason to grieve like the rest of humankind who have no hope (1 Thess 4:13), because it is the Lord of both the dead and the living who imparts hope beyond death into eternal salvation (1 Thess 4:17; 5:10). The Christian community in Thessalonica ought to embody the gospel of hope before the non-Christians to prove the credentials of the gospel. In Thessalonian correspondence, "the Lord" referring to Jesus Christ, the one who comes from above and is able to raise dead from their grave is the real Lord in contrast to Caesar, the Roman Lord, who kills but never can give life. For Paul, the Lord, who died and is raised from the dead, is the Lord of all things. On the final day, "the Lord Jesus will overthrow with the breath of his mouth and destroy [the lawless one] by the splendour of his coming" (2 Thess 2:8, parenthesis added).

5.1.3. The gospel active within a believer

Paul used twice the expression the *word of God* (1 Thess 2:13) synonymously to the *gospel* (of God) in the first letter to the Thessalonians.[14] The *word*, like the *gospel*, refers to "the oral telling of the story of Jesus as the story of God's salvation breaking into human history."[15] Unlike in the first thanksgiving section (1 Thess 1:5), where the Spirit actively involves in effecting the believers' life with the gospel, in his second thanksgiving section (1 Thess 2:13) a similar function is played by the *word* that they have

---

13 Newbigin, *Gospel in a Pluralist Society*, 232.

14 Donfried, "Theology of 1 Thessalonians," 134.

15 Witherington, *1 and 2 Thessalonians*, 71.

received. Paul reminds them that it is not "a human word, but as it actually is, the word of God" that is at work in them (1 Thess 2:13).

In the Genesis creation account, the *word* is a creative agent of God. The *word* actively participated in bringing forth the world into existence out of nothing (Gen 1:1–25). Later in the prophetic tradition, Isaiah speaks about the *word* proceeding from the mouth of Yahweh as surely destined to accomplish the desired purpose for which it is sent out (Isa 55:11). The creative function of the word of Yahweh is mentioned by drawing a parallel with "the rain and the snow" in the preceding verse. They water the field by falling down from heaven causing the land to produce fruit for the people (Isa 55:10). So also, the *word* proceeds from Yahweh's mouth with its creative power to produce "the juniper" "instead of the thornbush" and "the myrtle" in place of the "brier" (Isa 55:13). Similarly, in the Johannine tradition, it is the pre-existent word, the *logos*, that was active in the creation of everything in the world that is created, both visible and invisible (John 1:1–3). For John, the *logos* is Jesus, the incarnate word (John 1:14), in his preexistent state. Paul reminds his audience that the creative and transformative effects visible in the lives of the non-Christian Thessalonians after they have believed in the gospel is the creative function of the gospel within them. Interestingly, as Beale maintains, the desire to please God by living a life worthy of God (1 Thess 2:12) is engendered by the activity of the *word* within them.

Hence, Paul's thanksgiving to God is the result of his awareness that they are being prepared to inherit his kingdom by the gospel, of which Jesus Christ is the content. Another important aspect of making the gospel effective in the lives of believers is the role of the Holy Spirit. In the remainder of this chapter, we shall seek to understand the significance of Paul's pneumatology in the Thessalonian correspondence through the missional lens.

5.2. Missional pneumatology

It is one thing to discuss the doctrine of the Holy Spirit, the Third Person of the Trinity, based on the Bible, but it could be an entirely different exercise to view the being, role, and character of the Spirit within the church from a missional point of view. We might call such an exercise "missional pneumatology." The primary interest of missional pneumatology is not just to contemplate the ontological character of the Holy Spirit, but to also decipher how the Spirit is missional in his very being, role, and character. Such an exercise implies prioritization of missional-theological insights because the Spirit as one in the Triune Godhead participates in the universal mission of God to redeem and save the fallen creation. Thus, the

Holy Spirit's role is important in the life of the church because "the missional community confesses its dependence upon the Holy Spirit, shown in particular in its practices of corporate prayer."[16]

Paul recognized the significance of the Spirit in the formation, growth, and development of the church in Thessalonica. Hence, the evidence of teaching a positive role of the Spirit within the church is found right from one of his earliest letters, that is, the Thessalonian correspondence. In the letters (as also in words), Paul teaches his believers that no aspect of their life in God and Christ is untouched by the activity of the Holy Spirit. He indwells them and works through them for the spread of the gospel. Their salvation is accomplished by the sanctifying work of the Spirit. Hence, in every sense, they are dependent upon the Spirit. Probably, Paul wants them to acknowledge this fundamental truth clearly because as a missional community, they need to depend upon the Spirit to fulfill God's eternal plan to save the sick and the lost.

5.2.1. The Holy Spirit in the preaching of the gospel

Right at the outset of 1 Thessalonians, Paul gives the reason for his thanksgiving to God in prayer for the Thessalonian believers. Referring back to his first missionary visit in Thessalonica with the gospel, Paul says to them that God "has chosen you, because our gospel came to you not simply with words but also with power, with the Holy Spirit and deep conviction" (1 Thess 1:4–5). There are two important parts of it: (i) Paul's reference to the arrival of the gospel to them and its relationship with the following part of the verse, and (ii) the relationship between the three important words—"power," "Holy Spirit," and "deep conviction"—in the awkwardly constructed Greek sentence.

First, with regard to the former, the term *gospel* refers to the content of the message Paul and his companions (notice "*our* gospel," emphasis added) preached in Thessalonica. In 1 Thessalonians 2:8–9, he qualifies "gospel" twice with the genitive expression "of God," while later in 3:2, he mentions it as the "gospel of Christ." For him, they both are synonymous because God's election of the Thessalonians into his universal missional plan of saving all people is actualized only in and through Jesus Christ. Even the essence of the gospel they believed is "that Jesus died and rose again, and so we believe that God will bring with Jesus those who have fallen asleep in him" (1 Thess 4:14) when he returns from heaven (1 Thess 1:10). Further, along with the content of the gospel, Paul also emphasizes the agency by which they received the gospel, "*our* gospel" (emphasis

[16] Walter C. Hobbs, "Dependence on the Holy Spirit," in *Treasure in Clay Jars: Patterns in Missional Faithfulness*, ed. Lois Y. Barrett, The Gospel and Our Culture Series (Grand Rapids, MI: William B. Eerdmans Publishing, 2004), 117.

added). By this, he underlines the missionary team's role in preaching the gospel in Thessalonica. So, "the primary nuance of εὐαγγέλιον in this verse concerns the act of delivering the gospel," which means that it "should be understood as meaning 'our gospel preaching.'"[17] It means that the expression "our gospel" implies the act of preaching with a uniquely personal experience added to it. That is, the gospel preaching has saved them from the coming wrath of God. Nevertheless, Paul by saying the "gospel came to you not simply in words" does not reject human words in preaching the gospel. Instead, he means to say that the gospel preaching did not happen simply in human words, but there is something more to it, that is, it came "also with power" (1 Thess 1:5).

The unique act of gospel preaching with power validates Paul's claim for the genuineness of his preaching among the Thessalonians. Paul forcefully states by contrasting "in word alone" (*enlogōmonon*) with "in power" (*endunamei*) to validate his successful mission among them. Weima says that "the addition of the word *alone* . . . is important: it shows that the apostle was not denigrating the importance of presenting the gospel in word (i.e., preaching) but rather distinguishing his preaching, whose genuineness is attested by the accompaniment of 'power,' from the kind of insincere preaching that consists in word *alone*."[18] Thereby, he quashed the possible misunderstanding of him (1 Thess 2:1–12) by some in Thessalonica likening them with any other philosopher or sophist speaking in "words of flattery" (1 Thess 2:5). Paul maintained "that the genuineness of his preaching was verified by the presence of 'power.'"[19]

Second, the relationship between the three words—"power," "Holy Spirit," and "deep conviction"—is important to understand how the gospel came to the Thessalonians. Weima argues that the lack of a preposition, "in" (*en*), before the third word in several manuscripts, unlike its presence before the other two words mentioned earlier, breaks the seeming pattern of Paul's sentence formation. So, the latter two words must be treated merely as a qualifier of the first word *power*.[20]

If so, what is the meaning of *power* (*dunamis*)? How can one understand the missional significance of the coming of the gospel with power? Although the actual meaning of the word *power* is not evident to us in this context, it is generally understood as "referring to the miraculous signs and wonders that accompanied the preaching of the gospel."[21] In Romans 15:18–19, Paul speaks about his ministry of preaching among the gentiles

---

17 Wanamaker, *Epistles to the Thessalonians*, 78.

18 Weima, *1–2 Thessalonians*, 94.

19 Weima, *1–2 Thessalonians*, 94.

20 Weima, *1–2 Thessalonians*, 94.

21 Wanamaker, *Epistles to the Thessalonians*, 79.

as accompanied and attested "by words and deeds, by the power of signs and wonders, by the power of the Spirit of God." Wanamaker rightly points out that it would not be wrong to understand the term as referring to the gifts of the Holy Spirit (1 Cor 12:8–10). Even Jesus has performed such miraculous works, which he ascribed to the power of the Holy Spirit and even the early apostles in the first century have done so.[22] Paul's reference to power proves his positive evaluation of the role of miracles with the power of the Holy Spirit (cf. Mark 3:20–30) in mission. Here we find him recognizing and confessing the Holy Spirit as the source of his powerful ministry in Thessalonica.

Further, the consequence of the Holy Spirit-inspired powerful mission in Thessalonica is a "deep conviction" (1 Thess 1:5). It refers to a much deeper work of the Holy Spirit within the human self. Bruce rightly observes that "the reference is to the Thessalonians' deep inward persuasion of the truth of the gospel, a token of the Holy Spirit's work in their hearts, more impressive and more lasting than the persuasion produced by spectacular or miraculous signs."[23] This means, while the powerful works of the Holy Spirit could give the initial breakthrough in capturing attention by creating a certain level of positive response toward the gospel in the hearts of the audience, the real and long-lasting reversal toward God happens only by the "deep conviction" effected by the Holy Spirit (cf. John 16:8–9). But both the aspects of the Holy Spirit's work are vital in doing an effective mission. The twinned role of the Holy Spirit in effecting the election of God into the life of a new convert is recognizable here: (i) As discussed earlier, the miraculous visible exhibition of the work of the Holy Spirit in mission validates the act of preaching, and the message proclaimed. (ii) A "deep conviction" points to a much more effective two-dimensional invisible work of the Holy Spirit: (a) within the heart of a hearer and (b) placing of a divine seal upon the genuineness and sincerity of the preachers. Paul is convinced that the two-dimensional invisible function of the Holy Spirit together contributed to the turning of the Thessalonians' hearts toward the living and true God. To produce the result of turning a sinner toward God, the Holy Spirit works both within the hearer and the preacher of the gospel simultaneously. Commentators like Wanamaker have wrongly limited the meaning of the expression, a "deep conviction," in this context to the "manner of Paul's preaching of the gospel" alone. He argues that, with the use of "just as," from 1 Thessalonians 1:6 onward Paul actually "turn[s] to the effect of the mission on his readers."[24] However, it

22 Wanamaker, *Epistles to the Thessalonians*, 79.

23 Bruce, *1 and 2 Thessalonians*, 14.

24 Wanamaker, *Epistles to the Thessalonians*, 79.

is better to see the effect of the Spirit's power manifesting upon both the parties, the hearers and the preacher.

5.2.2. The Holy Spirit, the giver of joy

In 1 Thessalonians 1:6, Paul pitches "joy" and affliction" against each other. Paul reminds the Thessalonian believers of their unique experience of joy amidst the suffering they underwent at the conversion. The "inward joy," Paul mentions here, "is an enthusiastic happiness (Phil. 1:25)."[25] It defined their response to the gospel of Christ through which they became a community of God's elect. While the joy within them encouraged the new converts to stick to the new faith they received, the response of "joy" appears to have played a vital role in establishing and nurturing a missional community of a religious minority in Thessalonica, a Roman city. It helped to resist every possible element of disillusionment due to the gospel that has seemingly invited affliction to them from others. They now experience not just violent opposition like the churches in Judea, but also sociocultural and religious alienation that has resulted in their rejection by their families. Still, Paul says, they have received the gospel with joy. Rightly, Lightfoot comments, "the degree in which the believer is allowed to participate in the sufferings of his Lord, should be the measure of his joy."[26] Thus, the vitality of "joy" (*chara*) in the life of Paul's believers in the city can be measured only against the "affliction" (*thlipsis*) they underwent from the time they received the gospel.

An important aspect of the "joy" Paul mentions here is that it does not originate from within a human self, but it belongs to the Holy Spirit, who is the source of real joy. In Greek, the expression *meta charas pneumatos hagiou* can be literally translated as "with the joy *of* the Holy Spirit." The "joy" belongs to the Holy Spirit, which is now inspired in them by the Holy Spirit. The expression "with the joy *of* the Holy Spirit" must be understood as a genitive of source because the joy they experience within themselves is a Spirit-enabled reality. In Galatians 5:22, Paul mentions "joy" as the fruit of the Spirit, but it is activated only in all those who live by the Spirit (Gal 5:25). In other words, the joyful response of the Thessalonians to the gospel amidst afflictions proves not only that God elects them but it also exemplifies the reality of their existence in the sphere of the Spirit. For Gaventa, the "joy" they experience is "a characteristic of the kingdom."[27]

---

[25] James Everett Frame, *A Critical Commentary on the Epistles of St. Paul to the Thessalonians*, The International Critical Commentary (Edinburgh: T&T Clark, 1979), 83.

[26] J. B. Lightfoot, *Notes on the Epistles of St Paul: I & II Thessalonians, I Corinthians 1–7, Romans 1–7, Ephesians 1:1–14* (Indiana: Alpha Publications, n.d.), 14.

[27] Gaventa, *First and Second Thessalonians*, 17.

So, the joy amidst persecution is not merely a human emotion that is conditioned by external circumstances. Rather, it is inspired by the Holy Spirit, unconditioned by the surrounding circumstances, who enables the Thessalonian believers to face the negative circumstances positively. It is about this type of joy that Jesus was speaking to his disciples in John 16:22. Jesus spoke to them about the impending violent separation of him from them that will grieve them, but it will turn into joy that no one can take away from them when they see him again. What Jesus implies is that no opposition to the gospel or persecution of the little flock of Jesus, his disciples, by the Jewish authorities can destroy their joy after they see him again at the resurrection. Weima states it succinctly: "The joy that the Thessalonian Christians experience does not stem from a naïveté or blindness to the seriousness of their current situation of affliction. Rather, their joy originates from the Holy Spirit, who enables them to see beyond their present suffering to their future deliverance."[28]

Further, the Spirit-inspired joy in the Thessalonian Christians is founded upon vital Christian spiritual realities. In the midst of persecution, the Christians in Thessalonica can rejoice at least for three reasons, as Wanamaker would list: (i) The foundational reality that they are now members of a new community of God's elect people by which they wait in anticipation of their final salvation at the Parousia. (ii) Paul's teaching that God will vindicate them in the future by punishing their oppressors in full measure (1 Thess 1:10). (iii) In all probability, Paul and his early converts' belief in the imminent Parousia resulting in their ultimate redemption must have instilled vigor to face hardship at present.[29] The three vital Christian realities as the basis for the Spirit-inspired joy in the believers prove that the message of hope preached by Paul within the hostile context not only facilitated the inclusion of the new converts in the community of God, but it also functioned as foundational for their steadfastness in faith.

5.2.3. The Holy Spirit: God's eschatological blessing upon the church

Another fundamental truth about the Holy Spirit that Paul teaches the Thessalonian believers is that the Holy Spirit is a divine provision to them. In 1 Thessalonians 4:8, Paul warns his audience that the rejection of their instruction by anyone among them means their rejection of "the very *God who gives* you *his* Holy Spirit" (emphasis added). These emphatic words of Paul toward the end of the parenetic section, starting at 1 Thessalonians

---

[28] Weima, *1–2 Thessalonians*, 101–2.

[29] Wanamaker, *Epistles to the Thessalonians*, 82. See also D. Michael Martin, *1, 2 Thessalonians*, *The New American Commentary*, vol. 33 (USA: Broadman & Holman Publishers, 1995), 62.

4:1, proves the significant role of the Holy Spirit that Paul envisioned in the moral standing of the community. According to Burke, the inferential particle highlighting the divine will for the believers, "Therefore" in 4:8, allows the parenetic section to culminate connecting the prolonged activity of the Holy Spirit in the formation of the community from their conversion to the present.[30] The divine will for them "to live a holy life" is accomplished only by their sensitivity to sustain the work of the Holy Spirit among them mediated by their submission to the "instruction" given to them already (1 Thess 4:7–8).

The two vital realities that must be noticed in Paul's words are: (i) Divine provision of the Holy Spirit to the believers, and (ii) the belongingness of the Holy Spirit to God implied in the use of a genitive pronoun *autou* ("his"). While the latter reinforces the exact identity of the Spirit like no other but the same God's Spirit that has always been active in the community of God's faithful, the former is vital for us to recognize the vital implication of the indwelling presence of the Spirit in the Thessalonian believers.

Paul is emphatic that the Holy Spirit that was at work in their conversion, as Burke claims, is "the same Spirit whom God continues to give" so that they might actualize their holiness by the enablement of the Spirit.[31] It must have been encouraging for the believers to learn that their missional task to live as the elect community of God, requiring them to be holy as the disciples of the Lord in Thessalonica, is a divinely assisted process mediated by the Holy Spirit. In fact, *eishumas* ("into you"), at the end of verse 8, emphasizes the indwelling presence (location) of the Spirit in addition to his durative transformational role in the life of the believers (notice present participle form of *didonta* meaning "giving"). Here, Paul appears to make a significant advance on the Old Testament evidence of the intermittent activity of the Spirit in the past. For him, the same Spirit of the old covenant now resides permanently in the new converts.[32] However, Paul's words, seemingly, allude to the fulfillment of Yahweh's eschatological promise, the new covenant, to the nation of Israel: "I will give you a new heart and put a new spirit in you" (Ezek 36:26). In fact, Joel later spoke about the same experience of the Spirit of God in a much more charismatic sense (Joel 2:28–29). The idea of the indwelling-Spirit is coherent with Paul's reminder to the believers in Corinth: "Do you not know

30 Trevor J. Burke, "The Holy Spirit as the Controlling Dynamic in Paul's Role as Missionary to the Thessalonians," in *Paul as Missionary: Identity, Activity, Theology, and Practice*, ed. Trevor J. Burke and Brian S. Rosner (London: Bloomsbury T&T Clark, 2011), 151–52.

31 Burke, "Holy Spirit as the Controlling Dynamic," 153.

32 Burke, "Holy Spirit as the Controlling Dynamic," 153.

that your bodies are temples of the Holy Spirit, who is in you, whom you have received from God?" (1 Cor 6:19 cf. 3:16). Although specific nonterritorial reinterpretation of the "Temple" appears later in 1 Corinthians, the fact that the Holy Spirit indwells the Thessalonian believers, as a result of their turn toward the living God, explicitly implies the same. Unlike their pre-conversion life, the Thessalonians believers are made holy in Christ and are required to walk in holiness because the Spirit is residing in them. As a result, they ought to behave suitably to their corporate identity. "Such a distinct lifestyle would undoubtedly impact those outside the community and it's precisely this counter-cultural or alternative lifestyle that would produce a missionary effect which is nothing less than missional holiness."[33]

Further, also in 2 Thessalonians 2:13, Paul mentions the soteriological function of the Spirit through sanctification: "God chose you as firstfruits to be saved through *the sanctifying work of the Spirit* and through belief in the truth" (emphasis added). Paul wishes to highlight the fact that his readers are not saved by their human effort of "belief in the truth," but they are being saved through the continual sanctifying work of the Spirit. Hence, Menken states that "God's sanctifying work by the Spirit has precedence over the human activity of belief in the gospel."[34] The purpose of the divine provision of the Spirit for the Thessalonians is the Spirit's continual role in a believers life to keep them "blameless at the coming of our Lord Jesus Christ" (1 Thess 5:23). However, the overlapping sanctifying role of the Spirit and the "God of peace" (1 Thess 5:13) does not concern Paul because all the three persons are involved in the one and only universal mission of saving the estranged humanity. So, if, as Menken suggests, "'to sanctify' means 'to bring into the domain of God,'"[35] then the Spirit is the primary arm of God in culminating the incorporation of the new converts in Thessalonica into God's kingdom. In 2 Thessalonians 1:11, God sanctifies the believers in Thessalonica to make them "worthy of his calling."

5.2.4. The Holy Spirit and the charismatic gifts

In 1 Thessalonians 5:19–22, we find the earliest evidence for the charismatic nature of the earliest Christian community, apart from Luke's mention of the event of Pentecost in Jerusalem (Acts 2:1–13). Although we read more on it from Paul later in 1 Corinthians 12–14, the two negative imperatives in 1 Thessalonians 5:19–20 prohibiting them from doing

---

33 Burke, "Holy Spirit as the Controlling Dynamic," 153.

34 M. J. J. Menken, *2 Thessalonians*, New Testament Readings (London: Routledge, 1994), 121.

35 Menken, *2 Thessalonians*, 120.

certain things and the following three imperatives (1 Thess 5:21–22), exhorting them to do certain other things, signify the importance of the charismatic gifts of the Spirit in the life of the church in Paul's thought. In this passage, Paul particularly speaks regarding the gift of prophecy, but we can be sure that it reflects Paul's attitude toward the charismatic gifts, in general. In the context of possible misuse or "over-enthusiastic stress on the Spirit"[36] within the community, Fee's proposal that the teaching appears to be more of a preventive measure from Paul in the light of their similar background of religious ecstasy is probable. Fee maintains that

> the evidence from 2 Thessalonians 2: 1– 2, at least, might suggest that Timothy has already informed Paul of some tendencies in worship that needed "adjustment"— but not elimination. Thus, some months later (2 Thess 2: 2), even though Paul apparently does not know the precise source of the misrepresentation of his teaching, he does know that "the Spirit" (= "a prophetic utterance") is one of the possibilities. That is probably why in the same letter (2: 15; cf. 2: 5) he urges them to stay close to what has already been taught them during his first (and founding) visit and in our present letter.[37]

Paul's command not to put out the fire of the Spirit from among them is directly connected to the contemptuous attitude among some toward the gift of prophecy. For Paul, such an attitude out of suspicion toward prophecy (or even to other charismatic gifts of the Spirit) is harmful to the healthy growth of the church in Thessalonica. Paul explicitly states the reason in 1 Corinthians 12:7: "Now to each one the manifestation of the Spirit is given for the common good." In the same breath, a little later, Paul exhorts the believers in Corinth to "eagerly desire the greater gifts" (1 Cor 12:31). Thus, the solution for the possible misuse of the gift is not in prohibiting such spiritual practices in the worship, but it must be used with greater caution. Paul commands them to "test them all; hold on to what is good, reject every kind of evil" (1 Thess 5:20–21). In other words, "the apostle was not afraid of the principles of grace and liberty because he believed the indwelling Spirit, if allowed to govern without hindrance, would pastor and perfect the church."[38]

The missional significance of Paul's encouragement of the Thessalonians to practice the gift of prophecy is not mentioned here. However, reading his words here, in the light of 1 Corinthians 14:3, sheds greater light on why Paul could have encouraged a persecuted community of minority Christians in a Roman city to practice the gift of prophecy

---

36 Marshall, *1 and 2 Thessalonians*, 157.

37 Fee, *1 & 2 Thessalonians*, 218.

38 Don N. Howell, Jr., "Confidence in the Spirit as the Governing Ethos of the Pauline Mission," *Trinity Journal* 17, no. 2 (1996): 210.

in worship cautiously. Paul teaches the Corinthian believers that, unlike speaking in tongues, the words of prophecy strengthen, encourage, and comfort other believers. But when some would indulge in misguiding the church through false prophecies (2 Thess 2:2), others in the community ought to test them and reject the evil in them. In other words, Paul encourages a cautious practice of charismatic gifts within the church, although the threat of its possible misuse is present within the community. The reason is simple—despite the potential threat to the church by its misuse, the gifts are of great benefit for the church if practiced in line with the apostolic teachings (cf. 2 Thess 2:15). The encouraging and comforting words of prophecy amidst persecution and fear of violent death at the hands of the persecutors could embolden the church to stand steadfast in the faith. The indwelling Spirit's emboldening presence is sure to kindle great joy in them amidst pain and sufferings for the sake of their faith in God (1 Thess 1:6).

5.3. The Creative Word, the Spirit, and the *Charismata* for the Life and Mission of the Church Today

The church in India as God's agent to expand the offer of eternal salvation to the rest of humanity must become a community with pure motives to preach the gospel. The goal of the mission must not be a mere religious conversion of non-Christians leading to the numerical growth of Christian community in India, but it must become a pursuit of genuine offer of rescue to those destined to eternal damnation according to the gospel. It ought to be the gospel evidenced by the life of the church and not just preached in words. The Christian community ought to live in Christian hope fearlessly despite the violent resistance to the gospel and physical attacks from the right-wing extremist groups within our society. The violence unleashed to curb the gospel of God imparting hope of the future as a tool to impart strength in the present state of hopelessness must embolden the church to bear testimony of the hope in Christ. The story of Jesus, who died and rose up from the dead, must be demonstrated practically amidst communal hatred and hopelessness perpetuated by those who oppose the church.

Further, the persecuted church in India must participate in the plight of the marginalized communities, the dalits and the tribals, in imparting hope. The persecuted community of Indian Christians must reassure the oppressed and marginalized communities by practically demonstrating a lifestyle of living in hope in Christ and being filled with joy imparted by the Holy Spirit. Violence against them by cow vigilantes banning them from carrying out their traditional occupation pushes them into abject poverty and lack of hope for a better future. According to a recent report, apart from the thirty-six who died from religious minority communities, "about 280 people have been injured in more than 100 attacks between May 2015 and December 2018."[39] People in the cattle business have been attacked by Hindu mobs merely on suspicion of cow slaughter in recent years. In response, there has been a seemingly gross apathy shown toward the victims of gruesome violence from the state and its law enforcement machinery. In this context, the impact of the missional community of Christians in India must be visible declaring hope of the crucified Christ's return as the sovereign authority over every force of fear, death, and hopelessness through their very lifestyle. It must be clear that in the given situation the Christian witness and the authentic gospel must radiate from the way the community of the living God lives in the society at large and not merely in aggressive evangelization of the non-Christians. Christian solidarity beyond religious boundaries founded upon the gospel of hope in Christ is a venue of the church's missional engagement imparting love, hope, and joy to all.

However, is it possible for a threatened, attacked, and victimized minority community of Christians in India to practice their missional call more effectively? As Paul teaches in his Thessalonian correspondence, the community of God in India must recognize the fuller significance of the person and work of the Holy Spirit in its mission and witness in the society. In other words, there is an urgent need to speak about "missional pneumatology," that is, Christian pneumatology conceived through the missional lens.[40] The role of the Holy Spirit as the one who empowers the church to preach the gospel convincingly must be highlighted. In 1 Thessalonians 1:4–5, Paul reminds the Thessalonian believers regarding the empowering charismatic function of the Holy Spirit that accompanied their preaching in the city. The church in India in its self-recognition as an eschatological community of God must concede the need of embracing the Holy Spirit as God's eschatological gift. Mission as something originating, establishing, and continuing in the world as the activity of the Triune God requires us not to talk just about *missio Dei* or *missio Christi*, but also *missio Spiritus Sancti*.

---

39 Iain Marlow, "Cow Vigilantes in India Killed at Least 44 People, Report Finds," *Bloomberg.com*, February 20, 2019, accessed on July 24, 2019, https://www.bloomberg.com/news/articles/2019-02-20/cow-vigilantes-in-india-killed-at-least-44-people-report-finds. See also, "'Cow Vigilantes' Kill Three Men in India," n.d., https://www.trtworld.com/asia/cow-vigilantes-kill-three-men-in-india-28367. According to these recent reports, forty-four people have been killed by cow vigilantes since 2015.

40 Roji T. George, "Introduction," in *The Holy Spirit and Christian Mission in a Pluralistic Context*, ed. Roji T. George (Bangalore: SAIACS Press, 2017), 13–14.

Shaibu Abraham, analyzing the charismatic function of the Holy Spirit and its significance in the rapid growth of the pentecostal movement in a pluralistic and hostile context of India observes that "the dependence on the power of the Spirit and biblical mandate imparts internal strength and outward thrust of the movement in the difficult terrains of Indian mission."[41] In other words, "if the baptism in the Spirit empowers the believers for mission, the gifts of the Spirit act as instruments of mission activities" because the charismatic gifts of the Spirit "enable the believers to act in the world as Jesus acted."[42] They, as Abraham would state, "equip the believers to move beyond their ability in this world of spiritual as well as physical bondage, rescuing people through healing their body and mind and bringing them to the kingdom of God." The missionaries receive "new strength and vigour" "through the infilling of the Spirit, and the ability to use the gifts of the Spirit propel them to go out into the world to alleviate the suffering of the people, even though they themselves go through such situations. They carry out tasks beyond their capacity and bring great changes in the life of the suffering people."[43] Paul too reminds the believers in Thessalonica that during the initial days of his mission work among them the gospel was accompanied by its visible attestation by the power of the Spirit that enabled the believers in Thessalonica to be convinced of the salvific power of the gospel message. In fact, Paul's warning not to quench the fire of the Spirit or to treat the gift of prophecy with contempt, and that they ought to "hold on to what is good," rejecting everything evil (1 Thess 5:19–20) is also a warning to the church in India to consciously restore the lost emphasis upon the missional function of the charismatic gifts in Christian witness today.

In the context of denominational differences based on the doctrine of charismatic gifts of the Holy Spirit operational within the church today, the non-charismatic and non-pentecostal churches ought to reassess their pneumatology from a biblical and missional perspective. The history of Christian mission proves that a theology of mission that inadequately emphasizes the role of the Holy Spirit, including the significance of the charismatic gifts, is bound to weaken Christian witness in the world. Tracing the history of the importance of the charismatic role of the Holy Spirit in mission from the inception of the early church in Acts of the Apostles proves that, as Tennent argues, there was an "embarrassing gap developed between the church in Acts and the life and practice of many

41 Shaibu Abraham, "Holy Spirit in Pentecostal Mission Praxis in India: A Paradigm for Mission in Pluralistic Context," in *The Holy Spirit and Christian Mission in a Pluralistic Context*, ed. Roji T. George (Bangalore: SAIACS Press, 2017), 87.

42 Abraham, "Holy Spirit in Pentecostal Mission," 89.

43 Abraham, "Holy Spirit in Pentecostal Mission," 90.

churches around the world."[44] Since the patristic period to the post-Reformation era, the Western Protestant theology neglected to recognize the fuller understanding of the person and work of the Holy Spirit. Several theological traditions either denied entirely or spared a negligible space to the charismatic gifts of the Holy Spirit in their theological articulations. Interestingly, this embarrassing gap in theology and mission after the first-century church was filled by the pentecostal movement that considered the charismatic gifts of the Holy Spirit normative in the effective Christian mission and witness to others.[45] In other words, after the first century the person and work of the Holy Spirit received its due central position in Christian theology of mission in the pentecostal theology and practice.

To be a missional community of God is not just to preach the word, but to also interpret the word through the community. It requires the active presence of the Holy Spirit as the power that convinces the hearers of the gospel creatively active in the community of God. The gospel is the story of God working out the salvation of humanity in and through the Christ, who is the sole focus, the content, of Christian preaching. However, within a context, the gospel is convincing not just because of its prepositional claims, but also because of the powerful role of the Holy Spirit. The word of God, the *logos*, is creatively active in the believers through the sanctifying role of the Holy Spirit. A missional community for the sake of its effectiveness in fulfilling the universal purpose of God requires a greater participation of the Holy Spirit with his charismatic gifts in Christian witness. Hence, God has given the Holy Spirit to the church as an eschatological gift. Paul teaches that the church must not show contempt toward the charismatic activity of the Spirit but must hold on to it, though with a critical eye to shun evil that deceives. The encouraging presence of the Holy Spirit is vital for the survival of the persecuted community both in the first century and in the present. Paul teaches that the Thessalonian community as a persecuted people of God must persist amidst hostility without wavering because of the joy-giving role of the Spirit. It is only the Spirit that enables one to see the hope of future deliverance beyond the present suffering.

---

44 Tennent, "Holy Spirit and Christian Mission," 82.

45 Tennent, "Holy Spirit and Christian Mission," 66–70.

6

IMITATION: A PAULINE STRATEGY OF DISCIPLESHIP

A basic assumption in identifying the true missional congregation is to discern an identifiable pattern of discipling taking place within the congregation. Every member of a missional congregation is expected to be involved "in learning to become disciples of Jesus."[1] Without discipling pursued within a community of God actively, a firm biblical formation of a believer to fulfill God's eternal purpose of saving humanity through the mission is impossible. So, Paul wrote letters to overcome his physical absence and to continue the process of discipling. Paul's letters are missional in function because they seek not just to form a community of believers, but to also encourage discipling within the community through verbal and non-verbal aspects of both individual and corporate existence. The letters "continue the formation for apostolic witness that the first missionaries were doing in the weeks and months they spent in each newly formed congregation."[2] The first century Christians believed that "they existed for Christ's mission" and in order to fulfill that, "they were to live their life together 'worthy of the calling to which they had been called' (see 1 Thess 2:12; Phil. 1:27; Eph 4:1)."[3]

So, we ask: How did Paul seek to disciple his new converts through the letters in their unique situation? What is the key discernible pattern

1 Darrell L. Guder, "Biblical Formation and Discipleship," in *Treasure in Clay Jars: Patterns in Missional Faithfulness*, ed. Lois Y. Barrett, The Gospel and Our Culture Series (Grand Rapids, MI: William B. Eerdmans Publishing, 2004), 59–60, cited from 60.

2 Guder, *Called to Witness*, 128.

3 Guder, "Biblical Formation and Discipleship," 61.

of individual and collective behavior that, both in private and public, Paul prescribes to the Thessalonians? How do Paul's moral and ethical prescriptions reflect his missional intent? How do they equip our church to gain a biblically grounded missional self-understanding to fulfill her ultimate vocation? To answer these vital guiding questions, the ensuing discussion will first explain the interrelationship between Paul's idea of imitation and discipleship. Having established that the apostle's appeal to imitate does not exhaust the idea of discipleship but only forms a part of it, an attempt shall be made to study the available data within the letters to highlight Paul's missional purpose in the moral and ethical formation of the Christ-like community in Thessalonica.

6.1. Interrelationship between imitation and discipleship

For some reasons unknown to us, Paul does not use the term *disciple* (*mathētēs*), also meaning "a learner," in his letters. It is repeatedly used in the gospel narratives and the Acts of the Apostles in a technical sense, referring to the twelve apostles of Jesus Christ. However, there are also instances of its non-technical use in John 6:66: "From this time many of his disciples turned back and no longer followed him." John uses the term *mathētēs* speaking about many of Jesus's followers who are not counted among the twelve.

The earliest literary evidence for the use of *mathētēs*, as Wilkins mentions, goes back to the fifth century B.C.E., when Herodotus used it in a very casual sense. However, the term came "into prominence in the written literature of Greece in the classical period" that "denoted three types of people: a learner, an adherent, and a pupil."[4] Wilkins's study of its use among Greeks in the different periods of history concludes that the term was predominantly used for the adherents of a master or religious figure who welded higher authority upon others. It was in this sense that the term circulated in a technical sense among the early Christians for the twelve disciples of Jesus.[5]

In the Old Testament, although the term *disciple* is absent, the idea of discipleship is present in a limited sense in the two words, *talmîdh* and *limmûdh*, which signify a master-disciple relationship. Interestingly, the master-disciple relationship among the prophets did not signify a disciple as a trainee under a master, a prophet, but a relationship in commitment toward each other to serve Yahweh. This sort of relationship underwent a transformation during the post-exilic period when the master-disciple

4 Michael J. Wilkins, *Discipleship in the Ancient World and Matthew's Gospel*, 2nd ed. (Grand Rapids, MI: Baker Books, 1995), 12.

5 Wilkins, *Discipleship in the Ancient World and Matthew's Gospel*, 12–42.

relationship among scribes existed within a family where primarily the father taught his sons the skills of the profession apart from some skill acquired in the fellowship of professional scribes. Underlining the significance of the idea of discipleship in a master-disciple relationship structure, Wilkins states that "they are recognized to be part of various means of communicating to Israel the revelation of Yahweh, and as such, *promote a greater depth of discipleship to Yahweh within the national life*."[6] So, discipling of every young Jew to Yahweh was quite intentionally built into the socio-religious life during the New Testament times, despite the absence of the very term in the Jewish Scripture (OT). Even in the intertestamental Jewish literature, despite the absence of the group of imitation words, imitation of great people is found significantly. Sirach encourages his readers to sing the praises of the prominent figures in Jewish history like Enoch, Abraham, Moses, Phinehas, Elijah, Hezekiah, and others (Sirach 44–50). For example, Sirach says, "Enoch pleased the Lord and was taken up, *an example* of repentance to all generation" (44:16, NRSV Catholic Edition, 1993, emphasis added). 1 Maccabees 2:49–64 recounts the faithfulness of Abraham, Joseph, Phinehas, David, Caleb, and others, to Yahweh as a perfect model of imitation for the remaining generations.

Similarly, even in Paul's letters, the absolute absence of the term *disciple* does not mean that the idea of discipleship escaped the apostle's mind. Paul employs two important terms "imitate" (*mimeomai*) or "imitator" (*mimētēs*) and "model" (*tupos*) in the letters to the Thessalonians as a missional strategy to produce disciples of Christ. In the Hellenistic context, "imitate" (*mimeomai*) signified an "act of mimicking," "emulating another," or "the representation of reality in artistic activities," which could also be used in a derogatory sense to speak about "weak and unoriginal copying."[7] Nevertheless, Paul's objective was not to encourage a slavish replica of Christ in the Thessalonian context. Rather, it was to help them emulate Christ's ethics authentically in the local ecclesial context. The goal was to contextually articulate the newly gained Christian identity in a religious pluralistic missional context. It includes constructing a self-identity locally in ambivalent cultural terms, to attract attention by practicing the Christ modelled countercultural ethics as part of their missional existence, and to dissuade every unnecessary hostile response birthed out of a mistaken understanding of Christians from all others.

The relationship between the two terms *mathētēs* and *mimētēs* is constantly discussed and debated. Wilkins says that "the term *imitator* is one

---

6 Wilkins, *Discipleship in the Ancient World and Matthew's Gospel*, 43–91, cited from 91 (emphasis added).

7 Michael J. Wilkins, "Imitate, Imitators," *Anchor Bible Dictionary*, vol. 3 (New York: Doubleday, 1992), 392.

link between the disciples of Jesus in the Gospels and the believers of the early church."[8] Michaelis treats the two terms as "one and the same."[9] Scholars in the later discussions dispute this conclusion. Copan's historical survey of the two terms appearing together in a text and the term *mimētēs* appearing alone in some other texts seeks to bring an end to the ongoing debate regarding the link between the two terms. Copan argues that *mimētēs* distinctly stands for emulating an exemplar (a set pattern or the virtues emulated). The two terms have always maintained their difference, where imitation is not fully restricted to discipleship. However, following Larsson's lead in discussion, he maintains that it falls within the sphere of discipleship as something that is referring to an intentional following of Christ's example.[10]

If Copan's contention is acceptable, it helps us to conjecture the possible reason behind the absolute absence of the term *mathētēs* from Paul's letters. Paul, probably, avoided the term due to the technical nature it assumed in the post-resurrection ecclesial context, but he was not averse to the idea of discipleship. Paul appears to have valued *mimeomai* in his apostolic vocation due to its strategic missional significance in attaining the ultimate goal of Christian formation. Discipling, for Paul, was impossible in the earliest church, comprised of new converts from Jewish and gentile backgrounds, without encouraging them to adhere to the authoritative teachings by imitation and, thereby, fashioning their life to serve God's ultimate missional purpose through imitation.

Thus, the stage is ready for us to go deeper into the idea of imitation in Paul's thought. What is the significance of imitation in the life and mission of the Thessalonian believers? Why does Paul repeatedly mention the idea of imitation in his letters? Do Paul's appreciation and exhortation to imitate him and others underline the ultimate goal of his apostolic mission? What is the core of imitation in Paul's thought?

6.2. Discipling through Imitation in 1 and 2 Thessalonians

Paul uses *mimētēs*, a noun, twice in 1 Thessalonians 1:6; 2:14 out of its total six occurrences in the entire New Testament (Heb 13:7; 3 John 11). Similarly, the term *mimeomai* (a verb) appears two times in 2 Thessalonians 3:7 and 9, out of its total four occurrences in the New Testament. In addition to them, the term *tupos* meaning "model" or "example," has been used twice in the letters (1 Thess 1:7; 2 Thess 3:9), which

8 Wilkins, "Imitate, Imitators," 392.

9 W. Michaelis, "Μιμεομαι Κτλ," *Theological Dictionary of the New Testament* 4: 673.

10 Victor A. Copan, "Μαθητής and Μιμητής: Exploring an Entangled Relationship," *Bulletin for Biblical Research* 17, no. 2 (2007): 313–23.

elsewhere in Paul's letters appear with similar connotation (e.g., Rom 5:14; 6:17; 1 Cor 10:6; Phil 3:17). Getty maintains that with the aid of several other hortatory features, Paul underlines the significance of imitation of Paul or Christ to the Thessalonians. For example, Paul's use of:

1. Verbs in the imperative;
2. δει (1 Thess 4:1; 2 Thess 3:7);
3. warnings about persecution and criticism of opponents;
4. support of exhortation and prescriptions with explanations, reasons, purpose and motivation;
5. antithetical contrasts between Paul, other community leaders or members and addresses on one side and false teachers, persecutors, agitators on the other side.[11]

A closely connected theme is to live worthy of their calling/kingdom of God (1 Thess 2:12; 2 Thess 1:5, 11). Let's discuss them to understand discipleship as Christian formation among the Thessalonians in the apostolic mission of Paul.

6.2.1. Mimeomai / mimētēs

Interestingly, *mimeomai* and *mimētēs*, the two important terms, appear either in the initial thanksgiving section (1 Thess 1:2–10 except 1 Thess 2:14) or in the concluding section as part of the final ethical exhortation (2 Thess 3:6–15). As argued earlier, if the two letters sent to the Thessalonians are treated as written in the same canonical order, then these two blocks of material characterized by the imitation idea appearing in the beginning and end of the letters respectively form a parenthesis around all that Paul teaches in the letters. In other words, Paul's appeal to imitation is not only important for the Thessalonians' lives; it also sets the hermeneutical framework of the letters. While Jewett contends that the epistolary thanksgivings function to make known the central theme of the epistle,[12] Betz similarly concludes that the concluding section of the letter functions like a postscript. Betz states that it "contains the interpretive clues to the understanding of Paul's major concerns in the letter as a

---

[11] Mary Ann Getty, "The Imitation of Paul in the Letters to the Thessalonians," in *The Thessalonain Correspondence*, ed. Raymond F. Collins, *Bibliotheca Ephemeridum Theologicarum Lovaniensium*, vol. 87 (Leuven: Leuven University Press, 1990), 278, fn 11.

[12] Robert Jewett, "Epistolary Thanksgiving and the Integrity of Philippians," *Novum Testamentum* 12, no. 1 (1970): 40–53.

whole and should be employed as the hermeneutical key to the intentions of the apostle."[13]

Paul mentions the objects of the Thessalonian believers' imitation as: (i) Paul and his associates (1 Thess 1:6; 2 Thess 3:7, 9), (ii) "the Lord" (1 Thess 1:6), and (iii) "God's churches in Judea" (1 Thess 2:14). Although in his later letters Paul's own life emulating Christ appears to be a major object of imitation for his believers, never is the object of the call to imitation limited to himself in the Thessalonian correspondence. However, for Paul, imitating his example and of his associates in discipling is necessary (2 Thess 3:7, notice the use of *dei*) and inevitable. Even in Philippians, Paul includes his companions and some others in Philippi with him to present a model before the Philippian believers to imitate (Phil 3:17 notice the use of *symmimetai* meaning "co-imitators"). In Philippians, Paul, though a prime visible Christ-like model before his believers, is one among all others as a co-imitator.[14]

In 1 Thessalonians 1:6, Paul appreciates the Thessalonian believers that they have already imitated "us" and "the Lord." He appeals to himself and his associates as an example that is left behind in the vivid memory of the Thessalonians for their own sake: "You know how we lived among you for your sake" (1 Thess 1:6). While they have personally witnessed how amidst strong persecution, Paul and his fellow missionaries preached the gospel to them in Thessalonica (1 Thess 2:2), Jesus Christ's example of self-sacrificial suffering and death had been initially preached to them as part of *ton logon* (1 Thess 1:6), the word. Paul has not shied away from teaching his new converts in Thessalonica regarding the inevitability of persecution. In 1 Thessalonians 3:3–4, Paul says, "for you know quite well that we are destined for them. In fact, when we were with you, we kept telling you that we would be persecuted. And it turned out that way, as you well know." Paul prepared the Thessalonian believers to face persecution by telling them about the inevitability of persecution. Hence, the Thessalonian believers' true imitation of Paul, his associates, and of the Lord resulted in their steadfastness in faith amidst violent onslaught from the fellow non-Christian population in Thessalonica. Such steadfastness amidst suffering makes them automatically the "imitators of God's churches in Judea" (1 Thess 2:14). It explains the true content of the call to imitate.

13 Hans D. Betz, *Galatians: A Commentary on Paul's Letter to the Churches in Galatia*, Hermeneia: A Critical and Historical Commentary on the Bible (Philadelphia, PA: Fortress Press, 1979), 313.

14 Roji T. George, "'Join Together with Me in Imitating My Example': Reflection on Paul's Call to Imitate in the Letter to the Philippians," in *Bible, Mission, and Theology: A Festschrift in Honor of Rev. Dr. Simon Samuel*, ed. P. V. Joseph (Dehradun/Delhi: Luther W. New Jr. Theological College/ISPCK, 2018), 99–111.

Paul's call to imitation is not to enforce certain idiosyncratic behavior upon his believers. Or his interest is not to produce his true copies or replicas in Thessalonica killing diversity for the sake of welding authority over others by thrusting slavish sameness upon them. Instead, the central thrust of his call to imitation is the self-denying cruciformed life of Christ. Imitation is primarily to emulate the core of Christ's suffering and his attitude to do so for the sake of the salvation of sinful humanity. Paul himself has done a cruciformed mission for the benefit of his believers. He implies the same, speaking about their ministry in Thessalonica while placing himself along with "the Lord" as an object for others to imitate (1 Thess 1:6). Later, in 1 Thessalonians 2:8, Paul says, "we were delighted to share with you not only the gospel of God but our lives as well" (1 Thess 2:8). Bruce states that for Paul and his associates "to share their own lives involved utter self-denial, 'spending and being spent' in the interest of others (cf. 2 Cor 12:15)."[15] Gorman states that,

> the expression 'to share with you...our own selves' (Greek *metadounai... tas he autōn psychas*) is parallel to the pattern of Christ narratives that refer to Christ's death as self-giving or self-surrendering (Greek [*para*] *didonai heautōn*). The terminology and context of 2:8 suggest that Paul has adapted a Christological formula about Christ's self-giving death to the pastoral situation of interpreting his ministry to the Thessalonians. When Paul says he and his co-workers 'shared themselves' with the Thessalonians in love, he is saying that their ministry had the shape of cruciform love in imitation of their Lord.[16]

Further, suffering defines the identity of Christians contrary to what the world does to them. Mentioning Jews who persecuted Christians in Judea as "who killed the Lord Jesus and the prophets and also drove us out," Paul says that "they displeased God and are hostile to everyone" (1 Thess 2:15). While the sole reason of opposition is to halt the proclamation of the gospel of salvation to the gentiles, the net result of their sinful action is an accumulation of God's wrath upon themselves (1 Thess 2:16).

Another vital aspect of the cruciformed self-sacrificial lifestyle to be imitated by the Thessalonians is not becoming a burden to others even if it requires forgoing ones right to support (2 Thess 3:9) and to do hard labor (1 Thess 2:9; 2 Thess 3:8). In 2 Thessalonians 3:6–15, Paul exhorts some of the Thessalonian believers "in the Lord Jesus Christ" not to be busybodies but to earn their food. Paul had addressed the same issue earlier in 1 Thessalonians 5:14, which proves that the problem of idleness was seriously threatening the communitarian life. Hence, Paul gives them

---

15 Bruce, *1 and 2 Thessalonians*, 32.

16 Michael J. Gorman, *Cruciformity: Paul's Narrative Spirituality of the Cross* (Grand Rapids, MI: William B. Eerdmans Publishing, 2001), 194–95.

twofold instructions: (i) They must imitate the model Paul and his associates taught and displayed before them while in Thessalonica (2 Thess 3:7–11). (ii) Paul instructs the rest of the community members not to associate with busybodies who refuse to obey Paul's directive given in the letter (2 Thess 3:14–15; cf. 3:6). Paul expects that such disassociation would put them to shame. However, it is not to treat them as enemies but to reprimand them as a fellow believer.

First, Paul's contextual directive based on the rule that "the one who is unwilling to work shall not eat" (2 Thess 3:10) is based on a deeper christological principle of self-denial. In 2 Thessalonians 3:7–8, Paul boldly states that he has worked hard day and night to earn his bread while he did ministry in Thessalonica. The good intention behind such an act is not out of his ignorance regarding his own apostolic right to receive support from his believers. Instead, his choice to earn his bread is an act of Christ-like self-emptying (cf. Phil 2:6–7). Paul's cruciformity is in play here at its best. Paul says, "we did this, not because we do not have the right to such help, but in order to offer ourselves as a model for you to imitate" (2 Thess 3:9 cf. 1 Cor 9:4; 1 Thess 2:6). It was an intentional act, an acted-out parable, for the Thessalonians to read and interpret in their day-to-day life.

Second, Paul cautiously worded instruction in 2 Thessalonians 3:15 ("work with your hands" 1 Thess 4:11), while absolutely rejecting any space for idleness within the Christian community in Thessalonica reflects its missional significance. While idleness of some within the community could disrupt ecclesial life (1 Thess 5:14) in Thessalonica, Paul is careful not to destroy believers by a complete rejection. He desires the restoration of the erring ones by warning them as fellow believers. Even in 2 Corinthians 2:5–11, Paul, referring back to his directive on handling the case of incest that was brought to his attention earlier, says that now the person requires to be forgiven and shown love. He is careful about the spiritual reality that it might give room to Satan to outwit them. In other words, the goal of firm ethical instruction within the community is not expulsion and destruction of someone's life as eternally condemned. Instead, it is to restore the "lost sheep" (cf. Luke 15:3–7) with adequate instruction and warning. Such a restoration-oriented disciplining, in essence, is the process of discipling where Christian formation in love and forgiveness is the final goal of a missional community of God. It is not about losing a soul either by allowing someone to continue in sinful and an unethical lifestyle or by expelling someone from the church.

6.2.2. *Tupos*

Tupos ("model") belongs to the group of words associated with the idea of imitation in Paul's letters. Paul uses *tupos* once to speak of the

Thessalonians as a community of God becoming a model of imitation for others (1 Thess 1:7, notice the singular form of *tupos*), while on the other occasion, it is used for himself and his associates as a model of imitation for the Thessalonians (2 Thess 3:9). In the first instance, the Thessalonians becoming a model for "all believers in Macedonia and Achaia" (1 Thess 1:7) is the result (*hōste* clause in v.7) of their imitation of Paul, his associates, and the Lord in accepting the gospel amidst hostility. In other words, imitation of the right model leads to becoming a model for others to imitate. Here, Paul is speaking about an unending process of imitation and becoming a model simultaneously. Paul imitates the Lord (1 Cor 11:1) according to the gospel he preached and becomes a model of imitation for the Thessalonians (2 Thess 3:9). They, further, become a model of imitation for all the believers in Macedonia and Achaia by imitating Paul and the Lord (1 Thess 1:7).

The process of discipling is further attested in Paul's use of the word *topos*. The idea gets deeper if *tupos* is also understood as a "mould" that "is a pattern of something that has the purpose of reproducing more identical patterns."[17] It highlights the missional role of the Thessalonian believers because the shape that they acquired by imitating Paul and the Lord in joyously suffering for their faith now becomes a mould to shape or disciple others in Macedonia and Achaia. In other words, "the essence of discipleship is imitation"[18] because imitation of Paul and the Lord in the divine plan is to finally produce a Christ-like mould (i.e., the Thessalonians) to make disciples. Paul finds the believers in Thessalonica having performed well the missional responsibility by modelling. They further reproduced (i.e., "all the believers in Macedonia and Achaia") disciples in the exact Christ-like shape that they acquired earlier by imitating Paul and others.

The two important consequences of the Thessalonian believers becoming a model to others by imitation are missional. Paul says: First, "the Lord's message rang out from you...[and] your faith in God has become known everywhere" (1 Thess 1:8a, parenthesis added). It is unclear how "the Lord's message rang out" (1 Thess 2:13) from the Thessalonians. Did it spread due to their active preaching of the gospel like Paul preached to them? Or, did the gospel ring out from them to everyone as a result of their Christ-like model lifestyle? As Witherington observes, although the customary use of hyperbole in epideictic rhetoric is recognizable in Paul's words ("become known everywhere"), it is not unlikely that the news about their conversion and their steadfastness in faith amidst hostility could spread to the nearby cities easily. Thessalonica was situated in an important geographical location (the *Via Egnatia*) that facilitated easy

17 Beale, *1–2 Thessalonians*, 58.

18 Beale, *1–2 Thessalonians*, 58.

travel to all into different directions. It is not impossible that the news about their conversion and suffering with joy for the gospel must have spread through the travelling merchants.[19] Even some of the new converts of Paul themselves must have testified to others. According to Flemming, "the primary means by which it rang out from the Thessalonians is through their oral proclamation." He imagines a simple scenario of "Christians explaining the reason for their changed behavior to unbelievers visiting their household from other places."[20] Beale maintains that the gospel rang out from the Thessalonians because their lifestyle endorsed their preaching activity. Paul mentions them in the same order; their exemplary lifestyle is mentioned before their actual preaching activity.[21]

Second, positive report about their conversion among others and the reception they gave to the apostle facilitated Paul's mission (1 Thess 1:8b–10) in the rest of the cities. In 1:8b, Paul says "therefore we do not need to say anything about it" (parenthesis added). Paul's words prove the magnitude of discipling in its true sense that the Thessalonians have undergone already. It is again the result of (a *hōste* clause in 1:8) their imitation of the right model visible in Paul and his associates. Bale states, "the readers' faithfulness in tribulation not only made them a model for others but also resulted in relieving significantly the burden of Paul's further labor of evangelizing the area around Thessalonica and beyond."[22] Paul mentions their conversion story he has heard from others in a quiet Old Testament theological understanding. It is, then, added with the "jewel" of Christian faith, the "hope" of the future. 1 Thessalonians 1:9–10, like in the Old Testament understanding, contrasts the God known in and through the Lord Jesus Christ as the "living God" against the gods of the Thessalonians as "idols." The Old Testament firmly denies all except Yahweh as false gods (cf. Ps 115:3–8; Jer 10:10).[23]

Further, for Paul, the God of the Old Testament is the God in whom the Thessalonians have put their faith by believing in the gospel of Jesus Christ he preached. The offer of salvation in the gospel of Christ Jesus is the same plan of saving the fallen humanity through Israel in the Old Testament narratives. It is the universal mission of God in the Old Testament, continuing at present, to save the whole of humanity through the salvific death of Jesus Christ. Paul is part of the eternal mission of God, and the Thessalonians are those who are now saved by faith to become "the continuation of the true Israel to whom Jeremiah spoke," as Beale

---

19 Witherington, *1 and 2 Thessalonians*, 73.

20 Flemming, *Recovering the Full Mission of God*, 196.

21 Beale, *1–2 Thessalonians*, 59.

22 Beale, *1–2 Thessalonians*, 60.

23 Beale, *1–2 Thessalonians*, 61.

would say. Thus, they have turned away "from the idols of this world and to serve God until the end of time."[24] The Thessalonian believers serve the living God already both by becoming a disciple through imitation of Paul and of the Lord and by actively proclaiming the word of the Lord to all. Thereby, they, as a missional community, like Paul, participate in the universal mission of God.

However, unlike the Jewish faith in the first century, Paul reminds them of their historically founded hope of the Messiah's return. Paul says that they "wait for his Son from heaven, whom he [God] raised from the dead—Jesus, who rescues us from the coming wrath" (1 Thess 1:10, parenthesis added). Undoubtedly, while the unbelieving Thessalonians are destined to be condemned under the wrath of God, they who have believed in him have the hope of being rescued on the last day.

6.3. Missional Ethics

In Thessalonians, Paul places a lot of emphasis on the moral and ethical formation of the believers as disciples. In 1 Thessalonians 5:5, the identity of the Thessalonian believers is defined, saying, "you are all children of light and children of the day." Immediately, Paul continues to state it both negatively and positively overruling a possibility of understanding it in any other ways. While in 1 Thessalonians 5:5, Paul said, "we *do not belong* to the night or to the darkness," he quickly restates the fact saying "we *belong to* the day" (1 Thess 5:8, emphasis added). According to Beale, both in the Old and the New Testaments, the light either refers to God's attribute or his revelatory act. So, Paul addressing himself and his converts as "children of light" in contrast to those belonging to darkness vocalizes their new found status as a new creation in Christ. The contrast between the light and the darkness in the light of the Genesis account of creation where creation begins with the light shining forth into darkness (Gen 1:1–5) functions as a foil to amplify Paul's ethical demand from the Thessalonians.[25] The Thessalonian Christians are reminded that they ought to conduct themselves before others living in darkness in Thessalonica according to the discipline of the new creation status in Christ. Witherington states, "the light has already dawned in Christ, and the Thessalonian Christians are already children of light, transformed into new creatures."[26] The recognition of this great truth about their being in Christ requires paying close attention to the life and content of Paul's preaching.

---

24 Beale, *1–2 Thessalonians*, 62.

25 Beale, *1–2 Thessalonians*, 146.

26 Witherington, *1 and 2 Thessalonians*, 148.

Hence, Paul consistently worked in two ways to teach the Thessalonian believers to be what they are at present in Christ: first, he displayed a Christ-like lifestyle (to be imitated) before them during his stay among them (1 Thess 2:3–5, 10), and, second, he intentionally taught and exhorted them both orally and by writing letters (1 Thess 2:12; 4:1, 11; 2 Thess 2:15; 3:6 cf. 2 Thess 1:11). In 1 Thessalonians 2:3–7, he claims for the purity of motive in preaching the gospel among Thessalonians without flattery and greed, to have behaved as the approved men of God who are entrusted with the gospel, and as the one aiming only to please God and not men. Normally, scholars have understood Paul's words rhetorically as his attempt to distinguish "his own motives and practices with that of popular rhetors and philosophers and hucksters of that era and realm."[27] However, the underlying reason for Paul to do so, as Johnson would want us to think, is paranaetic. He argues that Paul "provides both an explanation for his continued absence as well as a pattern for the vocation of Christian leadership, a pattern that his audience is to implement in ordering their own life together."[28]

As a result, Paul appeals to their personal knowledge about him and his mission among them. He also invokes God as their witness to prove the veracity of his claims in 1 Thessalonians 2:5. In the same stretch of words, Paul repeats the claim for themselves with the aid of three important words—"holy, righteous and blameless"—saying, "You are witnesses, and so is God, of how holy, righteous, and blameless we were among you who believed" (1 Thess 2:10). In fact, Paul's prayer for them for the last day is that they "will be blameless and holy in the presence of our God and Father when our Lord Jesus comes with all his holy ones" (1 Thess 3:13 cf. 5:23). God's will for the Thessalonian believers is for them to "be sanctified" (1 Thess 4:3) through abstinence from sexual impurity and passionate lust. He says that "no one should wrong or take advantage of a brother or sister" (1 Thess 4:3–6). Carras argues that 1 Thessalonians 4:3–8 shares in common Jewish prescriptions regulating the ethical behavior of a convert. Paul uses the verb *paralambano* (1 Thess 4:1–2) and *peripato* to contrast the expected conduct of God's people against those who do not know God (cf. 1 Thess 4:4). His reference to God's will (1 Thess 4:3) motivating them to adopt a set pattern of behavior fashioned according to God's will proves that Paul's ethical exhortations are Jewish in character.[29] In other words, Paul is borrowing a different set of cultural

27 Witherington, *1 and 2 Thessalonians*, 78.

28 Johnson, *1 and 2 Thessalonians*, 59.

29 George P. Carras, "Jewish Ethics and Gentile Converts: Remarks on 1 Thes 4:3-8," in *The Thessalonain Correspondence*, ed. Raymond F. Collins, *Bibliotheca Ephemeridum Theologicarum Lovaniensium*, vol. 87 (Leuven: Leuven University Press, 1990), 306–15.

expectations founded upon the Jewish religious system to disciple the Thessalonian Christians.

However, how is it important in the context of Thessalonica? It may be argued like Carras that it has a social function in distinguishing the Thessalonian Christians morally from their non-Christian neighbors just as the Jews separated themselves morally from the gentiles.[30] However, for Paul, Christians in Thessalonica ought to intentionally pursue moral uprightness or holiness in every aspect of their Christian living because God's call upon them is "to live a holy life" (1 Thess 4:7). The divine call "to live a holy life" implies God's missional purpose and the reason for the existence of the community of God. They are not already a perfect community but should live up to the standard of their call and their identity in Christ as a new creation. The missional dimension of the divine call upon Christians is summarized well in Paul's singular and paramount demand from the Thessalonians; they ought "to live lives worthy of God" (1 Thess 2:12) or "to live in order to please God" (1 Thess 4:1). Rightly, Guder states,

> "Walking worthily" appears to be a key description of the life and conduct of these communities as they continue the apostolic witness that is their very reason for being. They are to walk worthy of God, of his call, of the Lord, of the gospel of Christ, of the calling to which they have been called. The missional congregation may be defined as the community that walks worthy of the calling to which it has been called.[31]

The other dimension of missional ethics to be practiced within the community seeking to live worthy of God is Christian mutualism. It has "to do with the ways in which the community practices its calling towards each other."[32]Amidst the ongoing persecution, Paul recognizes that the key to the survival of the new found minority Christian community is the practice of radical mutualism based on *agape* ("love") both within and outside the community. Jesus exemplifies the *agape* type of self-sacrificial love in his vicarious death, which typifies the Christian response toward others amidst conflict and persecution. The theological basis of Christian mutualism is, for Paul, rooted in the very salvific act of God that unites all, living or dead, with Christ (1 Thess 5:9–11). For Paul, Thessalonian believers ought to practice mutualism in love toward both outsiders and insiders: "for one another, and for all men" (1 Thess 3:12). Paul prays for divine assistance to them to "increase and abound in love" for them (1 Thess 3:12) and be "taught by God" (1 Thess 4:9). In fact, in 1 Thessalonians 5:11–15, Paul maintains that such united existence in/

30 Carras, "Jewish Ethics and Gentile Converts," 314.

31 Guder, *Called to Witness*, 130.

32 Guder, *Called to Witness*, 136.

with Christ mandates undergirding each other in: (i) encouragement, (ii) building up one another, (iii) appreciating and highly esteeming those who labor among them, (iv) living in peace with one another, (v) admonishing the erring ones, (vi) being patient toward all, (vii) practicing a non-retaliatory approach, and (viii) pursuing the common social good. This multi-pronged response draws special attention to the needs of the faint-hearted who doubt the veracity and vitality of the new found faith either due to the demise of their beloved ones (1 Thess 4:13) or the experience of persecution. It ensures social cohesion and survival amidst conflict and discord. Further, those who defy the manner of life worthy of God must not be either retaliated in equal measure ("evil for evil") or dealt with impatience. They must be dealt with pro-actively in the light of the common good of all. The "weak" (1 Thess 5:14) must be edified (1 Thess 5:11) and helped (1 Thess 5:14).

Interestingly, the visible model of practicing mutualism in its true spirit is evident in the ministry of Paul among the Thessalonians. Paul defines his relationship with the new converts by employing both male and female characteristics stated together within the parenthesis formed by the *paraklēsis* in 1 Thessalonians 2:3 and 11.[33] In other words, he is to them "father-mother," at the same time, without distinction.[34] While in 1 Thessalonians 2:7 Paul speaks about the ministry of his team as "we proved to be gentle among you, *as a nursing mother* tenderly caring for her own children" (emphasis added), in 1 Thessalonians 2:11, he states

33 Boring, *I & II Thessalonians*, 90.

34 The question of Pauline community as egalitarian or hierarchical is a bone of contention. Scholars have argued vehemently for both the positions. However, to me it is much more nuanced. Paul is a parent ("father-mother") to his children in Thessalonica (1 Thess 2:7, 11) but also their "brother" (1 Thess 5:12, 14, 25, 27). His unconventional stance of adopting both father's and mother's role, at the same time, in himself is insightful. His authoritative position as "father" in educating (shared with God the Father's role as their teacher in 1 Thess 4:9) is moderated (probably deconstructed) by a lesser authoritative position as "mother." This does not deny the fact that he is also their brother in Christ who, like them, operates in *agapē*. While to Thessalonians his parental role affirms his superiority, the practical manifestation is out of a complex combination of authority at two levels that simultaneously operates in him, self-sacrificial love toward his new converts, his children, and the reality of him being their brother. It is this complex egalitarian model of relationship, ridden with ambiguity, which he appeals his believers to imitate. Even Paul's exhortation to esteem those brothers who labor among the Thessalonians in 1 Thess 5:12-13 is based on *agapē*. For this reason, I disagree with Trevor J. Burke's contention that Paul established a hierarchical relation from the inception of the community. To me, it is an egalitarian, non-hierarchical relationship structure that is modelled by Paul. See for a social basis of asymmetrical authority model Trevor J. Burke, "Paul's New Family in Thessalonica," *Novum Testamentum* 54, no. 3 (2012): 275–78.

that "we were exhorting and encouraging and imploring each one of you *as a father* would his own children" (emphasis added). While the former emphasizes his Christ-like self-sacrificial mission of imparting lives out of fondness to his new converts, the latter implies his authority to command. He is well aware of the scope of their authority as the "apostles of Christ" (1 Thess 2:6) but claims to have exercised it as that which is derived from the Lord (1 Thess 4:2). Thus, among his converts, his fatherly authority is exercised in a manner of building them up to enter into the kingdom (1 Thess 2:12). According to Boring, "though Paul is capable of speaking as an apostle who commands, here his fatherly instruction is not a matter of blind obedience but of response to explicit, substantial teaching."[35] Within the Greco-Roman culture, while the mother traditionally functioned as responsible for nurturing the child, the father was responsible for imparting lessons on expected standards of social and moral conduct.[36] In other words, Paul in the "father-mother" hybrid model of a non-hierarchical relationship presents himself as a new model of communitarian relationship "in Christ."

Such a non-hierarchical relationship structure to practice mutualism represented in the ministry of Paul is contradictory to the imperial relationship structure built on the "top-down" model. Lopez, in her study of Roman imperial ideology, convincingly demonstrates that the Roman imperial relation with the nations, as represented in her visual tradition, was hierarchical.[37] It is in this context that Paul exhorts to practice radical mutualism of working for the good of all. The scope of love-mutualism in Paul's thought goes beyond the closed Christian community (1 Thess 3:12 cf. Gal 6:10). It is the way, as Paul would suggest, for the persecuted community to be strengthened in holiness by God so that they may be found "unblameable in holiness" in the coming of our Lord Jesus (1 Thess 3:13). So, Paul exhorts the believers not to repay evil for evil but to seek the welfare of all even when they persecute them. In other words, it is the responsibility of the wealthy Christians in Thessalonica to undertake the acts of benefaction toward their *politeia* being indifferent to the violence directed against them. This is contrary to the accepted pattern of behavior within the patron-client relationship structure that permeated the Roman world. In the then social world, every patron deserved a response of gratitude from their client. In the words of Seneca, any violation of such an established pattern of behavior by a client is the "crime of ingratitude" (Seneca, *Ben.* 1.10.4). Perhaps, for this reason, Paul does not want Christians to depend on anyone else without working with their own

35 Boring, *I & II Thessalonians*, 90.

36 Witherington, *1 and 2 Thessalonians*, 82.

37 Davina C. Lopez, *Apostle to the Conquered: Reimagining Paul's Mission*, Paul in Critical Contexts (Grand Rapids, MI: Fortress Press, 2008), 1–54.

hands and indulge in the business of their patron (1 Thess 4:11–12).[38] The subversive consequence of Paul's advice is evident in the light of Tacitus's testimony that the relation between aristocrats and plebs were established based on patronal ties (Tacitus, *Hist.* 1.4). In this sense, Paul wanted his readers to share a sociopolitical relationship only as patrons and to refrain from being clients.

6.4. Cultural ambiguity, strategic identity, and discipleship "in Christ"

An important idea that repeatedly occurs within the Thessalonian correspondence is Christ as the new location of activity of every Christian believer both in this life and after death (cf. 1 Thess 1:1; 2:14; 3:8; 4:16). In Thessalonians, Paul uses two variant expressions "in Christ" (1 Thess 2:14; 4:16) and "in the Lord" (1 Thess 3:8; 5:12) to refer to this Spirit-empowered transcultural mystical space of union "beyond" the imperial sphere of power, hierarchy, and marginalization. Although we do not find in 1 Thessalonians a bold, direct statement of Paul on Christian mystical union "in Christ" like in Galatians 3:28 and 2 Cor 5:17, it is evident that the mystical union idea is not absent from the letter.[39] Paul envisions the participation of all people, including Jews and Greek Thessalonians, in Christ. Apart from his reference to it in formal greetings (1 Thess 1:1; 2 Thess 1:1), he and his companions live by the standing firm of the Thessalonians "in the Lord" (1 Thess 3:8; cf. 3:12). Here, in this locale, they in the Lord Jesus and the Lord Jesus in them are mutually glorified (2 Thess 1:12). In fact, to Paul, one enters into this space by faith and is saved by the vicarious death of Jesus (1 Thess 1:8; 2:13; 5:5, 9–10), the man from Nazareth. Even God's will for the Thessalonians is known only in Christ Jesus (1 Thess 5:18). Further, Paul's apostolic mission of preaching and exhortation is carried out "in the Lord Jesus" (1 Thess 4:1; 2 Thess 3:12). No doubt, according to Paul, it is the sphere of both singular and ecclesial life of the Thessalonians.

E. P. Sanders has discussed, at length, the theme "participation in Christ" as part of Paul's soteriology without giving much attention to the Thessalonians Correspondence.[40] In Paul's theology, it is an imaginary space created by the Spirit, identical to the *ecclesia* in Christ, where Christ's offer of salvation from all forms of sociocultural binaries is actualized in non-essentialist terms. It is an imaginary space, transcending the sphere of colonial authority, important to articulate selfhood of the

38 Winter, "From Secular Clients to Christian Benefactors," 49–50.

39 Cf. Donfried, "Assembly of the Thessalonians," 151–53.

40 E. P. Sanders, *Paul and Palestinian Judaism: A Comparison of Patterns of Religion* (Philadelphia, PA: Fortress Press, 1977), 453–63.

colonized subjects. In Paul's imagination, at one level, for every believer Jesus Christ is the transcultural location of union with the crucified Messiah and, on the other, mutual participation among Christians.[41] In Galatians, this mystical space of identification is a dynamic space of subverting cultural binaries, mutual identification in non-hierarchical terms, and articulation of a hybrid identity. To me, Paul's participatory language refers to his imagined "christological-*ekklēsial* space."[42] In the words of Bhabha, "in Christ" transcultural hybrid space is "the Third Space of enunciation,"[43] where the Thessalonian believers are invited to actualize their new found status as the children of light and day untouched by the cultural, ethnic, gender-specific binaries. Thus, in this hybrid christological-*ekklēsial* space, to put it in the words of Bhabha, the "intersubjective and collective experiences of nationness, community interest, or cultural values are negotiated"[44] without valorizing relationships in essentialist cultural terms.

Such an articulation of complex identity may well have been evident in Paul, Silas, and Timothy to the Thessalonian believers. Luke presents Paul, Silas, and Timothy, in the book of Acts, as transcultural hybrid characters who affiliate-disrupt the cultural binaries, simultaneously. While Paul and Silas as Jew-Roman and Timothy as a Jew-Greek must have been visible examples of "a true hybrid Christian identity (Greek-Jew) in whom the ethnicity is 'mixed' inseparably," the "cultural specificities are retained (by undergoing circumcision) as a part of cultural adaptation without essentializing one over the other."[45] Probably, the visible Greek-Jew transcultural hybrid identity of Timothy grants him some relaxation to return to Thessalonica, a free Greek city under Roman rule, immediately

41 Cf. Lopez, *Apostle to the Conquered*, 17–19. Lopez explains "imagination" as "a powerful tool, when coming from the marginalized, not only to confront the imaginary as deceptive, dominant, and harmful, but also to identify voices that have been repressed and articulate new discourse and ways of being that overcome its power. . . . Imagination arises from a position of hope among the disenfranchised; it is the ability to envision a different world when that task seems overwhelming, implausible, and forbidden. Imagination is, in a sense, an often-coded revenge of the margins and the borders; it is often only vaguely familiar or intelligible to the imaginary while at the same time shattering its totalizing grip" (18).

42 See my book for a discussion in similar lines based on Galatians, George, *Paul's Identity in Galatians*, 250–53.

43 Homi K. Bhabha, "The Commitment to Theory," in *The Location of Culture* (New York: Routledge, 1994), 54.

44 Bhabha, "Commitment to Theory," 2.

45 Roji T. George, "A Postcolonial Reconstruction of Christian Identity and Human Rights Affirmation Amidst Threat to the 'Freedom of Religion': A Lucan Perspective," *Doon Theological Journal* 14, no. 1 (2017): 37. See also Eric D. Barreto, "Negotiating Difference: Theology and Ethnicity in the Acts of the Apostles," *Word World* 31, no. 2 (2011): 134–35.

after their expulsion. It is this model of transcultural hybrid identity that Paul invites them to imitate based on their firsthand knowledge of the lifestyle of the missionaries (1 Thess 1:5–6). Undoubtedly, their lifestyle is colored by their twin-forked gospel of salvation brought by Jesus, the King, "beyond" cultural binaries. Thus, an important aspect of Paul's call to imitate[46] a hybrid cultural model represented before them is to creatively occupy an "in-between" cultural locale amidst polar opposite discourses emanating both from the colonial "centre" and "margins," simultaneously, in Thessalonica. Paul exhorts his readers to articulate their imitation both by following the model of enduring suffering and persecution of the churches in Judea at the hands of their own people (1 Thess 2:14), and also to present themselves as "an example" to other Christian converts in Macedonia and Achaia (1 Thess 1:7).[47] Interestingly, the suffering of persecution by a hybrid subject is the evidence of his/her "sly civility,"[48] an ongoing process of affiliative-disruptive self-articulation. In this sense, the call to imitate the apostle, a transcultural hybrid postcolonial subject, is a critical attitude toward the colonial and native dominant cultures with an urge to be "*almost the same but not quite.*"[49]

If so, who are the opponents of Paul's mission in Thessalonica? A closer analysis of the cultural identity of "us" (1 Thess 1:6; 2:15) against the opponents of the gospel (both Jews and Thessalonians) in 2:14–16 proves that it is a conflict between those who defined identity in pro-imperial essentialist, oppressive, and exclusionary terms.[50] They oppose Paul and others, and thereby the gospel they preached, who threaten their ideological symmetry. They appear mimicking-mocking the imperial discourse in hybrid terms. The "Jews" who initiated opposition to Paul and his mission (cf. Acts 17:5) are identical to those who killed Jesus and also the Thessalonians who persecute Paul's readers (1 Thess 1:14). Acts 17:6 proves that they knew about the activities of the new preachers in the past,

46 In recent discussions on Paul's call to Thessalonians to imitate him and others, Malherbe and Gieschen demonstrate how important was the life and teachings of a teacher as a model to imitate both in Jewish and non-Jewish cultures. See Malherbe, *Paul and the Thessalonians*, 52–60; Gieschen, "Christian Identity," 6-12. Michael Martin, "'Example' and 'Imitation' in the Thessalonian Correspondence," *Southwestern Journal of Theology* 42, no. 1 (1999): 39–49.

47 See Gieschen, "Christian Identity," 3–18.

48 Homi K. Bhabha, "Sly Civility," in *The Location of Culture* (London: Routledge, 1994), 132-44. For Bhabha, it is a related term to postcolonial mimicry.

49 Bhabha, "Of Mimicry and Man," 127 (emphasis original).

50 The reference to the Jews, probably the zealot Jewish nationalistic movement embroiled in cultural imperialistic activity, in Judea replicates the colonizing 'self' within a postcolonial context as a parallel to the situation in Thessalonica. 1 Thess 2:14–16 may be treated as a pointer towards the ideological leniency of the opponents in the city.

probably, referring to the problems in Judea surrounding Christians and their subversive gospel. For Paul, it is they who are "hostile to all men" (1 Thess 2:15).[51] They intend to hinder the gentiles from sharing in the salvation brought through the death of Christ (1 Thess 2:16) on a colonial cross. For Paul, it is an ideological propagandist mission evoking from the (pro-)colonial "centre" to dominate, silence, and deprive the marginalized of articulating selfhood in the interstitial cultural space.

What is the political significance of participation "in Christ"? The idea of "salvation" formed an integral part of the Roman colonial discourse. Even the title *sōtēr* was a high title of Caesar. Archaeological evidence proves that Augustus was declared as the sole savior of the whole human race.[52] The early Christian gospel, like that of Paul, imitated the colonial discourse with a difference. It means that they mimicked-mocked the dominant discourse, simultaneously. In Paul's eschatological imagination, "beyond" Roman imperial sphere of authority, Jesus the victim of the imperial punishment is the locale of God's eschatological action where he reversed the ultimate expression of the Roman authority, death. Now those who participate "in Christ" are the ones who confess allegiance to him, that is, by faith, and they are saved by him "from the wrath to come" (1 Thess 1:10). The quick successive reference to Jesus's humanity and deity (the Son) in 1 Thessalonians 1:10 makes him a hybrid divine-human figure like the Danielic eschatological messianic figure, "the Son of Man" (Dan 7:4; 13–14).[53] Unlike Caesar deified posthumously,[54] for Paul, Jesus is a divine-human figure who comes from heaven. In other words, the salvation wrought by the hybrid figure Jesus, through his vicarious death on the cross under the Roman colonial rule, is actualized for all those who are "in Christ," the all-encompassing spiritual existence of the resurrected Jesus. In fact, unlike the salvation brought by Caesar through

51 Witherington, *1 and 2 Thessalonians*, 84–87.

52 Harrison, "Paul and the Imperial Gospel," 87; Keesmaat, "Crucified Lord," 71–72; N. T. Wright, *Paul: A Fresh Perspective* (Grand Rapids, MI: Fortress Press, 2005), 63, 71; John Pairman Brown, *Ancient Israel and Ancient Greece Religion, Politics, and Culture* (Grand Rapids, MI: Fortress Press, 2003), 78.

53 Cf. Keesmaat understands the subversive strength of 1 Thess 4:13–5:11 in the background of Dan 7:13–14. Keesmaat, "Crucified Lord," 89–92.

54 Helmut Koester, *Introduction to the New Testament Vol 1: History, Culture, and Religion of the Hellenistic Age*, Foundations and Facets: New Testament (Philadelphia, PA: Fortress Press, 1982), 367; Dominique Cuss, *Imperial Cult and Harmony Terms in the New Testament* (Fribourg: Fribourg University Press, 1974), 30; George, *Paul's Identity in Galatians*, 76. According to Gieschen, the divine and human status of Augustus in the Roman imperial discourse at Thessalonica was "visible not only from the presence of this temple but also from the fact that his head soon displaced that of Zeus on local coinage of this period." Gieschen, "Christian Identity," 5.

war and bloodshed, the Christians in Thessalonica already experience the eschatological salvation here and now in this imaginary location. In this context, not only the portrayal of Jesus—both as the resurrected Lord who ushers in the true universal salvation and the eschatological Christ who will return to save his people—is politically subversive (1 Thess 1:10; 3:13), but also even the claim to form a universal community "in Christ" with new identity, eschatological hope, and salvation is a subtle stab at the imperial claims.

In short, the call of the apostle to the Thessalonian believers to imitate is to creatively articulate a culturally subversive identity, modelled after them, within the interstitial space of the cultures. Jesus himself is to Paul a hybrid divine-human figure who in his spiritual existence is an all-encompassing locale of all "beyond" cultural, ethnic, and racial bipolarities. It is he who ushers in true salvation in his vicarious death contrary to Caesar's offer of salvation through violence and death.

6.5. Imitation for Discipleship and Christian Witness in India

The significance of discipleship within the community of God can be neither overlooked nor undermined because it formed the real content of Jesus's last command to his disciples before ascension (Matt 28:19). After his departure, the apostles were to baptize and teach others to obey all that Jesus commanded with the sole intention to make disciples. Discipling was integral to Jesus' call and formation of the band of twelve men around him. He was investing in them in order to prepare them to continue his discipling mission after he departs from the world. Hence, Jesus was intentional to command them to "make disciples of all nations" (Matt 28:19) just before he went back to the Father. Paul too considered discipling important in his mission to form and establish the authentic community of believers in God among the non-Jewish population in the first century. Undoubtedly, Paul employed "imitation" as a strategy of discipling even when he was physically far away from his believers. As a result, in his letters, he reminded them about the "model" that he and his companions left before their eyes to imitate. It helped Paul to inculcate certain vital traits of Christian lifestyle in them such as a cruciform life characterized by agape in a non-hierarchical relationship structure within the church. He considered such virtuous traits of being a Christian in a non-Christian context to glorify God.

The church in India ought to adopt Paul's strategy of the authentic Christian community formation consciously in order to create a vibrant missional community that is contextually relevant and adapted.

Like Paul reinvented "imitation" as a strategy of discipleship in a Greco-Roman cultural context, an effective contextually relevant strategy to create a missional community in India could be to adopt the Indian *gurukula pathashala* system. Instead of viewing the relationship between a pastor and a believer within a shepherd/leader and sheep/mute follower framework, we need to view the relationship within a *guru* ("master" or "teacher") and *shishya* ("follower" or "student") framework in order to cause inner transformation within a believer. It would demand the *guru* (pastor) to act as a source of learning by listening, observation and imitation for the disciple (believer) in every aspect of life toward attaining a Christlikeness. In this relationship model, the pastor of a community will cease to be merely a unique combination of preacher-teacher-administrator. Rather, he would be an authentic model of Jesus, the *mahaguru* (supreme teacher)— a model to imitate for the disciples within a church, a source of right learning by observation and listening. In the traditional Hindu *gurukula pathashala* system, a *shishya* not only obeyed the *guru's* instructions meticulously for spiritual vibrancy, but he also imitated the *guru* diligently in the path to attain divine knowledge through strict observation of the authentic lifestyle lived by his *guru*. In this way, spiritual discipline was inculcated within a student.

Although the effectiveness of virtues imitated by someone depends upon the ability of the individual's observation, repetition and also the ability of a *guru* to impart the right spiritual and ethical values before others, it establishes greater accountability on the church leaders, the Christian *gurus*, to replicate the right lifestyle and values before others. In the context of ever-increasing corruption and moral degradation with a lack of missional zeal among the clergy, the *guru-shishya* relationship structure will demand accountability from both the parties involved (the clergy and the laity).

A key contribution of such a contextually relevant relationship model within the church would be a right ethical formation coupled with accountability that, on the one hand, would not only encourage emulation of the Christlike lifestyle before others, it would also enable, on the other hand, an effective, ethical formation to the believers to live worthy of their calling. The ultimate focus of Christian spirituality, then, would not be merely to escape hell and go to heaven in a shallow individualistic sense. Instead, the goal of both the individual and corporate Christian existence would be to reflect the image of Christ based on the gospel and its demands within the concrete historical context to fulfill the divine missional mandate upon the church. An important aspect of developing Christlikeness in the church is to imitate the model of self-sacrificial cruciformed life of Christ in and through the community of believers among the poor, marginalized, and exploited members within and outside the church. The church in India involving missionally in the world will have to practice austerity and participation in the suffering of the masses inspired by the self-sacrificial agape exemplified in Christ the *mahaguru*.

Such a lifestyle leads us to recognize the need for creatively recalibrating the Christian identity within the sociocultural and religious-political pluralistic context. Paul's self-portrayal as "holy, righteous, and blameless" (1 Thess 2:10) ought to be lived out practically in ambivalent transcultural hybrid terms with a non-hierarchical character of the community to fulfill the divine missional purpose of God. While ethical purity must characterize the church in India by getting rid of moral degradation and economic corruption rampant within the church today, the community must consciously shun from the forming of a caste- or class-based hierarchical identity in a local context in order to foster absorption of people from every sociocultural and economic background into the church. This would be a prophetic missional function of the church within a caste and class-based divided society in India. The church ought to be that agent of transformation and disciplining that does not slavishly imitate the corrupt social patterns of relationship. Instead, the church must consciously seek to disrupt the social and cultural symmetry enforced coercively through the imposition of hierarchical relationships. The community must provide an alternative space of authentic self-articulation of Christian identity through discipleship based on the gospel of Christ. The church in India as found in Christ must be a space of liberation in between the cultures that resists caste, class, and racial bipolarities in order to articulate an inclusive identity in fluid, mixed, and impure terms. In other words, imitation for discipleship is not carried out by the coercive imposition of certain cultural values and systems upon the people of other cultures. Instead, discipleship is purely founded upon the ethical principles and moral standards imbibed in the teaching of Christ Jesus that is culturally relevant and contextually authentic.

To sum up, Paul encouraged imitation not as a means to exert coercive power upon his believers but to nurture Christlike Christian disciples in Thessalonica who lived an assimilative-disruptive pattern of life in Thessalonica simultaneously. As a founder of communities of God across the Roman empire, Paul recognized the necessity to disciple in establishing and sustaining them based on the teachings he imparted to them. Unlike in the gospel narrative of Jesus calling his audience to follow him, Paul sought to employ imitation as a key strategy to disciple others. In addition to the theological and ethical teachings, he exhorted them to conduct themselves both in private and public as partners in the mission of God, Paul also encouraged them to imitate him and the fellow companions to nurture Christlikeness in them. Paul constantly, in teaching a cruciform lifestyle of Jesus Christ, presented himself and his missionary companions as visible models before them. In other words, his unique idiosyncratic behavior is not the apostle's content of model that the believers ought to imitate. The content of imitation ranges from moral living to their right social living including doing labor with their own hands. In fact, Paul's encouragement to imitate him and his fellow missionaries does not imply a lack of interest in following a desired Christlike pattern of life. Instead, the believers in Thessalonica have already become a model to other churches in the region, while they have become like the church in Judea in suffering under their countrymen. Under the missional reading lens, Paul's exhortation to imitate ethical standards in becoming worthy of their call is missional by nature as their acts of *agape* spread beyond the limits of the church's boundary. Moreover, in imitating to become like Christ there is greater mutualism practiced in non-hierarchical terms that is countercultural in the context of the Roman system of benefaction. Such a culturally mixed pattern of imitation leads to a transcultural hybrid identity formation of a disciple in Christ that defies cultural essentialism within the church. In other words, Paul's Jewishness is not the content of imitation for discipleship, nor their gentile cultural patterns for the essence of identity articulation. Through the identity formed by imitation of others in nurturing Christlikeness within them, the Thessalonians were encouraged to imbibe the pattern of life based on the gospel of Christ within their cultural context. It is an authentic and subversive Christian identity that assimilates-disrupts the cultures within a pluralistic cultural context while walking worthy of the call.

CONCLUSION

In this study, an attempt is made to highlight the missional intent, content, and tenor of Paul's Thessalonian correspondence. Toward this goal, the dominant ideas and theological themes discussed by the apostle in addition to his ethical and spiritual directives to the newfound community of believers in the city are studied. An emerging trend of theological interpretation called missional hermeneutics is employed in doing the same. While the introduction states clearly to its reader the problem, plan, and purpose of the study undertaken, Chapter 1 discusses in detail the definition of the repeatedly used terms like "mission," "missional," and "church," the premise of missional interpretation, its nature and the four dominant trends currently in use among its proponents. Unlike the traditional approach of constructing the biblical foundation of mission or the biblical theology of mission, missional hermeneutics maintains that the mission mandate of God to the church is not merely found in the Bible. In fact, *missio Dei* is the reason for the origin and compilation of the Bible. The Bible recounts God's activity in human history in order to provide directives to its readers through the centuries to understand God's unique ways of intervention in human stories at different places, times, and cultures. In doing that, missional hermeneutics maintains that Scripture is the tool by which God moulds, commissions, and actualizes his universal plan of salvation through his elect community. The biblical text also informs and invites its readers in every era to collaborate voluntarily in the ongoing mission of God. Such an interpretive stance that prioritizes the missional metanarrative in one's theological engagement with the biblical text introduces a huge shift in the process of interpretation. It alters the way the biblical text is viewed, read, and interpreted in relation to the life of the church. The biblical text does not get treated as a repository of historical details of God and his community waiting to be exhumed by someone out of mere interest in reconstructing the history of the biblical communities or identifying the trajectory of the development of theology. Unlike in the historical critical interest of the scholars, the text is not understood merely as a piece of literature to be appreciated for its literary aesthetics and studied to determine its source, form, or literary character.

So, in the remaining chapters, we gradually move forward engaging hermeneutically with 1 and 2 Thessalonians from a missional perspective. In Chapter 2, an effort is made to reconstruct the sociocultural and religiopolitical context of the Thessalonian correspondence in addition to providing relevant clarifications on key issues regarding its general background. It is argued that owing to the Roman imperial context and the commercial significance of the city during the first century, the city of Thessalonica attracted people from all walks of life. The large influx of people not only created a pluralistic context, but also caused cross-pollination of different religions, cultures, and ethnic groups. An important component of the process of transcultural hybridization that took place was the Roman religiopolitical discourse and the imperial cult that naturalized the Roman domination over the native Greek populace. The direct consequence of Roman imperial power discourse crisscrossing within the city was the negotiation of power from the bipolar ends—the native citizens and the Roman power. While some from the former group succeed to acquire power by allying with the imperial power, the poor living in the city nurturing their hope of liberation from the oppression in and through the native Cabirus cult were further deprived by Rome assimilating the cult into its imperial religion.

It is in this complex situation that Paul entered into Thessalonica during his second missionary journey in 49–50 C.E. The gospel of the Lord Jesus Christ that he preached, according to Luke, was heard with a political significance that evoked stiff violent resistance both from the Jews and the native Greeks. Paul and his companions had to leave the city abruptly as a result of the opposition they faced. However, it appears that the persecution that broke out while Paul was in the city continued against the new believers in Christ in Thessalonica. Paul feared that this might cause some to fall from their faith, but he received an encouraging report from Timothy that they continue to stand firm in their faith facing all the odds. But, other major issues that required Paul's immediate attention were primarily threefold: (i) the ethical degradation among some within the church and the problem of some becoming busybodies due to wrong eschatological understanding. Such behavior did not fetch good testimonies to them before others. (ii) The fate of those who already died in Christ had worried some in the church due to the inadequate eschatological teaching they received after Paul abruptly left the city. This required urgent attention from the apostle. (ii) In the absence of Paul, some had found a route into the church with false teaching (an over-realized eschatology) that had potentially threatened the spiritual well-being of the congregation. Hence, in 50–51 C.E., Paul wrote from Corinth two quick letters successively to the church in the city both with a pastoral and missional purpose. Paul as the founder of the church desired to strengthen them in faith amidst all the negative circumstances, while he desired them to recognize their mission responsibility by being elected by God to be saved and to partner with him in the ongoing divine universal mission.

There is no doubt that in these two small letters, there are large blocks of eschatological material. But, it is much more important for us to note that eschatological language permeates the two letters. One cannot get the complete meaning of Paul's words in the Thessalonian correspondence without paying due attention to the eschatological language he uses, that is influenced by the Jewish apocalyptic thought. The reason is simple; he employs eschatology as a hermeneutical framework to encourage his readers to live a missional life in the city and to view their historical context through the lens of the last days. He reflects on his mission among them through the eschatological lens. As a result, the eschatologically conditioned vision fills the apostle with a sense of urgency to live with the utmost sense of genuineness toward God's plan, purpose, and will because the coming of the Messiah can happen any time. For him, amidst suffering and persecution from the fellow Thessalonians, the church has to retain the hope of God's retributive justice at the Parousia, and the joy of the Holy Spirit poured out upon them at their conversion. They are encouraged to live a missional life with firm faith in the hope of resurrection. The present suffering is said to come to an end when God provides rest in the eschatological time. The judgment day is a warning for all to live in loyalty toward the judge of all who has the power and authority to destroy the ultimate representation of evil personified. Hence, the present must be lived in complete responsibility recognizing the will and purpose for them as the elect community of God.

In Chapter 4, the discussion moves on to prove that the apostle's interest is not to teach them the doctrine of Trinity. Instead, while Paul invokes the Triune God indirectly by speaking about the Father, Son, and the Holy Spirit with their interchangeable and overlapping roles in the lives of the believers, he relates their conversion experience with the character of God as living and true. The Thessalonian believers are exhorted to persevere in their faith amidst suffering because unlike in their former life, they now belong to the living God who has elected them to share in the Abrahamic blessings. They are encouraged by saying that they are now the subject of God's love, and the one who has called them is faithful to rescue them from the impending wrath of God. Moreover, God is just and he will judge all on that last day. However, those elected by God in Thessalonica are united in God and Christ. The newfound community of the gentile believers called the church symbolizes God's promise to redeem their fellow citizens. The believers are the "firstfruits" of God's elect ones in the city who must pray that the message of the Lord will spread rapidly.

Further, the missional activity within the city beyond mere evangelization is threefold—work through faith, labor energized by love, and endurance by hope. Despite the hostile response from the native Thessalonians, Paul encourages the believers to act as benefactors within the city, demonstrate self-sacrificial cruciform lifestyle before others, and to persevere in hope amidst hopelessness. Nevertheless, they ought to be a community that takes risk as a missional community. The evidence of the risk-taking nature of Christian mission is evident in the extensive adaptation of the high imperial language of domination and power to articulate the gospel of Christ in political terms. Such subversive articulation of the gospel in political vocabulary invites not only a violent response from the center of power in a society, but it also allows the church to act fearlessly as the transforming agent of God toward justice and liberation. This is an important insight from the Thessalonian correspondence that from the eschatological perspective mere salvation of the soul is not the sole goal and purpose of Christian mission. Instead, the goal is to make relentless efforts for the establishment of the kingdom of God here and now despite the secret works of the evil one through the social structures.

It leads us to another important aspect of Paul's theology in the two letters, that is, the gospel and missional pneumatology. In Chapter 5, more than a mere identification of the christological content of the gospel, an attempt is made to explain the nature of ecclesia in Paul's thought using Newbigin's idea of community as the interpreter of the gospel. The study points out that in some sense, the Thessalonian community has become the interpreter of the gospel to others. Hence, Paul appreciates them for the good word that has spread about them in the surrounding cities. However, Paul encourages the Thessalonian believers to intentionally embody the essence of the gospel in order to interpret Christian hope in contextually relevant terms. Thereby, the social structure that contradicts the gospel must be envisioned as brought under Christ's sovereignty at the end. Paul reminds the readers that the gospel as the creative word of God is active in the lives of the believers to accomplish his missional purpose. Further escalating the idea of creative act of God, Paul explains the dynamic role of the Holy Spirit convincing them of the truth of the gospel they received at conversion. It came to them through the charismatic mediation of the Spirit and the experience of the Spirit imparted joy amidst suffering. In a sense, Paul's interest in the Thessalonian correspondence is to speak of the mission of the Holy Spirit itself. In addition, looking at the event of the reception of the Spirit by the Thessalonians through his eschatological framework, Paul teaches that the Holy Spirit is God's eschatological gift to the church in fulfilling its missional call faithfully and effectively. His role of sanctification to charismatic empowerment in prophesying ought to be desired with caution, to guard against the evil one's deception by fake imitation. For the apostle, the fire of the Holy Spirit must be carefully kept glowing within the church. Interestingly, in the missional hermeneutical study a missional community is characterized by its emphasis upon the role of the Spirit within the mission of the community.

Finally, as a missional community is considered to be a discipling community, Paul's interest in the Thessalonian correspondence is quite intentionally disciple making. Paul encourages discipling by his call to imitate him and his fellow missionaries. He also regularly appeals to the believers to become a good Christian model before others. In fact, his appreciation of the Thessalonians for already becoming models for others to imitate is his rhetorical device to encourage continuing in the same pattern of life in the future. In addition to this, he also exhorts them to avoid certain other patterns of faith and practice by presenting his opponents as bad models. No doubt, Paul was employing Hellenistic and Jewish cultural tools of character formation practiced by the masters or Rabbis with their respective disciples in the Greco-Roman world. However, for Paul, the ethical thrust of imitation and character formation as holy and blameless in righteousness is missional at the core. Paul's effort is not deification of a human nor the attainment of perfection. On the contrary, for him, right Christian ethical practice inculcated within an individual or a community by imitation or modelling is continuing of the apostolic testimony as a corporate body in a local set-up. Hence, it ought to be a community characterized by agape to both those who are within and outside the church. They must exist as a non-hierarchical community dealing with one another in patience and peace. Paul himself has modelled it to them playing different roles as father, mother, or a sibling. However, apart from the aspect of ethical formation of the disciples within the community, it is vital to notice that there could be a possibility of also imitating a cultural hybrid identity as represented by Timothy and Silas. They defy cultural essentialism of a true disciple within the universal community existing in God beyond all forms of cultural binaries. Such an identity formation by imitation of Paul's companions within a hybrid pluralistic cultural context of Thessalonica is vital for mission. For sure, a hybrid figure in the Thessalonian community is sure to send out positive vibes of Christian living to others with a goal of invitation to become partakers in God's eternal plan for them.

In short, a missional reading of Paul's Thessalonian correspondence enables us to appreciate the missional intention of the author in a very broad sense. Paul did not see the Thessalonians fulfilling the purpose of divine call upon them merely in the oral proclamation of the gospel, but to him the mission is lying right within the goal and purpose of their existence. Their being the firstfruits of the elect ones in Thessalonica is a missional promise of God to the rest in the city. Their participation in the Abrahamic blessing through election is not just an opportunity to claim a privileged status, but also to live a life pleasing to God. Paul never says that the Thessalonians must become a sending agent of God into the unreached world. On the contrary, by their very being, they ought to:

- participate in *missio-Dei* every moment through the enablement of God and the Holy Spirit;
- preach the gospel accompanied by the power of the Spirit;
- recognize the creative work of the gospel within a believer and in the community of believers;
- interpret the surrounding hostility to the gospel and the mission of God through the eschatological framework;
- read the Bible and accept its authority from the missional perspective as an equipping tool for the communities to become both partners with God and the arm of God in the world;
- trust in God and in his eschatological justice to retain hope amidst hopelessness.
- Intentionally become a community of disciple makers while maturing oneself to be a model for others; and
- become a community that interprets the gospel in and through its presence in the society. It ought to be a community that takes risks challenging the evil structures that do not envision Christ as the sovereign Lord over everything at the end.

BIBLIOGRAPHY

Abraham, Shaibu. "Holy Spirit in Pentecostal Mission Praxis in India: A Paradigm for Mission in Pluralistic Context." In *The Holy Spirit and Christian Mission in a Pluralistic Context*, edited by Roji T. George, 84–104. Bangalore: SAIACS Press, 2017.

Akkara, Anto. "Indian Campaign Against Church Corruption." *ChristianityToday.Com*, January 1, 2001, https://www.christianitytoday.com/ct/2001/januaryweb-only/14.0.html.

Allen, Roland. *Missionary Methods: Saint Paul's or Ours?* Grand Rapids, MI: William B. Eerdmans Publishing, 1962.

Ascough, Richard S. "The Thessalonian Christian Community as a Professional Voluntary Association." *Journal of Biblical Literature* 119, no. 2 (2000): 311–28.

———. "The Thessalonian Christian Community as a Professional Voluntary Association." *Journal of Biblical Literature* 119, no. 2 (2000): 311–28.

Aune, D. E. "Eschatology (Early Christian)." In *Anchor Bible Dictionary*, vol. 2, 594–609. Toronto: Doubleday, 1992.

Barram, Michael D. "'Fools for the Sake of Christ': Missional Hermeneutics and Praxis in the Corinthian Correspondence." *Missiology* 43, no. 2 (2015): 195–207.

———. "'Located' Questions for a Missional Hermeneutic: The Gospel and Our Culture Network," 2006, https://gocn.org/library/95/.

———. *Mission and Moral Reflection in Paul*. Studies in Biblical Literature, vol. 75. Frankfurt am Main: Peter Lang, 2006.

———. "'Occupying' Genesis 1–3: Missionally Located Reflections on Biblical Values and Economic Justice." *Missiology* 42, no. 4 (2014): 386–98.

———. "The Bible, Mission, and Social Location: Toward a Missional Hermeneutic." *Interpretation* 61, no. 1 (2007): 42–58.

Barreto, Eric D. "Negotiating Difference: Theology and Ethnicity in the Acts of the Apostles." *Word World* 31, no. 2 (2011): 129–37.

Barrett, Lois Y., ed. "So We Do Not Lose Heart." In *Treasure in Clay Jars: Patterns in Missional Faithfulness*, ix–xiv. The Gospel and Our Culture Series. Grand Rapids, MI: William B. Eerdmans Publishing, 2004.

———. "Taking Risks as a Contrast Community." *Treasure in Clay Jars: Patterns in Missional Faithfulness*, edited by Lois Y. Barrett, 74–83. The Gospel and Our Culture Series. Grand Rapids, MI: William B. Eerdmans Publishing, 2004.

Bartholomew, Craig G. "Theological Interpretation and a Missional Hermeneutic." In *Reading the Bible Missionally*, edited by Michael W. Goheen, 68–85. Grand Rapids, MI: William B. Eerdmans Publishing, 2016.

Bartholomew, Craig G., and Michael W. Goheen. "Story and Biblical Theology." In *Out of Egypt: Biblical Theology and Biblical Interpretation*, edited by Craig G. Bartholomew, Mary Healy, Karl Möller, and Robin Parry, 144–71. Scripture and Hermeneutics Series, vol.5. Milton Keynes: Paternoster Press, 2004.

Bauckham, Richard. *Bible and Mission: Christian Witness in a Postmodern World*. Grand Rapids, MI: Baker Academic, 2003.

———. "Mission as Hermeneutic for Scriptural Interpretation." In *Reading the Bible Missionally*, edited by Michael W. Goheen, 28–44. Grand Rapids, MI: William B. Eerdmans Publishing, 2016.

Bauer, W., F. W. Danker, W. F. Arndt, and F. W. Gingrich. *A Greek-English Lexicon of the New Testament and Other Early Christian Literature*. 3rd ed. Chicago/London: University of Chicago Press, 2000.

Beale, G. K. *1–2 Thessalonians*. The IVP New Testament Commentary Series. Downer Grove, IL: IVP Academic, 2003.

Beker, J. Christiaan. *Paul the Apostle: The Triumph of God in Life and Thought*. Philadelphia, PA: Fortress Press, 1980.

———. *Paul the Apostle: The Triumph of God in Life and Thought*. Philadelphia, PA: Fortress Press, 1980.

Betz, Hans D. *Galatians: A Commentary on Paul's Letter to the Churches in Galatia*. Hermeneia: A Critical and Historical Commentary on the Bible. Philadelphia, PA: Fortress Press, 1979.

Bhabha, Homi K. "Of Mimicry and Man: The Ambivalence of Colonial Discourse." In *The Location of Culture*, 121–31. London: Routledge, 1994.

———. "Sly Civility." In *The Location of Culture*, 132–44. London: Routledge, 1994.

———. "The Commitment of Theory." In *The Location of Culture*, 28–.56, London and New York: Routledge, 1994.

Boring, M. Eugene. *I & II Thessalonians: A Commentary*. 1st ed. The New Testament Library. Louisville, KY: Westminster John Knox Press, 2015.

Bosch, David Jacobus. *Transforming Mission: Paradigm Shifts in Theology of Mission*. American Society of Missiology Series, no. 16. Maryknoll, NY: Orbis Books, 1991.

Brown, John Pairman. *Ancient Israel and Ancient Greece Religion, Politics, and Culture*. Grand Rapids, MI: Fortress Press, 2003.

Brownson, James V. "Speaking the Truth in Love: Elements of a Missional Hermeneutic." *International Review of Mission* 83, no. 330 (1994): 479–504.

———. *Speaking the Truth in Love: New Testament Resources for a Missional Hermeneutic*. Christian Mission and Modern Culture. Harrisburg, PA: Trinity Press International, 1998.

Bruce, F. F. *1 and 2 Thessalonians. Word Biblical Commentary*, vol. 45. Waco, TX: Word Books, 1982.

Bultmann, Rudolf. "Is Exegesis Without Presuppositions Possible?" In *Existence and Faith: Short Writings of Rudolf Bultmann*, translated by Schubert M. Ogden, 342–51. London: Fortana Library, 1964.

Burke, Trevor J. "Paul's New Family in Thessalonica." *Novum Testamentum* 54, no. 3 (2012): 269–87.

——— "The Holy Spirit as the Controlling Dynamic in Paul's Role as Missionary to the Thessalonians." In *Paul as Missionary: Identity, Activity, Theology, and Practice*, edited by Trevor J. Burke and Brian S. Rosner, 142–57. London: Bloomsbury T&T Clark, 2011.

Carras, George P. "Jewish Ethics and Gentile Converts: Remarks on 1 Thes 4:3–8." In *The Thessalonain Correspondence* edited by Raymond F. Collins, 306–15. *Bibliotheca Ephemeridum Theologicarum Lovaniensium*, vol. 87. Leuven: Leuven University Press, 1990.

Carson, Donald A., Douglas J. Moo, and Leon Morris. *An Introduction to the New Testament*. Grand Rapids, MI: Zondervan, 1995.

Cherian, M. T. *Hindutva Agenda and Minority Rights: A Christian Response*. Bangalore: Centre for Contemporary Christianity, 2007.

Collins, Raymond F. "'The Gospel of Our Lord Jesus' (2 Thess 1,8): A Symbolic Shift of Paradigm." In *The Thessalonian Correspondence*, edited by Raymond F. Collins, 426–40. *Bibliotheca Ephemeridum Theologicarum Lovaniensium*, vol. 87. Leuven: Leuven University Press, 1990.

Copan, Victor A. "Μαθητής and Μιμητής: Exploring an Entangled Relationship." *Bulletin for Biblical Research* 17, no. 2 (2007): 313–23.

Cuss, Dominique. *Imperial Cult and Harmony Terms in the New Testament.* Fribourg: Fribourg University Press, 1974.

Donfried, Karl P. "1 Thessalonians, Acts and the Early Paul." In *Paul, Thessalonica, and Early Christianity*, 69–98. Grand Rapids, MI: William B. Eerdmans Publishing, 2002.

———. *Paul, Thessalonians, and Early Christianity*. Grand Rapids, MI: William B. Eerdmans Publishing, 2002.

———. "The Assembly of the Thessalonians: Reflections on the Ecclesiology of the Earliest Christian Letter." In *Paul, Thessalonica, and Early Christianity*, 139–62. Grand Rapids, MI: William B. Eerdmans Publishing, 2002.

———. "The Cults of Thessalonica and the Thessalonian Correspondence." In *Paul, Thessalonica, and Early Christianity*, 21–48. Grand Rapids, MI: William B. Eerdmans Publishing, 2002.

———. "The Theology of 1 Thessalonians." In *The Theology of the Shorter Pauline Letters*. New Testament Theology, 1–79. Cambridge: Cambridge University Press, 1993.

———. "The Theology of 1 Thessalonians: Reflections on the Ecclesiology of the Earliest Christian Letter." In *Paul, Thessalonica, and Early Christianity*, 119–38. Grand Rapids, MI: William B. Eerdmans Publishing, 2002.

———. "The Theology of 2 Thessalonians." In *The Theology of the Shorter Pauline Letters*. New Testament Theology, 81–113. Cambridge: Cambridge University Press, 1993.

Donfried, Karl P., and Johannes Beutler, eds. *The Thessalonians Debate:Methodological Discord or Methodological Synthesis?* Grand Rapids, MI: William B. Eerdmans Publishing, 2000.

Edson, Charles. "Cults of Thessalonica (Macedonica III)." *Harvard Theological Review* 41, no. 3 (1948): 153–204.

Fee, Gordon D. *The First and the Second Letters to the Thessalonians*. The New International Commentary on the New Testament. Grand Rapids, MI: William B. Eerdmans Publishing, 2009.

Flemming, Dean E. *Recovering the Full Mission of God: A Biblical Perspective on Being, Doing, and Telling*. Downers Grove, IL: IVP Academic, 2013.

———. "Revelation and the Missio Dei: Toward a Missional Reading of the Apocalypse." *Journal of Theological Interpretation* 6, no. 2 (2012): 161–78.

Flemming, Dean E. *Why Mission?* Reframing New Testament Theology 4, edited by Joel B. Green. 1st ed. Nashville: Abingdon Press, 2015.

Foster, Paul. "Who Wrote 2 Thessalonians?: A Fresh Look at an Old Problem." *Journal for the Study of the New Testament* 35, no. 2 (2012): 150–75.

Frame, James Everett. *A Critical Commentary on the Epistles of St. Paul to the Thessalonians.* The International Critical Commentary. Edinburgh: T&T Clark, 1979.

Franke, John R. "Intercultural Hermeneutics and the Shape of Missional Theology." In *Reading the Bible Missionally*, edited by Michael W. Goheen, 86–103. Grand Rapids, MI: William B. Eerdmans Publishing, 2016.

Friedrich, G. "Ευαγγελιζομαι Κτλ." *Theological Dictionary of the New Testament* 2: 707–37.

Frykenberg, Robert Eric. "Hindutva and the Aftermath of Ayodhya: Dangers of Political Religion and Religious Nationalism." *Nationalism and Hindutva: A Christian Response*, edited by Mark T. B. Laing. Delhi/Pune: ISPCK/CMS/UBS, 2005.

Garrow, Alan John Philip. "The Eschatological Tradition behind 1 Thessalonians: Didache 16." *Journal for the Study of the New Testament* 32, no. 2 (2009): 191–215.

Gaventa, Beverly Roberts. *First and Second Thessalonians.* Interpretation, a Bible Commentary for Teaching and Preaching. Louisville, KY: John Knox Press, 1998.

George, Roji T. "A Postcolonial Reconstruction of Christian Identity and Human Rights Affirmation Amidst Threat to the 'Freedom of Religion': A Lucan Perspective." *Doon Theological Journal* 14, no. 1 (2017): 28–43.

———. "Introduction." In *The Holy Spirit and Christian Mission in a Pluralistic Context*, edited by Roji T. George, 11–20. Bangalore: SAIACS Press, 2017.

———. "'Join Together with Me in Imitating My Example': Reflection on Paul's Call to Imitate in the Letter to the Philippians." In *Bible, Mission, and Theology: A Festschrift in Honor of Rev. Dr. Simon* Samuel, edited by P. V. Joseph, 99–111. Dehradun/Delhi: Luther W. New Jr. Theological College/ISPCK, 2018.

———. *Paul's Identity in Galatians: A Postcolonial Appraisal.* New Delhi: Christian World Imprints, 2016.

———. "Situation in Thessalonica and Paul's Advice to the Community in 1 Thessalonians: A Postcolonial Reading for Contextual Significance in India Today," 1–27. Paper presented at the Society for New Testament Studies Asia Pacific Lesioning Regional Conference, Kottayam, October 22, 2016.

Getty, Mary Ann. "The Imitation of Paul in the Letters to the Thessalonians." In *The Thessalonian Correspondence*, edited by Raymond F. Collins, 277–83. Bibliotheca Ephemeridum Theologicarum Lovaniensium, vol. 87. Leuven: Leuven University Press, 1990.

Gieschen, Charles A. "Christian Identity in a Pagan Thessalonica: The Imitation of Paul's Cruciform Life." *Concordia Theological Quarterly* 72, no. 1 (2008): 3–18.

———. "Christ's Coming and the Church's Mission in 1 Thessalonians." *Concordia Theological Quarterly* 76, no. 1–2 (2012): 37–55.

Gill, David W. J. "Macedonia." In *The Book of Acts in Its Graeco-Roman Setting*, edited by David W. G. Gill and Conrad Gempf, 397–417. *The Book of Acts in Its First Century Setting*, vol. 2. Grand Rapids, MI: William B. Eerdmans Publishing, 1994.

Goheen, Michael W. "A History and Introduction to a Missional Reading of the Bible." In *Reading the Bible Missionally*, edited by Michael W. Goheen, 3–27. Grand Rapids, MI: William B. Eerdmans Publishing, 2016.

———. *A Light to the Nations: The Missional Church and the Biblical Story*. Grand Rapids, MI: Baker Academic, 2011.

———. "A Missional Reading of Scripture and Preaching." In *Reading the Bible Missionally*, edited by Michael W. Goheen, 241–62. Grand Rapids, MI: William B. Eerdmans Publishing, 2016.

———. "The Urgency of Reading the Bible as One Story." *Theology Today* 64, no. 4 (2008): 469–83.

Goheen, Michael W., and Christopher J. H. Wright. "Mission and Theological Interpretation." In *A Manifesto for Theological Interpretation*, edited by Craig G. Bartholomew and Heath A. Thomas, 171–196. Grand Rapids, MI: Baker Academic, 2016.

Goodman, Martin. *The Roman World 44 B.C.–A.D. 180*. London: Routledge, 1997.

Gorman, Michael J. *Apostle of the Crucified Lord: A Theological Introduction to Paul and His Letters*. Grand Rapids, MI: Willliam B. Eerdmans Publishing, 2004.

Gorman, Michael J. *Cruciformity: Paul's Narrative Spirituality of the Cross*. Grand Rapids, MI: William B. Eerdmans Publishing, 2001.

Gowda, Aravind. "Bangalore: Pastor Held for Sexually Exploiting Minor Girls." *India Today*, June 19, 2011. https://www.indiatoday.in/india/south/story/bangalore-pastor-held-for-sexually-exploiting-minors-135890-2011-06-19.

Guder, Darrell L. "Biblical Formation and Discipleship." In *Treasure in Clay Jars: Patterns in Missional Faithfulness*, edited by Lois Y. Barrett, 59–73. The Gospel and Our Culture Series. Grand Rapids, MI: William B. Eerdmans Publishing, 2004.

———. *Called to Witness: Doing Missional Theology*. The Gospel and Our Culture Series. Grand Rapids, MI: William B. Eerdmans Publishing, 2015.

———. "Missional Theology for a Missionary Church." *Journal for Preachers* 22, no. 1 (1998): 3–11.

———. "The Implication of a Missional Hermeneutic for Theological Education." In *Reading the Bible Missionally*, edited by Michael W. Goheen, 285–98. The Gospel and Our Culture Series. Grand Rapids, MI: William B. Eerdmans Publishing, 2016.

Guthrie, Donald. *New Testament Introduction*. 4th ed. (rev.). Leicester: Apollos [u.a.], 1990.

Hafemann, Scott J. "Divine Judgement and the Completion of the Missionary Task: Paul's Motivation for Ministry in 1–2 Thessalonians." In *Paul's Message and Ministry in Covenant Perspective: Selected Essays*, 185–94. Bangalore: SAIACS Press, 2016.

Harrison, J. R. "Paul and the Imperial Gospel at Thessaloniki." *Journal for the Study of the New Testament* 25, no. 1 (2002): 71–96.

———. "Paul and the Imperial Gospel at Thessaloniki." *Journal for the Study of the New Testament*25, no. 1 (2002): 71–96.

Hedlund, Roger E. *Evangelization and Church Growth: Issues from the Asian Context*. India: CGRC McGavran Institute, 1992.

Hobbs, Walter C. "Appendix: Method." In *Treasure in Clay Jars: Patterns in Missional Faithfulness*, edited by Lois Y. Barrett, 154–72. The Gospel and Our Culture Series. Grand Rapids, MI: William B. Eerdmans Publishing, 2004.

———. "Dependence on the Holy Spirit." In *Treasure in Clay Jars: Patterns in Missional Faithfulness*, edited by Lois Y. Barrett, 117–25. The Gospel and Our Culture Series. Grand Rapids, MI: William B. Eerdmans Publishing, 2004.

Howell, Don N., Jr. "Confidence in the Spirit as the Governing Ethos of the Pauline Mission." *Trinity Journal* 17, no. 2 (1996): 203–21.

Hunsberger, George R. "Proposals for a Missional Hermeneutic: Mapping a Conversation." *Missiology* 39, no. 3 (2011): 309–21.

Jewett, Robert. "Epistolary Thanksgiving and the Integrity of Philippians." *Novum Testamentum* 12, no. 1 (1970): 40–53.

———. *The Thessalonian Correspondence: Pauline Rhetoric and Millenarian Piety*. Foundations and Facets. Philadelphia, PA: Fortress Press, 1986.

Johnson, Andy. *1 and 2 Thessalonians*. The Two Horizons New Testament Commentary. Grand Rapids, MI: William B. Eerdmans Publishing, 2016.

Judge, Edwin A. "Decrees of Caesar at Thessalonica." *Reformed Theological Review* 30, no. 1 (1971): 1–7.

Kanungo, Pralay. *RSS's Tryst with Politics: From Hedgewar to Sudarshan*. Delhi: Manohar, 2003.

Kaye, Bruce N. "Eschatology and Ethics in 1 and 2 Thessalonians." *Novum Testamentum* 17, no. 1 (1975): 47–57.

Keesmaat, Sylvia C. "Crucified Lord of Conquering Savior: Whose Story of Salvation?" *Horizons in Biblical Theology* 26, no. 2 (2004): 69–93.

Koester, Helmut. *Introduction to the New Testament Vol 1: History, Culture, and Religion of the Hellenistic Age*. Foundations and Facets: New Testament. Philadelphia, PA: Fortress Press, 1982.

———. *Introduction to the New Testament Vol 2: History and Literature of Early Christianity*. 3rd print. Foundations and Facets: New Testament. New York, NY: Fortress Press, 1984.

Lightfoot, J. B. *Notes on the Epistles of St Paul: I & II Thessalonians, I Corinthians 1–7, Romans 1–7, Ephesians 1:1–14*. Indiana: Alpha Publications, n.d.

Lopez, Davina C. *Apostle to the Conquered: Reimagining Paul's Mission*. Paul in Critical Contexts. Grand Rapids, MI: Fortress Press, 2008.

Lowry, Lindy. "The 10 Most Dangerous Places to Be a Christian." Open Doors USA, January 16, 2019. Accessed February 5, 2019, https://www.opendoorsusa.org/christian-persecution/stories/10-dangerous-places-christian-worldwatch- list/.

Malherbe, Abraham J. *Paul and the Thessalonians: The Philosophical Tradition of Pastoral Care*. Philadelphia, PA: Fortress Press, 1987.

———. *The Letters to the Thessalonians: A New Translation with Introduction and Commentary. Anchor Bible*, vol. 32B. New York: Doubleday, 2000.

Manson, T. W. "St Paul in Greece: The Letters to the Thessalonians." *Bulletin of John Rylands Library* 35, no. 2 (1953): 428–47.

Marlow, Iain. "Cow Vigilantes in India Killed at Least 44 People, Report Finds." *Bloomberg.Com*, 20 February 2019. Accessed July 24, 2019, https://www.bloomberg.com/news/articles/2019-02-20/cow-vigilantes-in-india-killed-at-least-44-people-report-finds.

Marshall, I. Howard. *1 and 2 Thessalonians*. New Century Bible Commentary. Grand Rapids, MI: William B. Eerdmans Publishing, 1983.

———. *1 and 2 Thessalonians: Based on the Revised Standard Version.* New Century Bible Commentary. Grand Rapids, MI: William B. Eerdmans Publishing, 1983.

Martin, D. Michael. *1, 2 Thessalonians. The New American Commentary*, vol. 33. USA: Broadman & Holman Publishers, 1995.

Martin, Michael. "'Example' and 'Imitation' in the Thessalonian Correspondence." *Southwestern Journal Theology* 42, no. 1 (1999): 39–49.

Menken, M. J. J. *2 Thessalonians.* New Testament Readings. London: Routledge, 1994.

Michaelis, W. "Μιμεομαι Κτλ." *Theological Dictionary of the New Testament* 4: 659–74.

Morris, Leon. *1, 2 Thessalonians.* Word Biblical Themes. Dallas, TX: Word Publishing, 1989.

———. *The First and Second Epistles to the Thessalonians.* The New International Commentary on the New Testament. Grand Rapids, MI: William B. Eerdmans Publishing , 1959.

Newbigin, Lesslie. *The Gospel in a Pluralist Society.* Grand Rapids, MI: William B. Eerdmans Publishing, 1989.

Oakes, Peter. "Re-Mapping the Universe: Paul and the Emperor in 1 Thessalonians and Philippians." *Journal for the Study of the New Testament* 27, no. 3 (2005): 301–22.

———. "Re-Mapping the Universe: Paul and the Emperor in 1 Thessalonians and Philippians." *Journal for the Study of the New Testamentum* 27, no. 3 (2005): 301–22.

Oommen, T. K. "Religious Nationalisms and Democratic Polity in India: Impossibility of Reconciliation." In *Nationalism and Hindutva: A Christian Response,* edited by Mark T. B. Laing, 35–52. Delhi/Pune: ISPCK/CMS/UBS, 2005.

Pelser, G. M. M. "Resurrection and Eschatology in Paul's Letters." *Neotestamentica* 20 (1986): 37–46.

Plevnik, Joseph. "1 Thess 5:1-11: Its Authenticity, Intention and Message." *Biblica* 60, no. 1 (1979): 71–90.

Richards, E. Randolph. "Ministering in a Tough Place: Paul's Pattern in Thessalonica." *Southwestern Journal of Theology* 42, no. 1 (1999): 17–38.

Riesner, Rainer. *Paul's Early Period: Chronology, Mission Strategy, Theology.* Translated by Doug Stott. Grand Rapids, MI: William B. Eerdmans Publishing , 1998.

Rulmu, Callia. "Between Ambition and Quietism: The Socio-Political Background of 1 Thessalonians 4:9–12." *Biblica* 91, no. 3 (2010): 393–417.

Sanders, E. P. *Paul and Palestinian Judaism: A Comparison of Patterns of Religion*. Philadelphia, PA: Fortress Press, 1977.

Schmidt, Daryl. "1 Thess 2:13-16: Linguistic Evidence for an Interpolation." *Journal of Biblical Literature* 102, no. 2 (1983): 269–79.

Sherwood, Harriet. "One in Three Christians Face Persecution in Asia, Report Finds." *The Guardian*, n.d. https://www.theguardian.com/world/2019/jan/16/one-in-three-christians-face-persecution-in-asia-reportfinds.

Simpson, J. W. "Thessalonians, Letters to The." In *Dictionary of Paul and His Letters*, 932–39. Downers Grove, IL: IVP, 1993.

Smith, Abraham. "Unmasking the Powers: Towards a Postcolonial Analysis of 1 Thessalonians." In *Paul and the Roman Imperial Order*, edited by Richard A. Horsley, 47-66. Harrisburg/London/New York: Trinity Press International, 2004.

Stacy, R. Wayne. "Introduction to the Thessalonian Correspondences." *Review & Expositor* 96, no. 2 (1999): 175–94.

Still, Todd D. "Eschatology in the Thessalonian Letters." *Review & Expositor* 96, no. 2 (1999): 195–210.

———. "Paul's Thessalonian Mission." *Southwestern Journal of Theology* 42, no. 1 (1999): 4–16.

———. "'Since We Believe That Jesus Died and Rose Again': The Gospel Paul Preached in Thessalonica as Evidenced by 1 Thessalonians." *Restoration Quarterly* 54, no. 1 (2012): 7–18.

Stott, John R. W. *Christian Mission in the Modern World*. Bombay: Gospel Literature Service, 1993.

Strandenaes, Thor. "Completing the Mission: Paul's Application of the Gospel to the Faith and Life of the Thessalonian Converts in 1 and 2 Thessalonians." *Svensk Missionstidskrift* 98, no. 1 (2010): 69–98.

Tennent, Timothy C. "Holy Spirit and Christian Mission in a Religious Pluralistic Context." In *The Holy Spirit and Christian Mission in a Pluralistic Context*, edited by Roji T. George, 60–83. Bangalore: SAIACS Press, 2017.

Thomas, Joy. "The Evolution of the Concept of Mission in the Bible." In *Bible and Mission in India Today*, edited by Jacob Kavunkal and F. Hrangkhuma, 38–52. Bandra, Bombay: St. Pauls, 1993.

Thomas, Maria. "The AP Blows the Lid off Decades-Long Sexual Abuse of Nuns by Catholic Priests in India." *Quartz India*, n.d. https://qz.com/india/1513007/how-catholic-priests-sexually-abused-nuns-in-kerala-india/.

Tyra, Gary. *The Holy Spirit in Mission: Prophetic Speech and Action in Christian Witness*. Downers Grove, IL: IVP Academic, 2011.

Wagner, J. Ross. *Heralds of the Good News: Isaiah and Paul in Concert in the Letter to the Romans*. Boston: Brill, 2003.

Wanamaker, Charles A. *The Epistles to the Thessalonians: A Commentary on the Greek Text*. The New International Greek Testament Commentary. Grand Rapids, MI: William B. Eerdmans Publishing, 1990.

Ward, Roy Bowen. "Ekklesia: A Word Study." *Restoration Quarterly* 2, no. 4 (1958): 164–79.

Ware, Phil. "The Coming of the Lord: Eschatology and 1 Thessalonians." *Restoration Quarterly* 22, no. 1–2 (1979): 109–20.

Weatherly, Jon A. "The Authenticity of 1 Thessalonians 2:13–16: Additional Evidence." *Journal of the Study of the New Testament* 13, no. 42 (1991): 79–98.

Weima, Jeffrey A. D. *1–2 Thessalonians*. Baker Exegetical Commentary on the New Testament. Grand Rapids, MI: Baker Academic, 2014.

Wengst, Klaus. *PAX ROMANA and the Peace of Jesus Christ*. Translated by John Bowden. Philadelphia, PA: Fortress Press, 1987.

West, J. C. "The Order of 1 and 2 Thessalonians." *Journal of Theological Studies* 15, no. 57 (1913): 66–74.

Wilkins, Michael J. *Discipleship in the Ancient World and Matthew's Gospel*. 2nd ed. Grand Rapids, MI: Baker Books, 1995.

———. "Imitate, Imitators": 392. *Anchor Bible Dictionary*, vol. 3. New York: Doubleday, 1992.

Winter, Bruce W. "From Secular Clients to Christian Benefactors: 1 Thessalonians 4:11–12 and 2 Thessalonians 3:6–13." In *Seek the Welfare of the City: Christians as Benefactors and Citizens*. First Century Christians in the Graeco-Roman World, 42–60. Grand Rapids, MI: William B. Eerdmans Publishing, 1994.

Witherington, Ben. *1 and 2 Thessalonians: A Socio-Rhetorical Commentary*. Grand Rapids, MI: William B. Eerdmans Publishing, 2006.

———. *The Acts of the Apostles: A Socio-Rhetorical Commentary*. Grand Rapids, MI: William B. Eerdmans Publishing, 1998.

Woodbridge, Paul. "Did Paul Change His Mind?: An Examination of Some Aspects of Pauline Eschatology." *Themelios* 28, no. 3 (2003): 5–18.

Wright, Christopher J. H. "Mission as a Matrix for Hermeneutics and Biblical Theology." In *Out of Egypt: Biblical Theology and Biblical Interpretation*, edited by Craig G. Bartholomew, Mary Healy, Karl Möller, and Robin Parry, 103–143. Scripture and Hermeneutics Series, vol. 5. Milton Keynes: Paternoster Press, 2004.

———. *The Mission of God: Unlocking the Bible's Grand Narrative*. Downers Grove, IL: IVP Academic, 2006.

Wright, N. T. *Paul: A Fresh Perspective*. Grand Rapids, MI: Fortress Press, 2005.

"Bishop Warns against Illegal Sale of Church Property | Allahabad News-Times of India." *The Times of India*, n.d. https://timesofindia.indiatimes.com/city/allahabad/Bishop-warns-against-illegal-sale-of-church-property/articleshow/19553793.cms.

"'Cow Vigilantes' Kill Three Men in India." n.d. https://www.trtworld.com/asia/cow-vigilantes-kill-three-men-in-india-28367.

"Land Scam of Rs 10,000 Crores Reported in Christian Organisations of Uttar Pradesh." *OpIndia*, July 16, 2019. https://www.opindia.com/2019/07/church-scam-fraudulent-land-deals-illegal-sale-of-over-10000-crores-reported-in-christian-organisations-of-uttar-pradesh/.